DRESS HISTORY

DRESS HISTORY

New Directions in Theory and Practice

Edited by

Charlotte Nicklas and Annebella Pollen

Bloomsbury Academic
An imprint of Bloomsbury Publishing Plc

B L O O M S B U R Y
LONDON · NEW DELHI · NEW YORK · SYDNEY

Bloomsbury Academic
An imprint of Bloomsbury Publishing Plc

50 Bedford Square	1385 Broadway
London	New York
WC1B 3DP	NY 10018
UK	USA

www.bloomsbury.com

BLOOMSBURY and the Diana logo are trademarks of Bloomsbury Publishing Plc

First published 2015

British Library Cataloguing-in-Publication Data
A catalogue record for this book is available from the British Library.

ISBN: HB: 978-0-85785-541-1
PB: 978-0-85785-640-1
ePDF: 978-1-47424-051-2
ePub: 978-1-47424-052-9

Library of Congress Cataloging-in-Publication Data
A catalog record for this book is available from the Library of Congress.

Typeset by Newgen Knowledge Works (P) Ltd., Chennai, India

To Louise Purbrick

CONTENTS

LIST OF ILLUSTRATIONS

Figures

Plates

PREFACE

Lou Taylor

have been enthralled by dress and textile history for my whole life, from my days as a fashion student at St Martin's School of Art in the early 1960s and then as a milliner, a dress curator in Edinburgh and Brighton museums and finally through all thirty years of my teaching at the University of Brighton. I have loved it all. I joined the slow struggle for acceptance of the field in university and museum worlds and now I watch with delight when I see how dress and textile history are respected and absorbed into so much interdisciplinary research and are taught at universities worldwide.

Leora Auslander believes 'the use of material objects is . . . not reducible to words' (2005: 1); Susan Pearce writes that objects tell us 'the stories of our lives in ways which would be impossible otherwise' (1993: 147); Kaori O'Connor is convinced that, within the history of fashion and dress, the close study of objects offers 'nuanced insights into the dynamism of society on many levels not easily arrived at by other means, if at all' (2005: 41). All these scholars offer persuasive accounts of the unique perspective provided by object-based study and its profound potential for enabling understanding of the world. Many other scholars agree. Anthropologists, business historians, economic and social historians, scholars of literature, film and photography – to name but a few – now frequently engage with the study of dress, each from their own disciplinary positions.

The truth about dress history is that all the approaches from these various disciplinary and subject areas – and others tackled in this fascinating publication – are valid. However, none is more valid than another, although enthusiasts in each corner may feel otherwise. Practitioners of each are correct in asserting that the specific focus of their research reaches dress history understandings that can be reached in no other way. But there is now little remaining dispute about the vital importance of interdisciplinarity across the field today. It has taken a lifetime of scholarly pioneering work by women and men over the last thirty or forty years for this situation to be achieved. It is obvious that, while none of us can, singly, be authorities in all these disciplines, we can and are working together – respecting and learning from each other's specialisms.

I know my absorption with dress history is shared both by the editors and contributors to this book. I thank Dr Louise Purbrick who, with a profoundly sympathetic and contemporary understanding of the subject, organized the 2011 Developments in Dress History conference, which brought together dress scholars from around the world. I thank Dr Charlotte Nicklas and Dr Annebella Pollen for continuing those conversations, and for starting others, in order to produce this volume; I thank them also for their generous account of my own work herein. Both the conference and book are perfect examples of the academic strength and vibrancy of dress history across museums and universities the world over today.

Personally, I remain as committed to the subject as when I started and feel so lucky to have found the subject of dress history early in my life. When I was fourteen and on holiday in South Wales we visited a dark, musty antique shop on the sea front at Tenby. At one point the owner, standing in front of a series of tall, dirty windows on the first floor, unrolled a length of material for us to admire. He said nothing about it and even if he had, I would not have understood his references. The gorgeous fabric, flung across the dusty floor, was more clear yellow than green, a piercingly bright, fresh colour like the inside of a fresh lettuce. Dusty rays of sunshine piercing through the gloom caught the fabric's shimmering surface and its beauty really took my breath away. It was a very real shock of delight. I realize now that it was a length of fashionable silk damask probably from about 1740–50 and would have been woven in Spitalfields or even in Lyon. That totally unexpected and glorious sight became a trigger for my work. I have been lucky to have had many similar shocks since – all over the world – and I look forward to more in the future.

References

Auslander, L. (2005), 'Beyond Words', *American Historical Review*, 110 (4): 1015–45.
O'Connor, K. (2005), 'The Material Culture of New Fibres', in S. Küchler and D. Miller (eds), *Clothing as Material Culture*, Oxford: Berg.
Pearce, S. (1993), *Museums, Objects and Collections: A Cultural Study*, Washington, DC: Smithsonian Institution Press.

NOTES ON CONTRIBUTORS

Jennifer Clynk completed her PhD in the Centre for Heritage and Museum Studies at the Australian National University in 2014. Her PhD explored how a family of Quaker drapers in colonial Hobart balanced faith and fashion in their clothing stores. Her main research interests are the social histories of dress, fashion and museums.

Aline T. Monteiro Damgaard studied visual and material culture at Universidade Federal de Goiás, Goiania, Brazil, where she completed her MA with a research-based dissertation on *traje de crioula*. Her work addresses both material and social aspects of nineteenth-century creole clothing and the circulation of printed fabrics in Brazil.

Jonathan Faiers is Reader in Fashion Theory at Winchester School of Art, University of Southampton, UK. His work explores the interface between popular culture, textiles and dress. His published work includes *Tartan* (2008), *Dressing Dangerously: Dysfunctional Fashion in Film* (2013) and chapters in *London Couture 1923–1975: British Luxury* (2015) and *Alexander McQueen* (2015).

Liza Foley is a doctoral candidate at the National College of Art and Design, Dublin, Republic of Ireland. Her thesis focuses on the culture of glove use in eighteenth-century England. Her main research interests include early modern dress, textile and consumption studies, particularly the production and consumption of leather.

Christine M. E. Guth is Senior Tutor at the Royal College of Art in London where she leads the Asian design specialism in the postgraduate History of Design Programme run jointly with the Victoria and Albert Museum. Her publications include *Art, Tea and Industry: Masuda Takashi and the Mitsui Circle* (1993), *Longfellow's Tattoos: Tourism, Collecting, and Japan* (2004) and *Hokusai's Great Wave: Biography of a Global Icon* (2015).

Jane Hattrick lectures in History of Art and Design at University of Brighton, UK, where she completed her PhD, 'A Life in the Archive: The Dress, Design and Identity of the London Couturier Norman Hartnell'. Publications include chapters in *Narrating Objects, Collecting Stories* (2012), *Love Objects: Emotion, Design and Material Culture* (2014) and *London Couture 1923–1975: British Luxury* (2015).

Charlotte Nicklas is Senior Lecturer in History of Art and Design at University of Brighton, UK. Her primary research interest is the dress and textiles of the nineteenth century. She has published in *Fashion Theory, Textile History, Journal of Design History* and in the edited collection, *Surface Tensions* (2013).

Alexandra Palmer is the Nora E. Vaughan Fashion Costume Senior Curator at the Royal Ontario Museum, Toronto, Canada. She has edited and contributed to numerous books, museum catalogues and journals and is the author of *Couture & Commerce: The Transatlantic Fashion Trade in the 1950s* (2001) and *Dior: A New Look, A New Enterprise 1947–1957* (2009).

Sharon Peoples is Convenor of the Museums and Collections Program within the Centre for Heritage and Museums at the Australian National University (ANU). She also lectures at ANU School of Art, and guest lectures for the Art History Department, ANU, where she completed her PhD, 'Military Uniforms in the Eighteenth Century: Gender Power and Politics'.

Annebella Pollen is Director of Historical and Critical Studies at University of Brighton, UK. Her writing on popular image culture and design history has appeared in a wide range of journals and collections and her monograph, *Mass Photography: Collective Histories of Everyday Life*, is forthcoming with I. B. Tauris. Her current AHRC Research Fellowship explores the cultural history of the British woodcraft movement.

Rachel Ritchie is an Associate Research Fellow at Brunel University, London. Her research focuses on women's magazines in the mid- to late-twentieth century, with a particular interest in fashion and beauty. She has published on *Woman* magazine and her research on glamour in 1950s women's magazines has appeared in *Women's History Review*.

Kala Shreen is a sociocultural anthropologist and filmmaker. As the Chairperson of the Centre for Creativity, Heritage and Development in Chennai, India, her research focus includes Indian material culture and heritage. She is also the Director of Cultural Dynamics and Emotions Network, Queen's University Belfast, UK.

Nicola Stylianou was awarded her PhD in 2013 for research into the little-known African textile collection at the Victoria and Albert Museum. Her PhD was funded by an AHRC Collaborative Doctoral Award between the Research Centre for Transnational Art, Identity and Nation at the University of the Arts London and the Victoria and Albert Museum. She currently works as a Research Assistant at the Open University.

Kimberly Wahl is Associate Professor in the School of Fashion at Ryerson University, Canada. Her first book is *Dressed as in a Painting: Women and British Aestheticism in an Age of Reform* (2013). She has also published work on alternative forms of dress in the print culture of the nineteenth century and contemporary fashion photography.

INTRODUCTION: DRESS HISTORY NOW: TERMS, THEMES AND TOOLS

Charlotte Nicklas and Annebella Pollen

Dress history has come of age. Too long ignored, overlooked, and even denigrated, the study of dress is now thriving. Today, scholars from disciplines ranging from anthropology to media studies engage with clothing and its meanings. There remains, however, much to be done, particularly in the investigation of the dress of those who have been marginalized due to ethnicity, geography, gender or social position, or simply because they did or do not fit neatly into pre-existing categories. *Dress History: New Directions in Theory and Practice* brings to light these untold stories. Through original research and innovative case studies, we argue that dress is a fundamental means, indeed sometimes one of the only available ways, by which groups and individuals express and negotiate their identities. The chapters in this volume, while spread across four centuries and a broad range of global locations, are united in their close focus on objects and images of dress and by the ground-breaking research that underpins them. As such, in its showcase of the latest research from around the world, this volume shows how to do cutting-edge dress history.

Dress history as the subject of study: names and positions

Terminology is a perpetual difficulty in the study of dress history: how should 'dress', 'fashion', 'clothing' (or 'clothes') and 'costume' be defined and distinguished from each other? In current scholarship, how do 'dress history', 'fashion history' and 'fashion studies' differ? The meanings of these words and phrases overlap and interconnect, their definitions continuing to challenge researchers

(Cumming 2004: 8, 15; Harte 2009: 176; Taylor 2013: 26). Joanne Eicher and Susan Kaiser both emphasize that 'dress' is an inclusive term, encompassing all adornment and modification of the body. 'Clothing' refers to the objects that are worn. 'Costume' commonly applies to dress worn for specific events, although this word is also used to describe clothing associated with a particular group of people or historical period (Eicher 2010: xiii; Kaiser 1998: 4–5). 'Fashion' implies change in dress over time, as well as the 'dynamic social *process*' by which this change occurs (Kaiser 1998: 4). So, to be in fashion, people wear certain clothes, but not all clothing or dress is fashion. We have used 'dress' in the title of this volume to signal the inclusivity designated by the term. Ranging from the garments of Tasmanian convicts to Norman Hartnell's private wardrobe, this book allows discussion of a very broad range of clothing and wearers, many of which have been hitherto neglected.

As well as considering terms for their subject of study, scholars of past and present fashion and dress must also address the question of what to call their activity. After decades of critique (Taylor 2002a: 67–8), historian Negley Harte recently pronounced 'dress history' a 'sub-discipline of history' (2009: 178). The term 'history', however, suggests certain methodological approaches, particularly the traditional reliance upon archival sources; our volume reflects these core methodological tools, with archives or museum collections featuring prominently across the chapters. Our contributors, however, often turn to unusual or unresearched historical sources and make special efforts to interrogate what is missing or unsaid.

The new research included here reflects the convulsions that history, as a discipline, has undergone in recent decades. After the dramatic refocusing provoked by the social historians of the 1960s, the discipline has experienced successive cultural, visual and material turns as scholars have continued to broaden the way they consider the past (Eley 2005; Tosh 2010). As Taylor argues, these developments helped to make the academic study of dress history possible (2002: 85). Christopher Breward has also noted that design history's focus on production and consumption, along with the growing awareness of the theoretical dimensions of identity and representation in the new art history, also influenced the development of dress history (1998: 302). Although curators have always considered objects crucial in their historical research, scholarly attention to material culture has been an important spur to dress history research outside museums (Küchler and Miller 2005); as will be discussed below, material culture approaches to the understanding of dress underpin much of this volume's content.

Closely related to 'dress history' is 'fashion history'. Peter McNeil and Giorgio Riello, in the introduction to their recent *Fashion History Reader: Global Perspectives*, note that, in research since the mid-twentieth century, 'it was *dress* not *fashion* that was at the centre of historical attention' (2010: 5). McNeil and Riello underscore the important theoretical influences of cultural studies and postmodernism on the growing interest in the study of fashion during the past few decades (2010: 7). They argue that the comparative study of fashion, with its emphasis on change in different periods and locations, provides insight into historical experiences of the passing of time itself (2010: 1–3). 'Fashion studies' has appeared relatively recently as a named academic field, as McNeil and Riello note (2010: 7). Avowedly interdisciplinary, fashion studies incorporates methodologies and critical approaches from fields ranging from history to media studies (Black et al. 2013; Granata 2012; McNeil 2010). Although fashion studies by definition seems to include everything, past and present, related to fashion, much (although not all) of the research that has appeared under this banner concerns the late twentieth and early twenty-first century and contains a strong thrust of critical theory. Many contributors to this volume discuss fashion in original and provocative ways, often working at (and querying) the boundaries between fashion and dress territories. Here, in addition, theoretical tools, from feminism and queer theory to postcolonialism, are fruitfully applied to a range of subjects, including the recent and contemporary. These chapters exemplify the innovative integration of critical theory and dress history.

As Lou Taylor points out, distinguishing these areas of study is challenging, as definitions of 'dress history', 'fashion history' and 'fashion studies' differ across countries, institutions and individuals (2013: 25). These difficulties of definition point to, in part, the ongoing academic debate about disciplinarity, particularly as negotiated in universities. Disciplines established in the late nineteenth and early twentieth centuries, from philosophy to biology, have experienced fundamental changes since the 1960s. In the questioning of disciplinary identities, James Chandler highlights the important role played by what he calls 'shadow disciplines' (2009: 735–7); for our newer area of academic study, the influence of disciplines such as cultural studies and film studies has been profound. Despite the stimulating recent debates about what to call our research, Taylor's preferred name for her work remains 'dress history'. Although keen for museums and the academic world to pay scholarly attention to fashionable clothing as a subject worthy of study, Taylor's term *dress* includes uniforms, work wear, children's garments, ceremonial costume and more within its generous remit. This volume follows her lead in using this term and, indeed – as is discussed below – in applying and extending her suggested methods.

As Jonathan Faiers argues in his chapter – which opens this volume and continues these debates – dress history has, from its inception, drawn on many sources and approached its subject in many ways. While there are methodologies that many dress historians use, there is no established set of practices that one must observe. In fact, Francesca Granata observes that '[i]t might become more precise to call the study of fashion multi-methodological rather than interdisciplinary' (2012: 75). While this wide open territory may be daunting, such inclusiveness allows scholars with many academic backgrounds and approaches to contribute to the ever-growing study of dress history and opens up a range of fertile new directions for new work, such as that contained in this volume, to explore.

As we asserted at the outset, dress and fashion are now well-established subjects of academic study, but some scholars feel that they are still marginalized, particularly within disciplines long-entrenched in universities (Lemire 2010: 1; McNeil 2010: 106; Kawamura 2011: 11). Although quantity of publications is not an index of quality, the sheer number of recent academic books and articles in scholarly journals certainly indicates interest in the topic of dress; indeed, it may be at an all-time high. These journals range from familiar names like *Fashion Theory* and *Costume* to those less frequently cited (by dress historians at least) such as *Comparative Sociology* and the *Journal of Global History*. Studies of dress appear to be in the pink of health; as such, the publication of *Dress History: New Directions in Theory and Practice* is timely. It offers a welcome place to reflect on this new-found – if hard-won – position and to present a range of the newest work from both established scholars and emerging voices.

Standing on the shoulders of giants: *Dress History*'s debts and influences

As noted above, the term dress history has come to prominence especially through the work of Professor Lou Taylor. Any discussion of the area must acknowledge her contribution; this volume is no exception. From a background in fashion design to a half-century-long career in research, curating, teaching and writing, Taylor's contributions to dress history scholarship are unparalleled and have been hugely influential for several generations of scholars, including those who have benefitted directly from her teaching (the present authors included) and those who have engaged with her many publications (all of the contributors to this volume). The most prominent of Taylor's works include 2002's *The Study of Dress History* and 2004's *Establishing Dress History*. These influential historiographies, rooted in her extensive experience in museums and academia, discuss the schisms, secessions and shifts of status in the study and display of dress. The subject, as Taylor repeatedly points out and is at pains to correct, has a long history of being marginalized and perceived as trivial not least because, despite its parallel rigour with the methods of fine art and architecture scholarship, examining clothes in great detail has been seen as merely 'women's work' (2002a: 59).

In Taylor's assessment of the state of the subject in 2002, burgeoning scholarly interest in dress had resulted in the application of an ever-broadening and increasingly interdisciplinary methodological toolkit of research and interpretation strategies; she later described this as a 'maze' (2004: 280). In Taylor's most recent review of dress history's theories and methods for *The Handbook of Fashion Studies*, she notes that there has been further 'escalation' or 'blossoming' in the seemingly limitless variety of theoretical approaches utilized (2013: 23, 40). These include 'performance studies, geography, urban studies, colonial and postcolonial studies, literature studies'. She concludes, happily, 'and on it goes'. From this plethora of possibilities, however, Taylor asks a key methodological question: 'What critical stances does the drowning researcher leave in, without overconfusing the story, and what can she/he leave out without compromising it?' (2013: 23) These are challenges debated and played out in practice through the contributions to this volume. In our opening chapter, Faiers addresses precisely these questions, head on.

The Study of Dress History and *Establishing Dress History* are both dedicated to evaluating, in detail, the practicalities and potential of older and newer methods of research and interpretation, with an underlying plea for the union of close observation and description (from the so-called catalogue tradition of dress collectors, enthusiasts and curators) with the scholarly, analytical approaches of, for example, cultural, social and economic history and museological theory. In pragmatic terms, Taylor warns that the aspiring scholar should not scrimp on study of the 'minute detail' of garments; this, she argues, is precisely what gives 'the required period identification which in turn provides the basis upon which cultural theory can later be viably applied' (2002a: 12). In other words, for Taylor, the 'actuality of clothing' (2002a: 98) must come first, and remain central, for the study of dress to be meaningfully and materially grounded; in each of the case study chapters of this volume, the artefacts – or the pursuit of them, when they are not readily available – are at the heart of the debate. There are few shortcuts that can be made in this painstaking yet creative process of knowledge acquisition, and Taylor argues that assumptions should not be made, nor, indeed, theory applied, until close attention has been paid to an artefact's core and sometimes subtle material aspects, including cut, construction and manufacture; in this, we aim to follow her lead.

Unsurprisingly, given her attention to detailed observation, grounded in experience, many of Taylor's key points of reference come from collectors and museum practice, the disciplinary approaches of anthropology and the associated methods of material culture studies. Igor Kopytoff's (1986) 'social biography of things' model and Claude Lévi-Strauss's (1966) dictum that 'things are good to think with' form more or less visible centrepieces of much of Taylor's writing and teaching. Their principles also underpin the research in this collection. Taylor's interest in ethnography (while not necessarily employing what would be strictly understood as an ethnographic methodology) is also evident in her longstanding interest in dress held in ethnographic and open air museum collections, her interest in clothing and nationality (2000, 2002b), in fashion outside of the dominant Euro-American context, and in hybrid objects that cross cultural boundaries. These are territories shared by the contributors to this volume.

Social history, particularly in its attention to those who have been excluded from historical posterity, is another of Taylor's core disciplinary influences. Frustrated by the dominant emphasis of dress publishing and exhibiting on elite clothing, Taylor complained that it seemed that '90 per cent of books on dress at the start of the new millennium are about the clothes of the two or three hundred women who can afford these garments' (2004: 1), or as she has put it elsewhere, 'the top 0.5 per cent wealthy of Europe and the USA' (2002: 51). The contributors to this volume respond to this challenge by looking further afield or by looking in different ways at the celebrated names. Inspired by 'history from below', Taylor has argued passionately for the study of mass-produced, ready-to-wear, working class and everyday clothing, and has collected examples of used, adapted and museum-rejected garments from these largely overlooked categories in the study of dress for the purposes of teaching and research throughout her professional life; several of our contributors do the same. The collecting practices of museums (and their exclusions) form a key part of Taylor's *Establishing Dress History*; in this volume the theme is taken up again and explored through the prism of a range of original and global examples.

Taylor's passion for social history's disciplinary approaches also extends to her promotion of one of its core research methods, that of oral history; several contributors to this volume also adopt this approach to explore the lived experience of dress. The grounded, personal insights that first-person accounts can generate also accords with Taylor's interest in the affective processes of memory, attachment and dress and the senses, all areas that she feels are neglected. As she has put it, 'One of the great voids of dress history has been its failure to establish emotional responses to clothing and appearance. Perhaps design/dress historians in their search for academic respectability have become over-nervous about departing from safely established academic methodologies, but in doing so they have missed a key approach to which others are increasingly turning' (2002a: 102). The deeply personal and affective sensual quality of garments, worn close to the body and literally and metaphorically porous, is taken up by several contributors in the case-study chapters that follow.

Acknowledging the potential analytical uses of a range of disciplinary perspectives, from sociology to semiotics, and cultural theories from subculture to feminism, Taylor has highlighted the necessity of combining theoretical and empirical studies of dress, albeit with some cautionary provisos. Giving short shrift to, for example, psychoanalytic and philosophical approaches that may offer theories of dress unrelated to or in opposition with dress-as-worn, and little impressed by studies that focus on the representations of clothing without integrated comparative analysis with actual clothing or its experience, Taylor is certainly dismissive of theory for its own sake. In terms of methodology, she has expressed uncertainty, for example, about where the fine line might fall between leading-out from objects to appropriate theories and the less preferable working-back from theories to objects. As she put it, back in 2002, the validity of such processes in dress studies is 'the essence of future debate' in the subject (2002a: 85). In the same year Taylor observed that the role new theoretical approaches may play in dress scholarship 'is a key question for the future of the field and one that may be resolved only through the reality of museum and other historical research and practice' (2002a: 74). Importantly, Taylor also indicated that future dress historians should not only adopt and apply existing theories, but also devise new strategies of their own (2002a: 85). *Dress History: New Directions in Theory and Practice* inhabits precisely that future and, from the volume's title onwards, takes up the gauntlet of Taylor's methodological challenges by gathering together the latest research and analysis in subject areas that specifically engage with and update these concerns, addressing gaps and advancing theoretical thinking, a decade after Taylor's key publications.

Developments in Dress History: a snapshot of current practice

In December 2011, the University of Brighton planned and hosted an international conference entitled Developments in Dress History. Convened by Dr Louise Purbrick, the event was designed to reflect on Taylor's contribution to the discipline of dress history through more than forty years of teaching and fifty years of curatorial experience, and to evaluate dress history's current academic position. From this departure point, contributions that explored the widest range of cultural and historical contexts for dress were invited. As a gathering of established and emerging scholars from across the globe, the contributors, topics, themes and analytical approaches included offer a telling snapshot of the state of dress history now.

More than seventy papers were presented and the conference was attended by 150 delegates from India, Brazil, Australia, New Zealand, Canada and the United States, as well as Poland, France, Greece, the Netherlands, Scandinavia, the Republic of Ireland and Great Britain; these included collectors, curators and academics of all stripes. The spread of subject areas extended the geographical territory even further, with case studies of regional and national clothing from Panama, Argentina, Korea, China, Qatar and Ethiopia. This spread is testament to the increasingly global identity of dress history in the twenty-first century and also new ways of thinking about dress and place. Significantly, many papers explored concepts of transnationality, postcolonialism, hybridity and ethnicity as core debates in their interpretations, challenging traditional ideas that fashion is a capitalist system based in modernity and conceived in the West that only later 'goes global'.

Dress was broadly understood by respondents to the conference invitation, and manifested itself in an eclectic range of subjects from military uniform and fancy dress to strait jackets and dance tutus; the reach even extended to dressed dolls and undressed mannequins. Contributors considered the humble, even unfashionable, nineteenth-century American 'Mother Hubbard' dress and 1950s British housecoat alongside the plainness of Mennonite and Quaker clothing. In contrast, others examined the spectacle and luxury of the wardrobes of monarchs and aristocrats or reappraised couturiers to the rich and famous. Time periods under scrutiny stretched from the early modern to the twenty-first century via seventeenth-century lace, the eighteenth-century silk industry, nineteenth-century dye technology and twentieth-century fashion shows, to name but a few examples.

In keeping with Taylor's embrace of a broad range of sources for the study of dress history, speakers explored not only surviving garments but also dress in paintings and photographic archives, press cartoons and magazine pages, engravings and illustrations, plays and autobiographies, diaries and personal letters, wills and inventories, business accounts and household expenses, retail sites and advertisements, moving image and statuary. Several dress historians examined the methodological challenges of working with gaps, with missing artefacts, mystery objects and family secrets. In response to Taylor's ground-breaking work on the role of dress in museums and galleries, contributors revisited historic dress exhibitions and pioneering collectors and analysed curatorial thinking in new strategies and forms of dress display. In dialogue with Taylor's particular engagement with terminology, several papers offered new approaches to contested definitions of fashion, dress, costume and their various conjunctions, antagonisms and spaces between. Through a wide range of explorations of the inherent relationship between dress and identity, speakers examined class, gender and generation; politics, spirituality and sexuality; health, ethics and morality. Histories of dress were enhanced and contextualized by histories of science, education and manufacturing. Research methods and theoretical approaches from ethnography and iconography, sociology and oral testimony were used to examine dress as a sensual and material phenomenon, as well as memory, myth and metaphor.

Dress History: themes, content and structure

Drawing initially from the deep pool of subject areas and methodological approaches explored in the context of Developments in Dress History, *Dress History: New Directions in Theory and Practice* presents a selection of new case studies that engage with pressing critical debates, and develop and reflect on research methods, in order to showcase the latest thinking in the field and new contributions to the expanding literature in dress history. Following Chapter 1 by Faiers, who examines the historiography of dress history to argue for new ways of thinking about interdisciplinarity, eleven chronological chapters provide a series of illuminating historical case studies, from the eighteenth century to the present, in order to explore a range of key issues in dress history today.

Over the past ten years, scholars have done much to move beyond dress history's traditional focus on the Northwestern European and North American elites (Taylor 2002: 51). Robert Ross (2008) and Patricia Rieff Anawalt (2007), for example, have published histories of dress that approach the subject as a global phenomenon. In addition to these wide-ranging studies, scholars are also addressing the history of clothing and fashion in specific locations outside Western Europe and North America, including Communist Europe (Bartlett 2010), Africa (Jennings 2011), Latin America (Root 2005) and particularly China (Finnane 2008; Wu 2009; Hua 2011). This research is often, although not always, related to work on ethnic and racial identities as expressed through dress and appearance. This volume also challenges the parameters of those usually considered deserving of attention and the usual privileges of geography and race, and includes Asia, Africa, Australasia and South America as well as Euro-American subject areas. Similarly, it examines lesser-known figures as much as celebrated designers, makers and collectors of clothes. Jennifer Clynk and Sharon Peoples, for example, in Chapter 3, explore the dress of transported convicts and emancipists in nineteenth-century Tasmania, explicitly seeking new approaches to address silences and historical erasures. Aline T. Monteiro Damgaard's research on the dress of Afro-Brazilian slaves and their descendants in eighteenth- and nineteenth-century Brazil, in Chapter 4, continues this theme in providing a new view of an area that has remained relatively unexplored. Studying subjects who lack status and who have left few remaining garments, both chapters wrestle with the challenges of exploring areas of dress history riddled with omissions and myths. In the case of Kala Shreen's case study in Chapter 12, the *sungudi* sari textile – which is her focus in present-day India – while apparently 'traditional' and regional is shown to be mobilized by a range of modern heritage discourses; at the same time, it communicates a new, global fashionable identity.

There is a rich tradition in anthropology of considering dress as material culture, pioneered by Joanne Eicher and Mary Ellen Roach (1965) and more recently substantially augmented by Daniel Miller in his work with Susanne Küchler (2005). Contributors to this collection similarly consider materiality as central to their analysis and utilize anthropologically informed methods. Liza Foley (Chapter 2) argues that the particular material conditions of the Limerick gloves that she analyses – made from the skins of aborted, stillborn or short-lived calves – transferred directly into their meanings as refined, rare gifts in the late eighteenth and early nineteenth centuries. The influence of anthropologist Igor Kopytoff's social biographical method (1986), as mentioned above in relation to Taylor's work, is also evident in Chapter 5, where Nicola Stylianou follows the journey of garments that once belonged to a nineteenth-century Ethiopian queen through a series of status changes and revaluations from colonial looted booty to postcolonial museological critique.

As well as examining new geographies, recent dress history also attends to historically marginalized and overlooked groups. Sophie Woodward, for example, has fruitfully applied ethnographic methods to her analysis of ordinary British women's clothing choices in the present day (2007), moving away from the conventional focus on the dress of the rich, privileged and white. Taking a longer historical view, John Styles (2007) has provided ground-breaking analysis of fashion and clothing of ordinary people in eighteenth-century England using a rich mix of archival and material sources, while Alison Toplis has investigated working-class acquisition of clothing in provincial Britain during the nineteenth century (2011). Contributors to this collection, such as Damgaard on slaves and Peoples and Clynk on convicts, explicitly investigate social groups with troubled histories who have been socially marginalized. In her discussion of *sungudi* craftswomen in Tamilnadu, Shreen shows how, despite efforts to elevate the status of their products, these makers are still clearly excluded from the design process; marginalization of women involved in the 'women's work' of textile-making thus continues to the present day. While dealing with a very different population, Rachel Ritchie (Chapter 10) highlights how some areas – the rural – have long been overlooked as sites of fashion. Reappraising the role of dress in a group often thought to exist outside of such concerns – housewives in 1950s and 1960s rural England – Ritchie demonstrates that even those far from fashion centres and arguably culturally marginalized could think very carefully about the meanings of their appearance. Related dress history research that has turned the spotlight away from spectacular and extraordinary has recently focused on common objects of dress, including the sunbonnet (Matheson 2009), the cotton dress (Boydell 2010) and the button (Edwards 2012) as a way of illuminating everyday dress practices. Alongside Ritchie, in this volume, Foley's appraisal of the glove and Annebella Pollen's analysis of the humble, sensible shoe (Chapter 11) utilize such unassuming artefacts as devices through which complex cultural stories can be told.

Gender has long provided a key point of interpretation in dress history (Kidwell and Steele 1989; Eicher and Barnes 1992), but as Christopher Breward pointed out in *The Hidden Consumer* (1999), men's fashion and dress history (unlike men's history) has been overlooked. Over the past decade, however, scholars have done much spadework to tackle this neglect, including the publication of not one, but two *Men's Fashion Reader*s (Reilly and Cosbey 2008; Karaminas and McNeil 2009). While the dress practices of Norman Hartnell, Raymond Duncan and Edward Carpenter (in Hattrick, Palmer and Pollen, respectively) form three focus points of this volume, each subject pushes at the boundaries of normative clothing styles and gender designations; menswear in these unisex or cross-dressed contexts challenges the category itself. The constraints of female gender roles in the late nineteenth century frame Christine M. E. Guth's examination of the interconnectedness of self, collections and display in the life and museum of Isabella Stewart Gardner (Chapter 7). Guth illuminates the way that dress and textiles can be used as a uniquely privileged means to self-fashion and perform public and private identities. In their chapters, Kimberly Wahl and Annebella Pollen also explore the role that dress has played in efforts at female emancipation. In another facet of the exploration of gender roles and dress, Shaun Cole has led the way in mapping the history of gay dress (2000). This subject has seen a recent efflorescence, demonstrated by Adam Geczy and Vicki Karaminas's *Queer Style* (2010) and a major exhibition at the Fashion Institute of Technology in New York (Steele 2013). Jane Hattrick, in Chapter 9 of this volume, argues that to ignore the gay sexual identity of her case study, London couturier Norman Hartnell, is to miss the central shaping factor in his life and his designs. By looking again at Hartnell's oeuvre and at a range of previously unanalysed archival sources, like several other contributors (Stylianou, Peoples and Clynk), Hattrick develops her argument by reading sources against the grain.

Alexandra Palmer's research on Raymond Duncan (Chapter 8), akin to chapters by Hattrick and Guth, explores the distinctive perspective of a single public figure through examining the role of dress in his life and work. While less well-remembered than Hartnell or Gardner, Duncan provides a pertinent and expansive example of the ways that cloth can be used as part of a complex, if eccentric, total system for living. Duncan's combination of historic revivalism with modernist ways of thinking, and the way in which these ideas were expressed in his dress and textiles, both fit within and stand defiantly outside existing design styles and schools of thought. Wahl (Chapter 6) and Pollen (Chapter 11) also examine the role of dress as aesthetic resistance. Wahl examines the ways in which nineteenth-century ideals of dress reform – comfort, creativity and freedom from convention – were played out differently in aesthetic clothing in visual and material form, while Pollen explores the contested status of fashion for British second-wave feminists. Clothing as rebellion has long held a central place in dress history, not least in the work of Elizabeth Wilson (2000, 2005); subcultural style also has a prominent position in cultural studies more broadly, from the influential work of Dick Hebdige (1979) to the second generation of subcultural scholars including David Muggleton (2000), Paul Hodkinson (2002) and, most recently, Yuniya Kawamura (2012). Chapters in this volume extend and add value to these discussions.

As Taylor has noted, collections of images of dress constituted the very first dress history texts in the sixteenth century (2004: 5). Aileen Ribeiro has done much to interpret dress in images, particularly paintings (1998). In recent years, scholars have interrogated the relationship between fashion and visual culture using a broad range of sources, from fashion photography (Shinkle 2008) to Impressionist paintings (Groom 2012). In this volume, Wahl and Damgaard, in different ways, engage with the challenges of comparing extant garments with their often better-known visual representations; similarly Guth and Hattrick examine the careful decisions made in dressing for paintings and photographs by their respective subjects. The methodological challenges of working across media and forms and with eclectic and sometimes elusive sources are tackled by many of our contributors, using a range of theoretical tools. Together these constitute a rich range of dress historical subjects, debates and critical approaches.

Worn by all but scrutinized by far too few, whether spectacular or humble, celebrated or ignored, cherished or discarded, dress has a uniquely expressive capacity to carry a range of cultural information and meanings, past and present. As contributors to this volume show, the privileged communicative capacity of dress applies across genders and geographies, occupations and ethnicities, and can encompass a range of philosophical and political positions. As such, dress and textiles offer a deeply productive means to explore a range of pertinent historical and theoretical concerns; however, it is important not to diminish clothing as merely a mouthpiece through which to discuss other issues. In each of our case studies, dress is deliberately the core focus of attention. The particular material qualities and affordances of clothing – sensual, intimate and proximate to the body, while simultaneously public, declarative and performative – place it at centre stage culturally as well as at the heart of lived experience. Materially and metaphorically, dress can variously conceal, embellish, envelop and shape ideas as well as bodies. Through its chapters, this volume weaves these diverse strands together to form a richly textured collection of new work and fresh perspectives. Dress history as an area of study, a research tool and a way of thinking offers exciting possibilities to its scholars and students. *Dress History: New Directions in Theory and Practice* revels in this richness and adds further substance to the scholarship.

References

Anawalt, P. R. (2007), *The Worldwide History of Dress*, London: Thames and Hudson.
Bartlett, D. (2010), *FashionEast: The Spectre that Haunted Socialism*, Cambridge, MA and London: MIT Press.
Black, S. et al. (eds) (2013), *The Handbook of Fashion Studies*, London and New York: Bloomsbury.

Boydell, C. (2010), *Horrockses Fashions: Off-the-peg Style in the '40s and '50s*, London: V&A Publishing.

Breward, C. (1998), 'Cultures, Identities, Histories: Fashioning a Cultural Approach to Dress', *Fashion Theory*, 2 (4): 301–14.

Breward, C. (1999), *The Hidden Consumer: Masculinities, Fashion and City Life, 1860–1914*, Manchester: Manchester University Press.

Chandler, J. (2009), 'Introduction: Doctrine, Disciplines, Discourses, Departments', *Critical Inquiry*, 35 (4): 729–46.

Cole, S. (2000), *'Don We Now Our Gay Apparel': Gay Men's Dress in the Twentieth Century*, Oxford: Berg.

Crowley, D. and Taylor, L. (eds) (2000), *The Lost Arts of Haslemere: The Haslemere Museum Collection of European Peasant Art: A Collection of Essays*, Haslemere: Haslemere Educational Museum.

Cumming, V. (2004), *Understanding Fashion History*, London: Batsford.

Edwards, N. (2012), *On the Button: The Significance of an Ordinary Object*, London: I.B. Tauris.

Eicher, J. (ed.) (2010), *Berg Encyclopedia of World Dress and Fashion: Global Perspectives*, vol. 10, Oxford: Berg.

Eicher, J. and Barnes, R. (1992), *Dress and Gender: Making and Meaning in Cultural Contexts*, New York and Oxford: Berg.

Eicher, J. and Roach, M. E. (1965), *Dress, Adornment and the Social Order*, New York and London: Wiley.

Eley, G. (2005), *A Crooked Line: From Cultural History to the History of Society*, Ann Arbor, MI: University of Michigan Press.

Finnane, A. (2008), *Changing Clothes in China: Fashion, History, Nation*, New York: Columbia University Press.

Granata, F. (2012), 'Fashion Studies In-Between: A Methodological Case Study and an Inquiry into the State of Fashion Studies', *Fashion Theory*, 16 (1): 67–82.

Groom, G. (ed.) (2012), *Impressionism, Fashion and Modernity*, New Haven and London: Yale University Press.

Harte, N. (2009), review of *The Dress of the People* (John Styles), *Costume*, 43: 176–8.

Hebdige, D. (1979), *Subculture: The Meaning of Style*, London and New York: Methuen.

Hodkinson, P. (2002), *Goth: Identity, Style and Subculture*, Oxford: Berg.

Hua, M. (2011), *Chinese Clothing*, Cambridge: Cambridge University Press.

Jennings, H. (2011), *New African Fashion*, Munich and London: Prestel.

Kaiser, S. (1998), *The Social Psychology of Clothing: Symbolic Appearances in Context*, 2nd rev. edition, New York: Fairchild Publications.

Karaminas, V. (2013), *Queer Style*, Oxford: Berg.

Karaminas, V. and McNeil, P. (eds) (2009), *The Men's Fashion Reader*, Oxford: Berg.

Kawamura, Y. (2011), *Doing Research in Fashion and Dress: An Introduction to Qualitative Methods*, Oxford and New York: Berg.

Kawamura, Y. (2012), *Fashioning Japanese Subcultures*, Oxford and New York: Berg.

Kidwell, C. B. and Steele, V. (1989), *Men and Women: Dressing the Part*, Washington, DC: Smithsonian Institution Press.

Kopytoff, I. (1986), 'The Cultural Biography of Things: Commodization as Process', in A. Appadurai (ed.), *The Social Life of Things: Commodities in Cultural Perspective*, Cambridge and New York: Cambridge University Press.

Lemire, B. (ed.) (2010), 'Introduction', in *The Force of Fashion in Politics and Society: Global Perspectives from Early Modern to Contemporary Times*, Farnham: Ashgate.

Lévi-Strauss, C. (1966), *The Savage Mind*, Chicago: Chicago University Press.

Matheson, R. J. (2009), *The Sunbonnet: An American Icon in Texas*, Lubbock: Texas Tech University Press.

McNeil, P. (2010), 'Conference Report: "The Future of Fashion Studies"', *Fashion Theory*, 14 (1): 105–10.

McNeil, P. and Riello, G. (2010), 'Introduction', in *The Fashion History Reader: Global Perspectives*, Abingdon: Routledge.

Miller, D. and Küchler, S. (2005), *Clothing as Material Culture*, Oxford: Berg.

Muggleton, D. (2000), *Inside Subculture: The Postmodern Meaning of Style*, Oxford: Berg.

Reilly, A. and Cosbey, S. (eds) (2008), *The Men's Fashion Reader*, New York: Fairchild.

Ribeiro, A. (1998), 'Re-Fashioning Art: Some Visual Approaches to the Study of the History of Dress', *Fashion Theory*, 2 (4): 315–25.

Root, R. (ed.) (2005), *The Latin American Fashion Reader*, Oxford: Berg.

Ross, R. (2008), *Clothing: A Global History*, Cambridge: Polity.

Shinkle, E. (2008), *Fashion as Photograph: Viewing and Reviewing Images of Fashion*, London: I.B. Tauris.

Steele, V. (ed.) (2013), *A Queer History of Fashion: From the Closet to the Catwalk*, New Haven and London: Yale University Press.

Styles, J. (2007), *The Dress of the People: Everyday Fashion in Eighteenth-century England*, New Haven and London: Yale University Press.

Taylor, L. (2002a), *The Study of Dress History*, Manchester: Manchester University Press.

Taylor, L. (2002b), 'The Wardrobe of Mrs Leonard Messel, 1895–1920', in C. Cox et al. (eds), *The Englishness of English Dress*, Oxford: Berg.

Taylor, L. (2004), *Establishing Dress History*, Manchester: Manchester University Press.

Taylor, L. (2013), 'Fashion and Dress History: Theoretical and Methodological Approaches', in S. Black et al. (eds), *The Handbook of Fashion Studies*, London and New York: Bloomsbury.

Toplis, A. (2011), *The Clothing Trade in Provincial England, 1800–1850*, London: Pickering and Chatto.

Tosh, J. (2010), *The Pursuit of History: Aims, Methods, and New Directions in the Study of Modern History*, Harlow: Longman; Pearson.

Wilson, E. (2000), *Bohemians: The Glamorous Outcasts*, London: I.B. Tauris.

Wilson, E. (2005), *Adorned in Dreams: Fashion and Modernity*, rev. edition, London: I.B. Tauris.

Woodward, S. (2007), *Why Women Wear What They Wear*, Oxford: Berg.

Wu, J. (2009), *Chinese Fashion: From Mao to Now*, Oxford: Berg.

1 DRESS THINKING: DISCIPLINES AND INDISCIPLINARITY

Jonathan Faiers

Why is the study of dress history so often encountered, investigated and understood as one half of an equation? The use of the ubiquitous *and* has become a dominant feature of the landscape of dress history, and indeed of dress studies and fashion theory. It is as if dress history is doomed to a partial existence in constant need of an additional field of study or context in order for it to assert its credibility. While dress history and studies revels in its self-perception as interdisciplinary, promising its students exciting excursions into alternative theoretical territories, it often as not comes as a poor relation to the table, invoking more 'well-connected' cousins such as anthropology, economics or psychology. Since Lou Taylor's pioneering work in the formation of dress history (2002, 2004), utilizing clothing as primary historical evidence, rather than as somehow secondary or additional, the field has been dazzled by an increasing number of seductive disciplinary additions. Interestingly, it is 'fashion and . . .' that occurs more frequently now, whereas 'dress and . . .' is more commonly incorporated into titles that preceded Taylor's publications, suggesting that her work provided a corrective to the methodology of dress studies if not to fashion theory. A brief and partial survey highlights this break: *Dress and Undress* (Ewing 1978), *Dress and Morality* (Ribeiro 1986), *Dress and Identity* (Eicher, Roach-Higgins and Johnson 1995), *Fashion and Fiction* (Ribeiro 2005), *Fashion and Psychoanalysis* (Bancroft 2012), *Fashion and Minimalism* (Dimant 2012) and *Fashion and Cultural Studies* (Kaiser 2013).

This chapter will suggest that in order for the field to develop and remain challenging, a similar debate needs to take place to that which has recently occurred concerning the relations among art, craft and design. The discrete territories implied by these terms have been explored, and the status of each tested by considering the impact of new technologies on our understanding of 'making'. An increasing number of exhibitions have been staged that blur disciplinary lines, such as those held at the Victoria & Albert Museum: *Out of The Ordinary* (2007), *The Power of Making* (2011) and the furniture design/art show *Telling Tales* (2009). Whether we regard an object as art, craft or design is no longer a case of consigning it to classificatory restrictions, but rather allowing it to inhabit all three, moving freely in and out of these aesthetic, economic and conceptual boundaries at will (Adamson 2007; Britton Newell 2007; Coles 2005, 2007). If interdisciplinarity is to mean anything it must count for more than the ceaseless search for the next fashionable alliance, and allow us to realize the potential of the *inter* of *inter*disciplinarity and situate dress history among, and at the centre of, critical enquiry rather than on one side forever fighting for its ascendancy.

Interdisciplinarity or indisciplinarity?

This chapter will consider some of the pioneering works in the field of dress history. Although these works predate any notion of interdisciplinarity, I believe they achieve an enviable 'indisciplinarity', a condition that offers an alternative to the contemporary disciplinary side-taking threatening to cannibalize our field. Before proceeding any further, however, it should be made clear that this chapter is in no way intended to be some sort of polemic against the current state of dress studies or history, or of fashion theory. Much exciting and challenging work continues to be produced and is pushing, and hopefully eroding, some of the boundaries that can too often territorialize the field and encourage internecine tension among its voices. However, it is also symptomatic of the current situation that so early into this text it is necessary to list and categorize our field as a history, a study and a theory, and to distinguish between fashion and dress. Here we might understand dress history or studies to be concerned with the close study of individual garments and their construction analysed as a means of tracing not only the changes in the manufacture of garments, but also as a means of comprehending wider political and socio-economic developments. Dress studies also implies a broader range of material than fashion, encompassing occupational, non-Western and everyday dress. Fashion is often, but certainly not exclusively, understood as Western, worn by the privileged and from the nineteenth century, at least, identified strongly with a notion of modernity. Elizabeth Wilson's *Adorned in Dreams: Fashion and Modernity* (1985) is widely regarded as instrumental in this understanding of fashion as 'modern'. When fashion is further complicated by the addition of the word theory we assume that a specific conceptual framework will be applied and form the basis of any subsequent analysis and interrogation of fashion and its multivalency.

Do these various terms constitute a discipline? Or are they just symptomatic of a taxonomic malaise that it is hard to resist, and which often leads to a form of negative litany, to state what dress history, studies or theory is not, rather than what it could be? This impulse is also responsible in part for the ubiquity of conjunctions, leading to a belief that the field can only become more meaningful, more universal, and more dare I say it, well-regarded, if it accessorizes itself with another branch of thought. As James Chandler suggests in his introduction to the special edition of *Critical Inquiry* devoted to 'The Fate of Disciplines': 'For a discipline to do its work it must have a home base and a sense of its identity over time; it must have a local habitation and a name' (2009: 734). Not only is the name of our field in constant flux, but its home might, according to the author's perspective, be the museum, the archive, the personal collection, the factory floor, the retail outlet, the novel, the film, the internet . . . the list of possible habitats is apparently endless.

It is as though the field has undergone the same journey that Gustave Flaubert's enthusiastic students Bouvard and Pécuchet took in his 1880 novel of the same name, sampling with eager excitement new disciplines, but all too swiftly finding the tenets of each too inflexible and too limiting, finding exceptions to, rather than, *the* rule. Indeed, their attempts to master the various disciplines' complexities prove ultimately impossible, and force Pécuchet to wonder: 'Where is the rule then, and what hope can we have of success or profit?' (1976: 56) Such a plea that might just as easily come from the contemporary student of dress history. Taylor's recent essay 'Fashion and Dress History: Theoretical and Methodological Approaches' echoes exactly the frustration felt by Flaubert's clerks and takes up the position of the contemporary 'bewildered incoming student' or 'drowning researcher' at a loss to know what critical positions to retain and which to leave out of any study of fashion and dress history (2013: 23).

While interdisciplinarity has become a linguistic talisman ensuring increased readership, increased student intake, and even increased funding opportunities, I am led to wonder how interdisciplinary the field really is. Can the addition of one other body of thought alongside dress, fashion or textiles really justify the 'inter-' of 'interdisciplinarity'? If we consider the prefix's most fundamental meaning; that is to be between, among, amid and so on, can the fitting of an additional prosthetic discipline really constitute this position? Surely it more often leads to an either/or situation, or a reaffirmation of the limits of dress, continually butting up against architecture, or museums or ethnography, an impasse no amount of conjunctive 'ands' can successfully clear away. Julie Klein in her pioneering *Interdisciplinarity: History, Theory and Practice* (1990) traces the origins of what we might understand the term 'interdisciplinarity' to convey. Although she concentrates largely on the sciences, she does illuminate one of the ultimate paradoxes of those who advocate interdisciplinarity: while they might consider themselves true interdisciplinarians, they are interdisciplinary *within* the limited terrain of their own specialisms and so in fact are often unaware, or choose not to avail themselves of the interdisciplinary approaches that colleagues in similar, but not identical, fields are exploring. As she argues: 'The majority of people engaged in interdisciplinary work lack a common identity. As a result, they often find themselves homeless, in a state of social and intellectual marginality'. She goes on to suggest: 'The cost of ignoring these commonalities are enormous. Instead of sharpened methodologies, broadened theories, and improved communication, there are disputed borrowings, aborted projects, frayed nerves, and continued scepticism about the whole interdisciplinary enterprise' (1990: 13–14).

Despite the passage of time, it seems that we still search for literary and textual boundaries, embarrassed by the limitless possibilities offered when we survey the territories of dress history. Whereas Bouvard and Pécuchet resign themselves at the end of the novel to intellectual defeat and content themselves with the prospect of copying out the various books and treatises that have bewildered them, perhaps the field under discussion could find a way of speaking about dress that neither consigns it to a museum case nor tries to keep up with its digital dissemination, that lets it trickle up *and* down, move fast *or* slow, and is sustainable not only in its production, but also in its discourse.

Dress history needs to regain some of its former flexibility, to be less concerned with seeking definitions or alliances, and to re-experience the pleasure, offered by considering what we chose and continue to choose to cover our bodies with. This might seem wilfully naïve, but it occurs to me that dress history needs to embrace indeterminacy and fluctuation. This need not mean anti-specialism, but rather multi-, or more precisely inter-specialism. This approach would encourage real interdisciplinarity and provide a way to speak about dress and its many representations. In this chapter I suggest that the state of disciplinary 'homelessness' that both Chandler and Klein identify as problematic for those who consider their work as interdisciplinary is in fact something that needs to be accepted, and not only accepted but celebrated and exploited. In order to do this I revisit some of the seminal moments in the history of dress history, the work of what I like to think of as the proto-interdisciplinarians, or, to borrow W. J. T. Mitchell's marvellous term, 'indisciplinarians'. Such a term implies the ability to be among disciplines but also to be outside of, oblivious to, or even unwilling to be 'disciplined', and to be more interested in 'forms of "indiscipline", turbulence or incoherence at the inner and outer boundaries of discipline'. As Mitchell puts it, '"indiscipline" is a moment of breakage or rupture, when the continuity is broken and the practice comes into question' (1995: 541).

Strangers in a strange land

James Laver was described in his obituary in *Costume* in 1976 as 'the man in England who made the study of costume respectable' (Gibbs-Smith 1976: 123–4). He might not have recognized himself as such, but certainly was well aware of the state of bewilderment that the necessary interdisciplinarity (or as some critics would suggest dilettantism) he adopted in order to pursue the development of dress history caused among his friends and colleagues. I am referring to Laver's own account of how he was regarded by his associates, which was quoted in his *Times* obituary subtitled 'A Polymath of Formidable Virtuosity': 'To my colleagues at South Kensington I had become a cigar-smoking, Savoy-supping, enviable but slightly disreputable character, hobnobbing with chorus girls and hanging round stage doors. To Gertrude Lawrence and her friends I was something "in a museum", engaged in mysterious and apparently useless activities quite outside their comprehension; a character out of "The Old Curiosity Shop", hardly fit to be let out alone' ('Obituary' 1975: 43).

Laver's 1969 *A Concise History of Costume* remains a classic 'beginner' text for the student of costume history, and since his death in its revised and updated form has been re-titled as *Costume and Fashion: A Concise History* (noticeably allowing for the apparently obligatory conjunction). While both Laver's and his contemporary C. Willett Cunnington's sartorial insights into the nascent field of dress history are widely acknowledged, their patriarchal attitude to women's dress is something that has also featured in accounts of their work. For example, Laver's celebrated establishment of the concept of the shifting erogenous zone being at least partly inspired by male scopophilia, as he termed it the 'bust, belly and behind business' (Gibbs-Smith 1976), has been commented upon by authors such as Elizabeth Wilson who notes that 'he argued that the back was eroticized because men were no longer turned on by legs' (2007: 92). Similarly, one only has to glance at Cunnington's *The Perfect Lady* to find abundant examples of the frankly lascivious prose and sustained trivialization of women to which subsequent feminist dress historians have objected, such as this description of 1870s women's fashion: 'Though the luscious curvatures of the late Seventies may be out of touch with modern taste, still they do not perplex us; their former fascination is quite understandable' (1948b: 2).

All this notwithstanding, Laver's *Style in Costume* (1949) remains, I argue, a dazzlingly interdisciplinary trailblazer for subsequent developments in dress history. The juxtaposition of trunk-hose next to Elizabethan table legs, top hats with chimneys and a disturbingly vacant image of a fashionable woman from 1928 dwarfing the Empire State Building not only seems the perfect realization of the surrealist desire for 'the chance juxtaposition of a sewing machine and an umbrella on a dissecting table' (Lautréamont 1978: 217) but a dazzling example of the indisciplinarity mentioned previously (Figures 1.1 and 1.2). It took an author such as Laver, equally versed in writing musical comedy reviews and poetry, expert in the occult, astrology and amateur mountaineering (to list just a few of his accomplishments), to produce such a deliriously surreal exploration of clothing's imbrication with the applied arts. It could easily be ranked alongside the most startling examples of present-day fashion image-making. *Style in Costume* selects examples of dress drawn from different eras and

FIGURE 1.1 'Top Hats' and 'Chimneys' from James Laver, *Style in Costume*, Oxford University Press, 1949.

aligns these with chronologically similar images of architecture, applied arts and elements of interior design, suggesting an inescapable link between changing tastes in clothing and technological and artistic developments. Laver describes his methodology as 'strictly non-scientific, which is a different thing from unscientific', and goes onto to state that this method of visual juxtaposition is 'a mere hint, a signpost into the Unknown, a reminder that we have by no means arrived at the city of knowledge, and that vast uncharted regions lie beyond' (1949: 7). This statement displays an admirable acceptance of both the limits and the possibilities of his fledgling discipline, or perhaps an early acknowledgement of its status as indiscipline.

Quentin Bell's *On Human Finery* was published in 1947, two years before *Style in Costume* and presented a post-war view of fashion roughly synchronous with Christian Dior's New Look. The second edition, published in 1976, gave Bell the opportunity to revise and make additions, including those to Chapter 8 where he predicts, or at least, hopes for, the end of fashion. This speculation generated much criticism at the time. Was this, and is this still, unthinkable? Bell concludes his foreword: 'Perhaps a final judgement of this matter cannot be attempted until another forty years have lapsed. The judgements of that future age are no concern of mine' (1992: ix). As those forty years have now almost elapsed it is an opportune moment to rethink, review and speculate upon the future of not fashion itself, as Bell imagined, but at least how we talk, write and understand fashion. Again the problematic term 'fashion' raises its ephemeral head (and may

FIGURE 1.2 'Lady of 1928' and 'Modern Skyscraper' from James Laver, *Style in Costume*, Oxford University Press, 1949.

even sit uncomfortably in the pages of this present volume with its focus on dress). Bell himself somewhat censoriously suggested, when musing on the catalysts for fashionable change (or as he puts it, the 'incredibly powerful evolutionary process'), that 'historians of dress tend to be vague upon this point; they produce secondary factors of undeniable importance, but insufficient to supply a complete answer' (1992: 29).

Overlooking Bell's apparent dismissal of historians, his preface lists many of the issues still occupying dress studies today: first, the selective/hierarchical status of material culture – only 'posh' clothes survive – something that we must remain indebted to Taylor for interrogating, with her emphasis on everyday wear, or at least clothing that tends to remain un-illuminated by the spotlight of museological display (2002). Bell then addresses problems of representation, for example that of fashion plates, which transport us to 'a fictitious world, prettier than life', as Bell puts it, quoting Doris Langley Moore, and the honorific idealizing imagery of the studio photograph (Bell 1992: xii). The abundance of underused film material also concerns Bell and which today is even more pressing, and further complicated by the appearance in the last few years of fashionfilm, a suitably compound noun that attempts to include moving representations of dress that are at once part promotional film, part record of a season's collection, part drama and perhaps ultimately none of these. Finally Bell understands sociological and anthropological approaches to dress as accompanied by their own inherent limitations. Citing Gerald Heard and his 1924 work *Narcissus: Anatomy of Clothes*, Bell suggests that unlike the evolutionary process in living things, fashion has evolved along specifically non-utilitarian lines and is often highly unfit for purpose, which runs contrary to animal evolutionary theories of survival of the fittest and therefore the application of evolutionary processes to fashion is, as he terms it, open to 'sweeping objections' (1992: 104).

Bell draws on Thorstein Veblen, the American economist and sociologist, and his work *The Theory of the Leisure Class* of 1899, to construct his primarily economic argument for the phenomenon of fashion. He is, however, fortunately unable, or unwilling, to remain within the strict parameters of Veblen's discussion of the fundamental roles fashion and adornment play in his 'Laws of Conspicuous Consumption', 'Vicarious Consumption' and 'Conspicuous Leisure'. Indeed Bell devotes a chapter of *On Human Finery* to 'Deviations from Veblen'. Bell constantly contradicts, wanders off the track or ignores Veblen at will, stating in the preface to his bibliography that 'this is not a work of erudition but of theory . . .' (1992: xiv). This is a contradictory claim perhaps to contemporary readers used to works of fashion theory being both erudite and theoretically specific, but maybe this is the point Bell is trying to convey. If one considers some of the earliest definitions of theory, it was not so much about seeking explanations and establishing definitive causes. In 1624 the word was defined as 'abstract knowledge, or the formulation of it: often used as implying more or less unsupported hypothesis' and in 1710 was more commonly understood as a 'mental view or contemplation' (Onions 1990: 2281).

I want to reassert, however, that I am not discrediting the list of invaluable works of dress studies and fashion theory that have chosen quite properly to understand what we wear (and perhaps why) by setting clothing within the rich and fruitful theoretical landscapes suggested by disciplines such as anthropology and psychology. Neither am I ignoring the significant contribution of those who have revealed so many insights into how we wore, and continue to wear, clothes by considering dress as an object of material culture. What I have been considering, however, is this idea of an indiscipline, an 'unsupported hypothesis' as the dictionary defines 'theory'. This is something that is in the process of becoming, an example of what we might understand as fashion or dress *thinking*, rather than history or theory, which the proto-indisciplinarians such as Laver, Bell and Langley Moore deployed.

Dress thinking

I am both prompted by the title of this book, *Dress History*, and wary of attempting to illustrate my topic by utilizing the analogy of the crinoline. I am immediately conscious that the word crinoline can of course refer to the material stiffened with horsehair, the crinoline skirt constructed with a succession of channels to receive supporting hoops, or the fully developed cage of light weight steel rings that were linked together by means of tapes and suspended from the waist. It is this last structure to which I allude here, for without the supporting structure of the crinoline, which can be considered the theory, the familiar silhouette of mid-nineteenth-century women's fashionable dress is unthinkable. We can perhaps understand this supporting structure as a manifestation of the rigid gender demarcations supporting nineteenth-century European and North American society, or as the patriarchal system that rendered its wearers incapacitated and fetishized, or as an articulating structure linking clothing to architecture and the construction of space: the list of possibilities is apparently endless. This endlessness returns us to the original point; that is by limiting ourselves to discussing and writing about *dress and* . . . we are in danger of running counter to the very aims of interdisciplinarity, which can never be a simple conjoining of terms, but an endless succession of 'ands' which fly from one another but always tie back to themselves. This echoes the rhizome that Gilles Deleuze and Félix Guattari (1992) employed so effectively when using this botanical structure to discuss the possibility of a way of thinking that is non-hierarchical and allows a multitude of entry and exit points; in application, this could become a form of 'dress thinking' or 'fashion thinking' that revels in its indisciplinarity.

There is a danger of course that this approach can lead to an unspecific and inconclusive pluralism, as Wilson (2003) states in *Adorned in Dreams*, a work that has repeatedly proved the merits of a way of thinking about fashion that provides multiple points of access and, indeed inspirational exit points for subsequent researchers. She, like Bell, considered herself 'an "*amateur*" in the original sense of that word, of an enthusiast, even an addict of fashion' (2003: vii). Also like Bell, she draws upon, and rejects, Veblen and finds a number of other theories unable to 'explain' fashion. Wilson arrives at 'modernity' as a more appropriate concept, a similar journey that led Bell to 'sumptuosity', a term he finds more useful to explore the phenomenon of fashion (Wilson 2003: 47–66; Bell 1992: 25–56).

As invaluable as *Adorned in Dreams* has proven to be since its publication in 1985, Wilson's exhortation to establish a field that 'endeavours to transcend the differences in approach that continue to traverse the discussion and study of dress' (2003: vii) may have led to an abundance of dress history or fashion 'readers' that, rather than traverse, in fact enshrine the differences in dress studies, or, ironically reinforce the theoretical boundaries that Wilson had so necessarily started dismantling. Readers are surely the perfect expression of interdisciplinarity, and in their bringing together texts from (hopefully) widely different voices and eras make conveniently available a range of material on a subject. They are, without doubt, invaluable teaching tools, but they also have the tendency to annexe and spotlight certain aspects of a writer's work, much as a museum spotlights key objects held in greater cultural esteem while letting others retreat into darkness. Jean Dubuffet, in his marvellous essay 'Asphyxiating Culture', warned:

> It is the nature of culture to cast a spotlight on certain productions. For the benefit of these productions, it drains the light from all others, without worrying about casting them into darkness. Because of this, all inclinations that do not have these privileged productions as their sources die asphyxiated . . . Only those who imitate, comment upon, exploit or study these productions can live . . . This is how culture, contrary to what is believed, is restrictive, reduces the field, generates night. What culture lacks is a taste for the anonymous, innumerable germination. Culture is smitten with counting and measuring; it feels out of place and uncomfortable with the innumerable; its efforts tend, on the contrary, to limit numbers in all domains; it tries to count on its fingers. Culture is essentially eliminating and thereby impoverishing. (1988: 13–14)

It is interesting to consider that many of Dubuffet's ideas were formulated after the Second World War, at the same moment as the fledgling field of dress studies was emerging in Britain, and were the expression of the belief in the need to start again, post-Auschwitz, in year zero. The flowering of British dress studies in this post-war period is still remarkable today when one considers the list of seminal works published between 1947 and 1949, including Langley Moore's *The Woman in Fashion* (1949b) and *Gallery of Fashion 1790–1822* (1949a), Bell's *On Human Finery* (1947), Laver's *British Military Uniforms* (1948) and *Style in Costume* (1949) and C. Willett Cunnington's *The Art of English Costume* (1948a) and *The Perfect Lady* (1948b). If we understand the work of the pioneers in our field as a similarly radical attempt to understand society via its dress, then following Dubuffet's observations, is the contemporary plethora of readers an indication of culture's desire to 'count on its fingers'? Repeatedly assembling the correct number of established and recognized texts, re-presenting and re-shuffling these same texts as opposed to finding those which so far have received less 'light' and yet are equally capable of illuminating our field, might unfortunately be understood as denying the field's capacity for 'innumerable germination' (Dubuffet 1998).

To return to the analogy of the crinoline, if we were to take away its support altogether, what would be left? The 'unsupported' skirt is still a garment, it still serves many of the same purposes as the original supported garment, that is to clothe the naked form and to provide a degree of warmth, but it now looks very different. In place of the familiar dome-shaped skirt we would be looking at a skirt falling into voluminous folds that drop from the waist, and in addition, due to the excess of unsupported material, it would move and behave very differently from the original. It is still a skirt, however, and perhaps what we might now focus on would be the fabric itself, its construction from gores or how it is fastened, sits on the waist, is attached to the bodice. Might we be made newly aware of the burdens that nineteenth-century fashionable dress imposed on its wearers, a different emphasis on the weight of fashion perhaps without its familiar and spectacular supporting structure of social and fashionable conventions? This analogy attempts to signal the part that the study of material culture has played in the development of dress history and fashion theory. The desire to understand dress, how it changes and most importantly how it was and continues to be worn both theoretically and in actuality has of course, been actively and passionately promoted by Taylor. In *The Study of Dress History* she draws attention to the often jealously guarded specialisms and approaches of the various theorists, collectors, commentators and manufacturers of dress, and how this excitingly diverse group of thinkers about dress has often worked if not in opposition, then certainly often in isolation from one another, even though, as Taylor suggests in her introduction 'clothing provides a powerful analytical tool across many disciplines' (2002: 1). Taylor's book provides a valuable assessment of some of the most innovative work being carried out in each of the various approaches she examined, and leads her to suggest that 'cultural conversations . . . are dependent upon open-minded interdisciplinary approaches that are not skewed by personal prejudice, by obsessive reliance on one field of study or by over-reliance on the latest theoretical fad' (2002: 272).

Ancestors and pioneers

Whether an open-minded interdisciplinary approach *has* been adopted is one of the issues that confronts us now, and I am sure the merits of a pluralistic approach versus the rigour of a single theoretical methodology will continue to be hotly debated. We need, alongside these discrete disciplinary explorations, to reconsider earlier approaches to dress and textiles that transcend, or rather exceed the formal limitations of cloth and cut and to utilize the figure of the rhizome once more. This starts with an inquiry into an initial piece of stuff, and then proliferates; sending out shoots in every direction, but still echoes its origins and returns to that point armed with fresh insights.

I am thinking of those works that seem so prophetic to our field and yet predate any such recognition of terms such as dress history, studies or, indeed fashion theory. These include works of fiction that take the reader along the less well-trampled literary driveways of Jane Austen's fashionably dressed characters, and should take their positions alongside Bulwer Lytton's celebrated 'men in black'.

I refer here, of course both to Edward Bulwer Lytton's celebrated 1828 novel *Pelham; or, Adventures of a Gentleman*, an enormously influential text which helped establish the custom for men to wear black for evening dress, and to John Harvey's seminal study of men's fashion *Men in Black* for which Bulwer Lytton's text provided a crucial reference (Harvey 1995).

Less well-known literary texts equally deserving of the 'light' that *Pelham* has received should include the erotically fixated textile detail of James Fenimore Cooper's *Autobiography of a Pocket Handkerchief* (1843), a marvellous combination of political tract, record of post-Revolutionary fashions in accessories and linen production in France narrated via the pocket handkerchief's 'vegetable clairvoyance'. Or Emile Zola's *The Dream* (1888), an ecstatic textile fantasy centred on the art of nineteenth-century ecclesiastical embroidery techniques, hagiology and nascent sexuality, where the detailed description of sewing implements, stitches and threads of gold and silver become a litany for the doomed Angélique; the innocent embroiderer who dies of a broken heart in saintly textile ecstasy. While no consideration of protean dress history would be complete without the often cited, but rarely scrutinized, *Sartor Resartus*, in which Thomas Carlyle treats his readers to such vestimentary delights as his account of aprons, episcopal, military and legal and then uses the garment to launch an attack on the authority of journalism, or his recognition of second-hand or 'old clothes' as he calls them as emotional repositories: 'Silent are they, but expressive in their silence: the past witnesses and instruments of Woe and Joy, of Passions, Virtues, Crimes, and all the fathomless tumult of Good and Evil in "the Prison called Life"' (Carlyle 1999: 183). Surely this is one of the most perceptive descriptions of dress and its emotional connectivity to its wearers, a topic that has recently been reconsidered in the context of emotionally durable design and sustainability (Fletcher 2008; Chapman 2005).

Increasingly, the works that I have found to be the most illuminating and relevant to the field of dress history today are those invariably not written by an 'expert' (whatever that term might convey), or perhaps, more accurately, are by experts in fields other than dress studies. Mark Wigley's (1995) *White Walls, Designer Dresses,* written by an architectural historian, paved the way for the succession of fashion and architecture productions that followed its publication (Quinn 2003; Hodge and Mears 2006). Wigley's book never falls into the trap of just being about the visual overlap between the two disciplines, and encompasses ideas about health and hygiene, façade and interior, why most seminal twentieth-century architects engaged with the practice of fashion, and how architecture at the beginning of the century can be understood as a form of clothing. More recently, architectural historian and designer Nicholas de Monchaux's (2001) *Spacesuit: Fashioning Apollo* ostensibly tells the story of the spacesuits worn by Buzz Aldrin and Neil Armstrong when they stepped onto the surface of the moon in 1969. The book, however, is much more than an account of these pioneering suits. As the description on the book jacket puts it:

> In *Spacesuit* Nicholas de Monchaux tells the story of the twenty-one layer spacesuit in twenty-one chapters addressing twenty-one topics relevant to the suit, the body, and the technology of the twentieth century. He touches, among other things, on eighteenth-century androids, Christian Dior's New Look, Atlas missiles, cybernetics and cyborgs, latex, JFK's carefully cultivated image, the CBS lunar broadcast soundstage, NASA's Mission Control, and the applications of the Apollo-style engineering to city planning.

To this I would add the imbrication between the space suit's development and brassiere design technology. In the field of textile studies Michel Pastoureau's *The Devil's Cloth: A History of Stripes and Striped Fabric*, written in 1991 and translated into English in 2001, remains an inspired text, written not by a textile historian, but by an authority on medieval heraldry. Commencing with a detailed account of the approbation with which the medieval world regarded stripes, the book then finds innumerable points of textile-related departure to allow discussions of, among others, pyjamas, zebras, awnings and flags all the while tracking stripes as they shift from being a sign of the devil, of the revolutionary, of the prisoner, as the mark of the oppressed and on into social acceptability and sobriety (Pastoureau 2001).

I am all too aware that this highly partisan discussion of interdisciplinarity within the published field of dress studies has made little mention of that most expert and simultaneously eclectic pioneer, who like Laver was also deeply interested in, and aware of, the potential to be found in the relationship between dress and photographic media. Doris Langley Moore published *The Woman in Fashion* in 1949 and it remains today a veritable 'gold mine' of possible approaches to dress history and, especially, its representation. Of course Moore was no outsider to dress history, and many experts, including Taylor, have assessed her enormous influence on the development of object-based dress studies. While it is entirely possible to regard *The Woman in Fashion* as literary proof of Moore's position within the British post-war cultural establishment – as nascent museum curator, collector, dealer, ballet writer, Byron scholar, and central figure in British theatrical, intellectual and artistic society at the time – the work is still remarkable for its ground-breaking and often startling approach. Its photographs of leading actors, ballerinas, writers and couturiers of the day dressed in garments from Moore's own collection are well known. Beyond the obvious enjoyment afforded by spotting Lynn Redgrave as a child modelling a mid-Victorian outfit, the forgotten British couturier Matilda Etches in Callot Soeurs, and even Moore herself billed as 'The Collector' in a dress dated as c. 1903 (which she suggests could just have easily been an illustration for Quentin Bell's discussion of Veblen's theory of conspicuous consumption), the illustrations are a perfect example of the meta-textual richness that characterizes Moore's work (Figures 1.3, 1.4 and 1.5). Elsewhere Moore's eclecticism is evident in her text littered with literary references and anecdotes including those found in the early essay *Fashion in Theory* with a postscript acknowledging Bell's work but with the addition that 'he appears to disapprove of fashion, which I regard as a delightful and even beneficent influence on civilized life' (Moore 1949a or 1949b: 15).

Moore's observation points to a significant difference between dedicated dress historians and writers such as Bell who could be accused of being guilty of dismissing fashion (while writing about it) as frivolous and ultimately meaningless, one of those who attempted to 'explain it away' to use Wilson's criticism of much early dress history (Wilson 2003: 47). A further example of the radical indisciplinarity that characterizes and makes *The Woman in Fashion* such an inspirational text is the moment in the book's essay on 'Fashion in Practice' when the reader is stopped short by a page which contains nothing more than a diagram of a circle in outline demonstrating graphically Moore's famous debunking of the impossibly small Victorian woman's waist circumference: 'the seventeen-inch waist is a myth'

FIGURE 1.3 Photograph ('Miss Lynn Redgrave'), from Doris Langley Moore, *The Woman in Fashion*, Batsford, 1949. Reproduced with kind permission of B.T. Batsford, part of Pavilion Books Company Limited.

FIGURE 1.4 Photograph ('Miss Matilda Etches'), from Doris Langley Moore, *The Woman in Fashion*, Batsford, 1949. Reproduced with kind permission of B.T. Batsford, part of Pavilion Books Company Limited.

(1949b: 19). Such audacious approaches to the subject seem once again to result from the author's readily acknowledged inclusiveness, encompassing photographic recreation and daring graphics, and being less concerned with presenting a comprehensive overview but relishing in the 'turbulence or incoherence at the inner and outer boundaries of discipline' to recall Mitchell's definition of indiscipline discussed at the beginning of this text. As Langley Moore herself puts it in the foreword to *The Woman in Fashion*: 'the book does not pretend in any way to be comprehensive, but it has been my constant object to make it representative' (1949b: v).

Moore's unapologetic stance is instructive for those engaged in the field today, allowing for the admittance of useful material from wherever it might hail. As Taylor invoked him in her introduction to *The Study of Dress History* it seems appropriate to let the historian Raphael Samuel have the final word. Samuel argued

FIGURE 1.5 Photograph ('The Collector'), from Doris Langley Moore, *The Woman in Fashion*, Batsford, 1949. Reproduced with kind permission of B.T. Batsford, part of Pavilion Books Company Limited.

in his seminal work *Theatres of Memory* that 'history is not the prerogative of the historian, nor even as postmodernism contends, a historian's "invention". It is rather a social form of knowledge; the work, in any given instance, of a thousand different hands' (1996: 8). Laver, Bell, Moore and other proto-interdisciplinarians such as C. Willett Cunnington, to whom my text only fleetingly refers, recognized that dress or fashion history is a 'social form of knowledge', and used a variety of disciplines to present that knowledge.

These pioneers also displayed a prophetic understanding of the powerful attraction between dress and what, at the time they were working, could certainly be regarded as new media. Doris Langley Moore's series of programmes entitled *Men, Women and Clothes* broadcast in 1957 as the first colour television series produced by the BBC is still under-researched as a pioneering work of dress history, as is the *Clothes-Line* series Laver produced some twenty years earlier with Pearl Binder. A series of six television programmes first broadcast by the BBC in 1937, *Clothes-Line* discussed the development of fashion using garments drawn from Cunnington's costume collection. Binder, herself a versatile artist and writer, expert on stained glass, pioneer of children's television, traveller, champion of the Pearly Kings and Queens and, of course, mother to Lou Taylor, is another significant example of an indisciplinarian, whose wide-ranging interests and talents were perfectly suited to the study, understanding and pleasures of dress, and whose career in the light of this current volume's subject it would now be instructive to explore.

These pioneering mid-twentieth-century figures saw the edges of their disciplines not as limits, but as bridges to further territories, affording routes and vistas to further study. A reassessment of their methods, of their readiness to seize the potential of what were then new modes of communication coupled with a healthy disregard for theoretical boundaries seems increasingly relevant to the advancement of our field today. The widely regarded and upheld interdisciplinarity of dress and fashion studies today is in danger of becoming institutionalized, and rather than continue on the search for the next 'and' we need to dispense with the disciplinary barriers that require yet another conjunction and revel in the opportunity that the study of dress offers. Like Laver, Bell and Langley Moore, we should aspire to indisciplinarity.

References

Adamson, G. (2007), *Thinking Through Craft*, Oxford: Berg.
Bancroft, A. (2012), *Fashion and Psychoanalysis*, London: I.B. Tauris.
Bell, Q. (1992), *On Human Finery*, London: Alison and Busby.
Black, S. et al. (eds) (2013), *The Handbook of Fashion Studies*, London: Bloomsbury.
Britton Newell, L. (ed.) (2007) *Out of the Ordinary: Spectacular Craft*, London: V&A Publications.
Carlyle, T. ([1833–4] 1999), *Sartor Resartus*, Oxford: Oxford University Press.
Chandler, J. (2009), 'Doctrines, Discourses, Disciplines, Departments', *Critical Inquiry*, 35 (4): 729–46.
Chapman, J. (2005), *Emotionally Durable Design*, London: Earthscan.
Coles, A. (2005), *DesignArt*, London: Tate Publishing.
Cooper, J. F. ([1843] 2006), *Autobiography of a Pocket Handkerchief*, London: Hesperus Press.
Cunnington, C. W. (1948a), *The Art of English Costume*, London: Collins.
Cunnington, C. W. (1948b), *The Perfect Lady*, London: Max Parrish.
De Monchaux, N. (2011), *Spacesuit: Fashioning Apollo*, Cambridge: MIT Press.
Dimant, E. (2012), *Fashion and Minimalism*, New York: Collins Design.
Dubuffet, J. (1988), *Asphyxiating Culture and Other Writings*, New York: Four Walls Eight Windows.
Eicher, J. B. (1995), *Dress and Identity*, Oxford: Berg.
Ewing, B. (1978), *Dress and Undress*, London: B.T. Batsford.
Flaubert, G. ([1880] 1976), *Bouvard and Pécuchet with The Dictionary of Received Ideas*, London: Penguin Books.
Fletcher, K. (2008), *Sustainable Fashion and Textiles*, London: Earthscan.
Gibbs-Smith, C. (1976), 'Obituary for James Laver', *Costume*, 10: 123–4.

Harvey, J. (1995), *Men in Black*, London: Reaktion Books.

Hodge, B. and Mears, P. (eds) (2006), *Skin + Bones: Parallel Practices in Fashion and Architecture*, London: Thames and Hudson.

Kaiser, S. B. (2013), *Fashion and Cultural Studies*, London: Bloomsbury.

Klein, J. T. (1990), *Interdisciplinarity: History, Theory and Practice*, Michigan: Wayne State University Press.

Langley Moore, D. (1949a), *Gallery of Fashion 1790–1822*, London: B.T. Batsford.

Langley Moore, D. (1949b), *The Woman in Fashion,* London: B.T. Batsford.

Lautréamont, Comte de ([1869] 1978), *Maldoror and Poems*, London: Penguin Books.

Laver, J. (1948), *British Military Uniforms*, London: Penguin Books.

Laver, J. (1949), *Style in Costume*, London: Oxford University Press.

Laver, J. (1969), *A Concise History of Costume*, London: Thames and Hudson.

Mitchell, W. J. T. (1995), 'Interdisciplinarity and Visual Culture', *Art Bulletin*, 77 (4): 540–4.

'Obituary James Laver: A Polymath of Formidable Virtuosity' (1975), *The Times*, 4 June: 43.

Pastoureau, M. (2001), *The Devil's Cloth*, New York: Columbia University Press.

Quinn, B. (2003), *The Fashion of Architecture*, Oxford: Berg.

Ribeiro, A. (1986), *Dress and Morality*, London: B.T. Batsford.

Ribeiro, A. (2005), *Fashion and Fiction*, London and New Haven: Yale University Press.

Samuel, R. (1996), *Theatres of Memory*, London: Verso.

Taylor, L. (2002), *The Study of Dress History*, Manchester: Manchester University Press.

Taylor, L. (2004), *Establishing Dress History*, Manchester: Manchester University Press.

Taylor, L. (2013), 'Fashion and Dress History: Theoretical and Methodological Approaches', in S. Black et al. (eds) (2013), *The Handbook of Fashion Studies*, London: Bloomsbury.

Wigley, M. (1995), *White Walls, Designer Dresses: The Fashioning of Modern Architecture*, Cambridge: MIT Press.

Wilson, E. (2003), *Adorned in Dreams: Fashion and Modernity*, London: I.B. Tauris.

Zola, E. ([1888] 2005), *The Dream*, London: Hesperus Press.

2 GLOVES 'OF THE VERY THIN SORT': GIFTING LIMERICK GLOVES IN THE LATE EIGHTEENTH AND EARLY NINETEENTH CENTURIES

Liza Foley

Made from the aborted skins of unborn calves, lamb or kid, Limerick gloves were a distinctive style of glove celebrated across Ireland and England during the late eighteenth and early nineteenth centuries. Originally produced in Limerick, a city on the River Shannon in mid-west Ireland, these exquisitely crafted gloves were specifically prized for their supremely delicate texture and, according to William Hull, author of *The History of the Glove Trade*, for rendering the hand of the wearer soft and smooth (1834: 64). Esteemed articles of aristocratic dress, they were distinctly characterized by the Anglo-Irish Attorney General John Fitzgibbon in 1789 as gloves 'of the very thin sort' (Fitzgibbon 2005: 43–4). This fineness was further demonstrated through their typical encasement inside two halves of a walnut shell (Plate 1).

According to a nineteenth-century commentary, 'a single nut with such a kernel' was deemed to be 'a very costly fruit indeed' and made from rare and precious leathers; a pair of Limerick gloves was once considered a 'significant present from a gentleman' (*Belfast Newsletter* 1874: 1). Currently held by numerous museums across Ireland and England, including Limerick City Museum; The National Museum of Ireland; Dents Glove Museum, Warminster; the Museum of London; the Museum of Leathercraft, Northampton; Hereford Museum and Art Gallery and Berrington Hall, Leominster, the number of surviving examples of these gloves testifies to their former significance and acclaim. Produced at a time when, according to dress historian Valerie Cumming, gloves became an 'indispensable accessory' (1982: 38), their position as an important fashion artefact is confirmed by their recurrent depictions in fashionable magazines such as *La Belle Assemblée or, Bell's Court and Fashionable Magazine Addressed Particularly to the Ladies* (1806–37) and *The Repository of Arts, Literature, Commerce, Manufactures, Fashions and Politics* (1809–28), also known as *Ackermann's Repository*. Illustrated in hand-coloured costume plates depicting various fashionable and leisurely pursuits that included walking, riding and going to the opera, they were celebrated as 'those selected by the female of taste and propriety' (*Belle Assemblée* 1807: 275) and became a requisite accessory of fashionable recreation (Figure 2.1).

Despite their former celebrated status, until this research (Foley 2014), very little scholarly attention has been paid to these objects. With the exception of a one-page article by leather historian, John Waterer (1966), in addition to some brief references included in more general studies on dress and accessories by historians Cumming (1982, 2010) and Mairéad Dunlevy (1982), their historiography to date has mainly comprised short, limited descriptions, featured in earlier studies of the glove trade, most notably by authors such as Hull (1834), Samuel Beck (1883) and Willard Smith (1917). Such limited study is reflective not only of Limerick gloves' overlooked place within dress history, but

FIGURE 2.1 Fashion plates ('Opera Dress' and 'Walking Dress') depicting Limerick gloves, *Ackermann's Repository*, 11 (May 1814): plate nos 30 and 31. Images from Los Angeles County Museum of Art.

also of the marginalization of gloves in general. Compared to other accessories such as pockets, shoes and fans, gloves have received only minimal scholarly attention. To date, Cumming's book, *Gloves* (1982), which was published as part of Batsford's *Costume Accessories Series* over thirty years ago, represents the only comprehensive study dealing with the subject.

As Lou Taylor (2002) has noted, the study of dress history has embraced an increasingly broad range of interdisciplinary enquiry in recent decades, including research in sociology and anthropology. Some of this work has placed new emphasis on the cultural relevance of dress by adopting a material culture approach and using what Taylor has described as 'consumption and the interpretation of objects as a means of examining "society" and "culture"' (2002: 72). Essential to this approach is a consideration of the materiality of objects themselves; a quality that, as anthropologists Victor Buchli (2002) and David Howes (2006) have argued, is accessed not only through a physical examination of the object, but also one that considers a sensory analysis.

Thus, inspired by these developments and adopting a material culture approach, this chapter will explore the cultural meanings ascribed to Limerick gloves by focusing on the materiality of the gloves and examining their role as tokens of late-eighteenth and early-nineteenth-century gift exchange. Drawing on anthropologist Marcel Mauss's influential theories of reciprocity and gift exchange whereby giving is conceived as an act that forges a relationship between the parties involved, this chapter demonstrates how the gift of Limerick gloves served to materialize important social and emotional connections. In doing so, it moves beyond Limerick gloves' traditional role as fashion accessories and, instead, attempts to bring to light their more elusive qualities as tokens of exchange.

The chapter begins by addressing the significance of the Limerick gloves' materiality by placing them within the context of late-eighteenth-century leather production and considering their physical and conceptual transformation from dead animal skins to luxury articles of refinement. While former studies of glove and leather production have tended to focus on the mechanical processes of manufacture (Ellis 1917; Smith 1921), this study is written from a perspective that takes into account the significance of the materiality of leather by highlighting its position as a complex and unstable raw material. Having outlined the general context of leather production, this chapter then turns its attention to examples of Limerick gloves within three different contexts of gift exchange and, drawing on a range of sources that include artefacts, letters and literary sources, demonstrates the ways in which they were involved in creating and maintaining important social relations.

Although only a handful of studies have examined the cultural significance of gloves, these investigations have been ably executed by scholars such as Peter Stallybrass and Anne Rosalind Jones (2001), Ariel Beaujot (2008, 2012), Susan Vincent (2009, 2012) and Steven Bullock and Sheila McIntyre (2012). Both

Beaujot and Vincent highlight the glove's cultural capacity by examining its role within the context of nineteenth- and twentieth-century middle-class femininity, while Stallybrass and Jones, as well as Bullock and McIntyre, focus on its position as a token of seventeenth- and eighteenth-century gift exchange. Each of these approaches have shed new light on the cultural agency of the object, but it is Stallybrass and Jones's study in particular that has offered fascinating insights into approaching the study of gloves. They consider how gloves, imparted as gifts, operated as what William Pietz called 'external organs of the body' (Stallybrass and Jones 2001: 116). In examining how these objects reach out and extend 'the prosthetic hand of affection' (118–19), Stallybrass and Jones have not only illustrated the significance of the material properties of gloves, but they have also called attention to the significance of their immaterial qualities also.

Historians Marcia Pointon (2001) and Arianne Fennetaux (2008) have pushed this approach even further in their respective examinations of other formerly trivialized objects such as miniature portraits and pockets. By focusing on the materiality of the objects and considering their roles as gifts or repositories for gifts, both scholars have convincingly highlighted the 'emotionally charged functions' (Fennetaux 2008: 329) of these artefacts. In explicating these heightened functions, both Pointon and Fennetaux emphasize the significance of tactility and body-object proximity and in doing so, demonstrate the ways in which these objects served to reinforce notions of the self in addition to physically and metaphorically securing connections between the self and other.

If we consider gloves, imparted as gifts, as materialized social connections, within the context of the studies outlined above, we begin to recognize them as deeply significant items of dress. As prosthetic extensions, intimate tokens or private interior spaces, gloves become enhanced by their capacity to evoke a sense of touch that is embodied, but contains an absence; a sense that is socialized yet remains deeply personal. As poet and critic Susan Stewart has argued, 'Of all the senses, touch is the one most linked to emotion and feeling' (1999: 31). It is this conception of touch, therefore, echoed throughout the layered meanings of the glove, that gives Limerick gloves their affecting potential as gifts and, like pockets and miniature portraits, enhances their position as 'emotionally charged' objects.

Producing 'slinks' and skins

Although leather was essential for the production of a wide range of eighteenth-century objects, including gloves, very little consideration has been given to the significance of the materiality of leather itself. As historian Giorgio Riello has shown, leather was a scarce material in pre-Industrial England. 'Confined to the natural world and to a stable cattle asset' (2008: 77), its production largely depended on the meat market, which, in the case of sheep, and to a greater extent cattle, accounted for the main value of a slaughtered animal (Clarkson 1966; Riello 2008). Adding to its relative scarcity, its production was also governed by archaic legislation, much of which had, what was described at the time as a 'fossilizing influence' (Proctor 1801: 18) on the industry. As leather conservationist Roy Thomson (1983) has argued, this prevented any major technological advancements in the leather trades until the early- to mid-nineteenth century.

As a result, the physical process of turning a dead animal skin into a quality piece of leather remained what contemporary writer, Robert Campbell, described in *The London Tradesman* as 'a nauseous dirty Business' that required 'great strength' in all its branches (1747: 217). It was also an expensive and time-consuming business, consisting of between 'seventy-two and eighty-six different processes' (Cumming 1982: 9) and taking anywhere from twelve to fifteen months to complete. Some of these processes are illustrated in plates that accompanied an article on leather making in Diderot's *Encylopédie* in 1763 and, as the images portray, included repeated bouts of washing, rinsing, pounding, fleshing (the removal of excess fat and flesh), paring, staking (softening the skins by rubbing them over various blunt edges), polishing, drying and dying (Figure 2.2). Even today, the production of leather is a complicated process, the quality of which is dependent on a variety of biological and environmental factors, ranging from the diet and condition of the animal (including the method by which it is slaughtered and flayed) to the quality of the water used and the climatic temperature in which it is produced (Sterlacci 2010). Given the technical constraints of production in a pre-industrial age, it is not surprising to find that the leather produced was often of inconsistent quality, an issue that posed considerable concerns for 'light' leather manufacturers such as glovers.

Such issues are clearly demonstrated in the letter book of Timothy Bevington (1726–1802), a Quaker and Worcester-based glove-maker, leather-dresser and, as historian Richard Coopey (2003) has noted in his study of the Worcester glove industry, owner of Beckett & Co. Although it has not been possible to ascertain whether Bevington was involved in the manufacture of Limerick gloves, his letters to suppliers reflect some of the difficulty involved in procuring decent quality skins for the purpose of glove-making. For example, on receiving a delivery from a Salisbury-based supplier in 1778, he complained:

> Thy skins are come to hand and had they appeared a fair collection we should have sent a bill for their charge, but instead of being better than they appeared to me when at Sarum [Salisbury] [. . .], they are very worst thou ever sent us in divers respects. We appeal to thy own conscious in this case, who cannot but know what a prodigious number of poor worthless dabs are in them [and] that ought not to have been counted according to the general custom in trade. (1778, n.p.)

FIGURE 2.2 Illustration showing leather production: 'Chamoiseur et Mégissier', *Encylopèdie ou Dictionaire raisonné des sciences, des arts et des métiers*, Paris, vol. 2 (1763): plate nos 1 and 2. Image courtesy of the ARTFL Project, University of Chicago.

Urging his supplier to reconsider his former charges and to 'act according to the golden rule: do as thou wouldst be done by', he concluded by adding 'we may also complain of bad drying and damage by the grubs' (1778: n.p.). Also known as ox warble flies, grubs were a form of larvae that caused considerable harm to cattle hides. Infesting the animal's hair as eggs, they created deep holes in the skin causing irreversible puncture wounds to the hide. Such wounds greatly affected the overall value of the skin, particularly if a hide had been subject to multiple invasions, which was often the case (Bennet 1909; Waterer 1946).

Grubs, however, formed only one of Bevington's many complaints. As his letters suggest, skins were also damaged in transit and he often rebuked suppliers for the carelessness of their handlers and carriers. Such carelessness typically included dispatching 'badly-sorted skins' (1781: n.p.), delivering samples in 'wretched, nasty conditions' (1782: n.p.) or including within his orders skins that were 'very small and broken' (1782: n.p.). For Bevington, the purchasing of leather required constant negotiation and he was often forced to return skins due to their substandard quality and size. For example, in 1783, on returning a delivery to London-based supplier, Thomas Hodgson, he explained: 'I would readily oblige thee in taking some of thy kidskins but really, the leather is gone in quality and almost perished that I cannot use them without offending my customers' (1783: n.p.). Of all his suppliers, however, it was Walter Morgan, a leather dresser from Brecon, to whom he expressed his greatest ire regarding poorly manufactured skins. Expressing his disapproval of a delivery in which whole skins (heads) had been substituted with smaller skins (halves) in a letter dated 12 August 1780, he curtly wrote:

I wish my friend Walter Morgan would make his leather what he calls them. These kids he calls 'head', whereas there was three dozen of the gloves skin in the fifteen dozens which were but halves [. . .] and there are among thy gloves lambs a dozen or two in every hundred that will not cut gloves. (1780: n.p.)

Such issues of quality were even more problematic given the desirability of fine leather gloves during this period. As Cumming (1982) has noted, French kid gloves were particularly favoured among the fashionable elite because of their quality and elasticity, which were essential in ensuring a neat fit. According to Beck (1883), their superiority stemmed from France's exemplary kid-rearing techniques, which placed considerable emphasis on the animal's diet, age and seclusion. Raised exclusively on milk and confined to pens to protect their hides, they were slaughtered at the tender age of six months. Such precautionary measures helped to produce leather that offered not only a high textural quality, but also an immaculate appearance – another highly prized feature of aristocratic gloves.

In their respective nineteenth- and early-twentieth-century publications on the glove trade, authors Beck (1883), Smith (1917) and Ellis (1923) have each asserted that the 'perfect glove animal' is one that is 'milk-fed – and – necessarily short-lived' (Smith 1917: 82). Although Limerick gloves were not necessarily produced from animals that were milk-fed, having been obtained from very young or unborn offspring, they were derived from sources that were, undeniably, short-lived. According to Beck, there were two sources for these extremely delicate skins: cows that had already died, or parturient cows that were purposely slaughtered. However, given that cattle were typically slaughtered to supply meat rather than to produce leather (Riello 2008), the production of slinks, as these foetal or stillborn skins were called, must have been somewhat limited. This is certainly suggested in the correspondence of Timothy Bevington. For example, of the approximately thirty leather suppliers recorded in his letter book between 1778 and 1785, only four suppliers are recorded as providing slinks, indicating a comparatively small pool of suppliers. In addition, over half of the letters referring to slinks detail some sort of issues of quality, suggesting that, in comparison to more mature skins such as sheep or lamb, the leather derived from slinks was even more complicated to produce adequately and even more susceptible to damage.

Bevington's letter book provides one source and the number of slink suppliers reflected in his letters may be a result of any number of external factors. However, as Coopey (2003) has noted, Bevington was a prominent Worcester glove-maker who enjoyed an extensive range of trade contacts, from leather manufacturers across Ireland and Great Britain, to merchants and glovers in London. Considering his repeated frustrations with his supplies of slink leather, surely, had more reliable suppliers been available, they too would have been included in his significant trade network. This suggests, therefore, that sourcing and producing quality slinks was a difficult task during the late eighteenth century. Certainly, calves' underdeveloped skins posed considerable manufacturing challenges in an industry that was already rife with production quality issues. Though it was precisely the prematurity of these skins that gave slink leather (and thus Limerick gloves) their superior fineness, it was also the same quality that made these skins particularly liable to deterioration and damage. Exceptionally difficult to flay, tan, cut and sew, it is ironic that the skins considered most ideal for fine leather gloves were, at the same time, most unsuitable for the production process. This irony frames the relation between the supply and demand of Limerick gloves, particularly during the latter half of the eighteenth century, when their distinctive materiality, combined with their limited production and availability, made them unique and exclusive items. This exclusivity in turn enhanced the gloves' desirability, particularly within a consumer society that sought luxury and novelty (Berg 2005).

The demand for perfect leather skins, as depicted in the correspondence of Bevington's letter book, may also be read to reflect a broader concern with the cultural refinement of the self. As historians Sarah Richards (1999) and Mimi Hellman (1999) have argued in their respective studies of eighteenth-century ceramics and furniture, 'Refined consumer goods played a significant role in constructing and reinforcing this condition' (Richards 1999: 1). As objects of polite consumption, Limerick gloves also served to facilitate this sense of refinement. Enveloping the hands and displacing the skin, they too 'encouraged and controlled the delicate management of the body' (Richards 1999: 97). This 'process of purification' (Richards 1999: 98) in which body and gesture are, as the etymological roots of the lexeme 'polite' suggests, 'polished' (Watt 2003: 32) and made smooth, reflects the production and purification process of fine leather itself, in which dead animal skins are pared, smoothed and polished into soft and supple materials of refinement.

The casing of a walnut shell

Unlike French kid gloves, an essential characteristic of Limerick gloves was the walnut shell in which they were encased. Part of an ancient gloving custom (Beck 1883: 98), it is unlikely that the practice of encasing gloves within nutshells originated in Limerick. However, based on the provenance of Limerick gloves, it is possible that the tradition was reincorporated into the trade by Limerick glove-makers, sometime during the mid-late eighteenth century (Cumming et al. 2010: 121). Acting as a sort of test, the successful encasement of a pair of Limerick gloves demonstrated the remarkable skill and dexterity of the glover; reinforcing their position as a well-crafted item made of the finest leather. A rich symbolic item, it also added to the gloves' metaphorical connotations whereby, as Lucia Impelluso (2004) has shown, its 'quality of enclosing the kernel in a shell, which in turn is protected by a hull, has often been interpreted in a favourable light as the protection of precious contents' (2004: 172). Representing a symbol of fertility in Ancient Rome, the French also associated walnuts with marriage – the two halves of a shell representing unity and solidarity, fitting together as one (Impelluso 2004).

The notion of protecting something precious combined with the physicality of the hollow shell is perhaps why the walnut was employed as a seemly receptacle for other miscellaneous curios. For example, in eighteenth- and nineteenth-century Europe, walnuts were commonly outfitted as etuis or *nécessaires*: tiny treasure troves of multiple curiosities that pertained to writing, sewing, the toilette and other uses. Numerous varied examples of these artefacts have survived; a typical walnut etui dating from the mid-nineteenth century offers a good example (Plate 2). Mounted on hinged silver rims, it is fitted with an inscribed solid silver interior, in which an assortment of miniature implements including a gilt scissors, a silver thimble, a silver needle case and a red glass perfume bottle complete with a hinged silver cap, are securely held in place.

Small enough to be held in the palm of the hand, yet sufficiently large enough to accommodate a pair of Limerick gloves, the size of the walnut is an important aspect of the gloves' materiality, and, as such, makes an important contribution to the gloves' cultural meaning. In her *Narrative of the Miniature* (1993), Stewart argues that 'A reduction in dimensions does not produce a corresponding reduction in significance' (1993: 43). She affirms that, on the contrary, values become condensed in the miniature whereby, 'minute description reduces the object to its signifying properties, and this reduction of physical dimension results in a multiplication of ideological properties' (1993: 47). In terms of the Limerick gloves, it was the walnut casing that reinforced the signification of the gloves as a token of affection. Although gloves in general represented tokens of affection, it was the miniature presentation of the gloves that compressed this symbolism in the walnut shell, which itself possessed connotations of unity and togetherness.

Gifting Limerick gloves

The capacity of Limerick gloves as particularly persuasive agents is convincingly captured in detailed correspondence between two prominent political figures: the Attorney General John Fitzgibbon (1749–1802), a wealthy member of the Protestant Anglo-Irish elite, and his friend and political ally William Eden (1745–1814) a British statesman and diplomat. The letters, dated between 1786 and 1789, revealingly convey how, in exchange for some Limerick gloves, Fitzgibbon carefully inveigled Eden into utilizing his connections with the court of Louis XVI and negotiating a commission of Sèvres porcelain on his behalf.

Dated 10 January 1786, Fitzgibbon's initial letter to Eden begins: 'Lees tells me that Mrs. Eden and you want some Limerick gloves but that you will not apply to me under the apprehension that I am too gallant a gentleman to open a debtor and creditor account for them' (Fitzgibbon 2005: 43–4). Informing Eden that he was unlikely to get the gloves 'for several months', unless he used his own personal acquaintance with the glover, Fitzgibbon subsequently instructed Eden to send him details of a suitable size and let him know 'what number [he] would have' (Fitzgibbon 2005: 43–4). Careful not to unveil the motive behind his proposition at first, it is only in the closing lines of his letter that Fitzgibbon reveals his true intentions, writing: 'In an article of their price, set your conscience at rest, when you are settled in Paris, I will in return give you a commission to send me over a service of dessert China' (Fitzgibbon 2005: 43–4).

Established as the Manufacture Royale de la Porcelaine de France in 1759, Sèvres was widely regarded as the best and most exclusive porcelain available during the late eighteenth century. As curator Ronald Fuch (2010) has noted, given the significance of dining as means of exercising status within the eighteenth-century elite, in addition to Fitzgibbon's own wealth and fondness for French style (Kavanaugh 1997), his desire to obtain such an extravagant dessert service was not surprising. Earlier correspondence indicates, however, that Fitzgibbon had sent gloves to the Edens on numerous occasions, so it is interesting to note that it was specifically Limerick gloves he had offered to secure in exchange for the French porcelain. Certainly, such a request could be regarded as a substantial and lengthy task, one that involved selecting, securing and sending an expensive order of china from Paris to Dublin. However, it was Fitzgibbon's offer of Limerick gloves in exchange for undertaking this task, which suggests their position as a particularly significant and luxurious item. In order to expedite his request from Eden, a man of equal wealth and influence, Fitzgibbon needed to provide him with something not only that he did not have, but also that was exceptional. Clearly, this is why he chose Limerick gloves. He was confident in the pleasing effects that the gloves would administer and satisfied that, like Sèvres, they represented the very best in terms of quality and workmanship.

Further evidence suggests that Eden was adamant about paying Fitzgibbon for the Limerick gloves as, on at least three occasions, he addressed details of a remittance. However, it appears to have been six months before Fitzgibbon finally agreed to accept payment for the gloves, writing to Eden on 26 August 1786: 'That you may not again accuse me for not allowing you to pay for Mrs. Eden's gloves, I now tell you that they cost five pounds, four shillings, Irish currency. If you can reduce this to the coin of England of France, pray deduct it from the price of my china' (Fitzgibbon 2005: 51).

Consisting of 116 pieces that ranged in price from 21 livres to 264 livres each (Fuch 2010), the cost of Fitzgibbon's dessert china clearly outweighed the cost of Eden's Limerick gloves. During the mid- to late eighteenth century, gloves were, in general, relatively inexpensive items that could be purchased at varying prices and qualities, ranging from two pence to five shillings per pair. Between 1789 and 1814, Limerick gloves are recorded as costing three and four shillings per pair respectively (Plumptre 1814; Cumming et al. 2010), indicating their position within the higher levels of the market. This position might be further elevated if one considers the comparatively short life span of these delicate objects and the frequency with which they would have been replaced. Yet, Eden's insistence of payment is especially pertinent when considered in relation to Mauss's theory of gift-giving. In *The Gift*, (2002) Mauss asserts that gifts are never free; they are bound by reciprocal obligation. Not only is the recipient obliged to receive the gift, but also, 'we must give back more than we have received' (2002: 84). Thus, the act of giving creates a gift debt, whereby 'the unreciprocated gift makes the person who has accepted it inferior, particularly when it has been accepted with no thought of returning it' (2002: 83). Perhaps this is why Eden was determined to pay Fitzgibbon for the gloves as, to accept them otherwise would have rendered him beholden to Fitzgibbon. Equally, had Fitzgibbon requested assistance from Eden without the offer of Limerick gloves, something he knew Eden already desired, then he too would have been indebted to Eden. In this instance, however, it would appear that both men clearly understood the implications involved in the act of giving, which, as Mauss has argued, is simultaneously governed by 'generosity and self-interest' (2002: 87).

A deeper analysis of the relation between the materiality of Limerick gloves, the porcelain and the social mechanism of gift exchange reveals a powerful metaphoric interplay. First, the multiple and complex stages of leather production are reflected in the complex web of interaction required in negotiating social exchange. This complexity is then refined in the emergence of gloves as objects of polite consumption, just as the act of exchange demands a refined adherence within a broader social convention. A final layer of this analysis shows how the careful handling and wearing of these refined and delicate objects mirrors the careful handling and maneuvering that is inherent to gift exchange, particularly in the delicate balance of generosity and self-interest.

The act of giving and receiving Limerick gloves is also portrayed in Maria Edgeworth's 'The Limerick Gloves', a short story written by the prolific Anglo-Irish novelist in 1799. Set in England in the town of Hereford, Herefordshire, it tells the tale of a young Irish glover named O'Neill, who seeks the affection of Phoebe – the daughter of O'Neill's main antagonist. Central to the story is a pair of Limerick gloves that are bestowed on Phoebe by O'Neill, in an attempt to gain her attention and subsequent affection. Throughout the story, Edgeworth also engages with the symbolic associations of the gloves, one of which she presents as an invitation to a ball. For example, when Phoebe first receives her pair of Limerick gloves, she is unaware of their meaning:

'And, Phoebe, have not you received a pair of Limerick gloves?'

'Yes, I have', said Phoebe; 'but what then? What have my Limerick gloves to do with the ball?'

'A great deal', replied Jenny. 'Don't you know that a pair of Limerick gloves, is as one may say, a ticket to this ball? For every lady that has been asked has had a pair sent to her along with the card'. (1804: 257–8)

As is demonstrated here and below, this story provides a vivid account of the evocative qualities of the gloves and demonstrates their role as a powerful material agent. It also corroborates Mauss's assertion that objects are never completely separated from those who exchange them. Instead, he proposes, the identity of the giver is invariably bound up with the object, creating a social bond that compels the recipient to reciprocate (2002). As a gift therefore, gloves alluded directly to the presence of the giver, not only through the act of giving, but also through the tactile associations that were present in the gloves themselves. The origin of the materiality of the glove is inextricably bound with the skin as a living and breathing organ of touch. The material relations of touch that emerge from the reciprocal nature of the gift's exchange between hands echo the original sensation of touch that emerged from within the organic matter of the gloves' leather.

Such a notion is carried explicitly throughout Edgeworth's text. For example, as a consequence of an angry confrontation with her lover, we learn that Phoebe refuses to wear her Limerick gloves, which are subsequently 'thrown' into a drawer without further consideration. There, the gloves remained until 'favourable sentiments of the giver of those gloves were revived' (1804: 266). Edgeworth describes how, while being reminded of the glover, Phoebe 'laid the gloves perfectly smooth, and strewed over them, whilst the little girl went on talking of Mr. O'Neill, the leaves of a rose which she had worn on Sunday' (1804: 266). These sensual aspects of the gloves are reinforced in the closing lines of the story when we told that, upon reconciliation: 'Phoebe appeared the next day at Mr. Marshall's in the Limerick gloves; and no perfume was ever so delightful to her lover as the smell of rose-leaves in which they had been kept' (1804: 308).

Another symbolic associations of the gloves, according to the English antiquarian, Charles Wade, includes an unusual Cornish custom that simultaneously relates to both marriage and death. Donated by Wade to the National Trust in 1921, a pair of Limerick gloves in Berrington Hall is accompanied by a handwritten note that was allegedly written by Wade himself. Describing the custom, it reads: 'Of the finest softest leather. In accordance with an old custom such gloves contained in a walnut shell were deposited in the church of Kilhampton, Cornwall by the bridegroom whose fiancée died before his wedding'. In this instance, if this caption is to be believed, the gloves can be read as an example of what cultural historian Louise Purbrick refers to in her work on wedding gifts as a 'ritually preserved thing' – an object that becomes so invested with heightened significance under certain circumstances that it is difficult to find another appropriate moment to use them again (2007: 97). As such, objects can transcend their functional qualities and instead become what Purbrick calls 'guardians of memory' (2007: 103). Certainly, the walnut's former associations of marriage and unity, in addition to the glove's connotations of amity and affection, make this artefact a particularly suitable token for such a poignant and bittersweet custom.

Conclusion

The examination of Limerick gloves as gifts helps to illuminate the place of these objects in the late eighteenth and nineteenth centuries. As this chapter has demonstrated, not only did these gloves represent a fashionable and valuable article of superior skill and craftsmanship, but imparted as a gift, they also personified a meaningful gesture of love and affection.

Bound by reciprocal relationships, the offer of Limerick gloves induced a weighty return, whether it be a favour from friends, as the case with Fitzgibbon and Eden, or used as a narrative device to symbolize commitment between lovers as illustrated by the fiction of Maria Edgeworth. Thus, from their production to their reception, Limerick gloves were a costly fruit in more ways than one. Through the lens of Mauss's theories, this was a cost that was incurred, not only by the giver of Limerick gloves, but one that was equally borne by their receiver.

As demonstrated, the materiality of leather, threatened by a variety of biological infestations, manufacturing irregularities and the complexities of production, meant that the skins from which Limerick gloves were made carried with them unique peculiarities. The leather skin, once a vibrant and vital organ of an animal's interaction with the world, is touched by a violence that would ultimately be refined and remade into a rare, delicate and expensive garment.

From this material basis, significant meanings emerge. In the wearing of animal skins on human skin, an organ is transferred and transformed. The production of luxury products from the skins of aborted foetuses, stillborn or short-lived calves carries a deeply symbolic and even emotive charge. In the case of Limerick gloves, the wearing of fine, pale leather on the hand and their presentation as highly precious gifts within social groupings, intensified by the difficult means of their production and their miniature walnut shell casing, adds further dimensions to their symbolic and even mythological significance.

References

Beaujot, A. (2008), *The Material Culture of Women's Accessories: Middle-Class Performance, Race Formation and Feminine Display, 1830–1920*, PhD thesis, University of Toronto.

Beaujot, A. (2012), *Victorian Fashion Accessories*, London and New York: Berg.

The Belfast Newsletter (1874).

La Belle Assemblée (1807).

Beck, S. (1883), *Gloves, Their Annals and Associations: A Chapter of Trade and Social History*, London: Hamilton, Adams.

Bennett, H. (1909), *The Manufacture of Leather*, London: Constable.

Berg, M. (2005), *Luxury and Pleasure in Eighteenth Century Britain*, Oxford: Oxford University Press.

Bevington, T. (1778), Letter Book of Timothy Bevington, Bevington Papers, Worcestershire Record Office, Worcester, 899:749 BA 8782/44H23.

Buchli, V. (2002), 'Introduction', in V. Buchli (ed.), *The Material Culture Reader*, Oxford and New York: Berg.

Bullock, S. and McIntyre, S. (2012), 'The Handsome Tokens of a Funeral: Glove-Giving and the Large Funeral in Eighteenth Century New England', *The William and Mary Quarterly*, 69 (2): 305–46.

Campbell, R. (1747), *The London Tradesman*, London: T. Gardner.

Clarkson, L. A. (1966), 'The Leather Crafts in Tudor and Stuart England', *Agricultural History Review*, 14 (1): 25–39.

Coopey, R. (2003), 'The British Glove Industry, 1750–1970: The Advantages and Vulnerability of a Regional Industry', in J. Wilson and A. Popp (eds), *Industrial Clusters and Regional Business Networks in England 1750–1970*, Aldershot, Hampshire: Ashgate.

Cumming, V. (1982), *The Costume Accessories Series: Gloves*, London: B.T. Batsford.

Cumming, V., Cunnington, C. W. and Cunnington, P. E. (2010), *The Dictionary of Fashion History*, London: Berg.

Dunlevy, M. (1989), *Dress in Ireland*, London: B.T. Batsford.

Edgeworth, M. (1804), 'The Limerick Gloves', in *Popular Tales by Maria Edgeworth*, vol. 1, London: C. Mercier.

Ellis, B. E. (1921), *Gloves and the Glove Trade*, London: Pitman.

Fennetaux, A. (2008), 'Women's Pockets and the Construction of Privacy in the Long Eighteenth Century', *Eighteenth Century Fiction*, 20 (3): 307–34.

Fitzgibbon, J. (2005), 'A Volley of Excrations': The Letters and Papers of John Fitzgibbon, Earl of Clare, 1772–1802*, D. Fleming and A. Malcomson (eds), Dublin: Irish Manuscripts Commission.

Foley, L. (2014), '"An Entirely Fictitious Importance?" Reconsidering the Significance of the Irish Glove Trade: A Study of Limerick Gloves', *Costume*, 48 (2): 160–71.

Fuch, R. (2010), 'John Fitzgibbon and His Order of a Sèvres Porcelain Dessert Service', The French Porcelain Society, http://www.thefrenchporcelainsociety.com/asp4/pdf/sum10.pdf, accessed 5 August 2011.

Hellman, M. (1999), 'Furniture, Sociability and Leisure in Eighteenth Century France', *Eighteenth-Century Studies*, 32 (4): 415–45.

Howes, D. (2006), 'Scent, Sound and Synaesthesia: Intersensoriality and Material Culture Theory', in C. Tilly et al. (eds), *Handbook of Material Culture*, London: Sage.

Hull, W. (1834), *The History of the Glove Trade*, London: Effingham Wilson.

Impelluso, L. (2004), *Nature and Its Symbols*, Stefan Sartarelli (trans.), Los Angeles, CA: J. Paul Getty Museum.

Kavanaugh, A. (1997), *John Fitzgibbon, Earl of Clare*, Dublin: Irish Academic Press.

Mauss, M. (2002), *The Gift: The Form and Reason for Exchange in Archaic Societies*, 2nd edition, London and New York: Routledge.

Plumptre, A. (1817), *Narrative of a Residence in Ireland*, London: Henry Colburn.

Pointon, M. (2001), 'Surrounded with Brilliants: Miniature Portraits in Eighteenth Century England', *The Art Bulletin*, 83 (1): 48–71.

Proctor, A. (1801), *Principles of Leather Manufacture*, Piccadilly: W. Desmond and J. Hatchard.

Purbrick, L. (2007), *The Wedding Present*, Hampshire: Ashgate.

Richards, S. (1999), *Eighteenth-Century Ceramics: Products for a Civilised Society*, Manchester: Manchester University Press.

Riello, G. (2008), 'Nature, Production and Regulation in Eighteenth-Century Britain and France: The Case of the Leather Industry', *Historical Research*, 81 (211): 75–99.

Smith, W. (1917), *Gloves: Past and Present*, New York: Sherwood Press.

Stallybrass, P. and Rosalind Jones, A. (2001), 'Fetishizing the Glove in Renaissance Europe', *Critical Enquiry*, 28 (1): 114–32.

Sterlacci, F. (2010), *Leather Fashion Design*, London: Laurence King Publishing.

Stewart, S. (1993), *On Longing: Narratives of the Miniature, the Gigantic, the Souvenir, and the Collection*, Durham and London: Duke University Press.

Stewart, S. (1999), 'From the Museum of Touch', in M. Kwint, C. Breward and J. Aynsley (eds), *Material Memories*, Oxford: Berg.

Taylor, L. (2002), *The Study of Dress History*, Manchester: Manchester University Press.

Thomson, R. (1983), 'The 19th-century Revolution in the Leather Industries', in R. Thomson and J. A. Beswick (eds), *Leather Manufacture through the Ages*, proceedings of the 27th East Midlands Industrial Archaeology Society Conference, October, Northampton.

Vincent, S. (2009), *The Anatomy of Fashion: Dressing the Body from Renaissance to Today*, London: Berg.

Vincent, S. (2012), 'Gloves in the Early Twentieth-Century: An Accessory after the Fact', *Journal of Design History*, 25 (2): 190–205.

Waterer, J. (1946), *Leather in Life, Art and Industry*, London: Faber and Faber.

Waterer, J. (1966), 'Leather Objects of Interest in the Limerick Museum', *North Munster Antiquarian Journal*, 10 (1): 78–9.

Watts, R. J. (2003), *Key Topics in Sociolinguistics: Politeness*, Cambridge: Cambridge University Press.

3 ALL OUT IN THE WASH: CONVICT STAIN REMOVAL IN THE NARRYNA HERITAGE MUSEUM'S DRESS COLLECTION

Jennifer Clynk and Sharon Peoples

In the nineteenth century, the laundry was often the destination of disadvantaged women helped by charities. The wash house was metaphorically the site for cleansing their criminal or sinful pasts (Preston 2004). Convict women in Australia suffered the same plight. The dress of such women has rarely been considered worth studying. This is not only due to the few surviving pieces in museum collections, but also because it is only in the last thirty years or so that public and academic interest in convict women has developed. The so-called convict stain was for a long time a shameful mark of personal and national identity in Australia. Tasmania, originally called Van Diemen's Land (VDL), is the southern island state of mainland Australia, and was where 72,500 convicts were sent between 1803 and 1853 (Alexander 2010). Here, the metaphor of the convict stain endured, unlike most of the clothing worn by convicts (Young 1988).

From the end of convict transportation to Australia in 1868 until the 1950s, a silence about the convict past in the public imagination, family history, institutions and academic scholarship prevailed in Australia (Smith 2008). The convict past was concealed by the omission of convicts from national celebrations and school history textbooks, the demolition of convict buildings, re-naming of convict places and destruction of other material evidence of their existence (Smith 2008). In her conclusion to *Australia's Birthstain*, historian Babette Smith (2008: 341) called for others to 'recover the lost world of convict society', making it a significant feature of twenty-first-century historiography. This chapter argues that the study of dress is one avenue of interdisciplinary scholarship which can heed Smith's call.

Another inspiration for this chapter was Lou Taylor's paper 'Doing the Laundry? A Reassessment of Object-based Dress History' (1998). In this and subsequent texts, Taylor (2002, 2004) suggests methods for researching dress history with dress and when garments do not exist. There have been a number of studies describing convict clothing using extant garments, or written and visual sources which focus on uniforms (Young 1988; Maynard 1994; Clark et al. 2012). This paper, however, looks at the challenge posed by the convict stain for object-based research in the setting of the Narryna Heritage Museum (Narryna), in Hobart, Tasmania. There are no convict uniforms in this museum but, we argue, there is great potential to uncover the dress of female ex-convicts (also known as emancipists).

Narryna was founded in 1957 in a colonial Greek Revival style town house built between 1837 and 1840. The museum, now under the management of the Tasmanian Museum and Art Gallery (TMAG), was established as the Van Diemen's Land Folk Museum, the first folk museum in Australia. Australian folk collections narrate local pioneer stories by representing domestic life, trades, agriculture, industries, Aboriginal culture, military or maritime histories. Originally, the museum collected only free settler dress and artefacts. Convict material culture was unwanted; however, the collection holds valuable artworks of so-called gentlemen convicts Charles Constantini, Thomas Bock and Knut Bull, and two inconspicuous objects, a wooden clothes brush and chair, most likely made by convict craftsmen. A nation-wide, but especially potent Tasmanian cultural and historiographical bias influenced the collection. For the museum, the convict past was its dirty laundry. Unfortunately, many items within Narryna's large nineteenth-century dress collection have limited or no provenance. This suggests that convicts, ex-convicts or their families could have worn some of these garments. A counter-narrative of the convict past can be interpreted through what was initially only thought of as free settler dress. While extant convict uniforms are rare, civilian or fashionable dress associated with convicts is potentially bountiful, yet overlooked.

Without identified convict or ex-convict garments in the Narryna collection, this study utilizes alternative primary sources such as museum documentation, digitized records and photographs of ex-convict women, as well as newspapers, to expand current research by historians and dress historians on the dearth of identified ex-convict dress. We applied an inductive approach based on observations of Narryna's nineteenth-century women's dress collection and its acquisition documentation, including Museum Committee Reports from the main period of dress collecting from 1956 to the 1970s. Although not always revealing in their contents, museum minute books and acquisition records can indicate the shifting approaches to collecting dress in the past. We also consulted digitized editions of mid-nineteenth-century Hobart newspapers such as the *Colonial Times* (1828–57) in the TROVE database of Australian newspapers that discussed female convicts and dress. We accessed the Female Convicts in Van Diemen's Land database (FCVDL database) as well, an initiative in progress that collates convict records and photographs from professional and amateur historians. Photographs of convict or ex-convict women are limited in the database, either through lack of preservation, provision by descendants, or the fact that studio portraits would have been limited to ex-convicts who went on to enjoy some material success. Nevertheless, a pattern of female convict or ex-convict access to fashion – especially among domestic servants or married, wealthier emancipists – emerged in published public opinion and photographs. This evidence led us to question how and why this pattern was not acknowledged in the Narryna dress collection. In lieu of identified surviving dress belonging to convict or ex-convict women, we argue that digitized visual, archival and newspaper sources offer promising opportunities to address silences in dress collections.

After considering the metaphor of the convict stain in Australian historiography, this chapter describes convict clothing and how it came about, why extant convict clothing is rare and how such dress was excluded in museum collections. This chapter discusses the better-known examples of convict uniforms, emphasizing that the dress worn by female convicts and ex-convicts is comparatively lesser known. The convict experience is narrated mostly through male uniforms; however, fashionable dress played a significant part in the lives of these men and women, particularly for emancipists who achieved financial security and social status. We explore the significance of dress in colonial society in negotiating identity, how convict identities have been silenced in the Narryna Heritage Museum, and how they might yet be heard.

The convict stain

This study extends historian Stefan Petrow's 2009 study of the convict stain and Narryna by suggesting ways in which its effects can be overcome or reinterpreted, especially in relation to dress. The metaphor of the convict stain relates to a social stigma dating from the 1840s, when anti-transportationists in VDL began a fierce political and moral campaign against convict transportation to the colony. The stain metaphor was a nineteenth-century term applied by historians from the 1850s through to the early twentieth century, and still explored today. VDL's penal past has left an indelible mark on the national historical record. It has had an overwhelming impact on historiography, including the representation of history in museums. From the mid-nineteenth century, peaking around 1901 (when the six colonies united to form Australia), people were ashamed of the brutality of the convict system, the individuals and their crimes (Smith 2008). Historian Alison Alexander (2010: 136) argues that the few who admitted their convict past did so because their social marginality meant they had 'nothing to lose'. A general amnesia neutralized and distorted the past in favour of a narrative of imperial triumph (Griffiths 1994). This reconsideration has been and continues to be part of the effort by scholars to diversify the narrative of Australian history by including a broader range of voices, including those from Aboriginal and non-white communities.

In current historiographical debate, there are two main theories of the origins of the convict stain. The first theory is that it had a colonial origin, created by anti-transportationists who thought the sentence of transportation was ineffective for convict reform. The second theory about the convict stain finds its origins abroad. Alexander (2010: 129) argues that the convict stain was the product of 'British contempt for the convict colonies'. The convict stain encompassed emotive language, such as 'dirty', 'unclean', 'tainted', 'tarnished' or 'filthy'. Many anti-transportationists feared that criminality, like smallpox or typhoid, was contagious and that it could contaminate free society, a concern that continued through to the 1960s (Smith 2008). In the nineteenth century, clothing was seen as a vehicle of contamination. The stigma of stained clothing as a shameful mark upon the wearer has been described by cultural theorist, Jenni Sorkin (2012: 223) as 'a form of reproach and silencing'.

For generations, the stain was a silent, repressed memory. Convicts themselves or families of convicts obscured their origins by not discussing the past; in what historian Tom Griffiths (1994: 16) calls the 'protective manipulation of family reputations'. Secrets of convictism were buried, hidden from view. This eventually

FIGURE 3.1 Installation photograph of *Costume to the 20th Century*, exhibition at Narryna Heritage Museum, 2010. Courtesy of Narryna Heritage Museum.

changed. From 1951, family historians gained access to archives of convict records. A new attitude developed by the 1960s which increased by the 1980s as Australia headed towards its Bicentennial celebrations. Genealogists, both professional and amateur, were uncovering unknown convict ancestors, or finding significant gaps or discrepancies in the lives of those in their family tree (Smith 2008). However, if the families who gave the earliest donations to the dress collection at Narryna had made such discoveries, they were not noted in museum records. Some collectors valued convict dress as examples of imperial history, but Narryna conformed to typical dress collecting biases of the time which valued elite women's fashion (Taylor 2004) as depicted in Narryna's *Costume to the 20th Century* exhibition of 2010 (Figure 3.1). Despite its organization as a folk museum, Narryna, like larger Australian institutions, did not recognize the significance of non-fashion or utilitarian dress to social history, leaving the collecting of such material to a few private collectors.

Clothing the colony

British colonization of Australia began with mass transportation of convicts in a series of fleets, the First Fleet being the first group of eleven British ships that arrived in Botany Bay in New South Wales in 1788. Over 750 convicts were carried on board. After an eight-month voyage, the convicts' clothing, packed into the hulls and on the backs of the thousand or so British passengers, must certainly have been in a poor state. Subsequent fleets, the Second and Third Fleets, were sent with more convicts and provisions, but did not arrive for two years.

The provision of adequate clothing for convicts was promoted by prison reformers such as Elizabeth Fry and John Howard (Ash 2010). Historian Carol Liston (2008) notes that by 1830, the transportation system was standardized and clothing was supplied, although women could bring their own. Fashion was not the business of government contracts; hence utility no doubt prevailed over style, adding to the wearers' willingness to relinquish such outfits through freedom or newly acquired wealth. As an example, the 199 convict women who sailed on the *Asia* from Ireland in 1830 were provided with only basic dress: 'two bed gowns (one grey baize or brown serge and the other striped cotton), two petticoats (one grey baize and the other of drugget), two linen shifts; two linen caps, one check apron; two pairs of black stockings, two handkerchiefs, one pair of shoes and one straw hat or bonnet' (Liston 2008: 30). Baize and drugget were old-fashioned textile terms and their use by government officials implies either the basic knowledge of officials on dress, or the utilitarian, unfashionable nature of the clothing itself. Being denied current styles reinforced the women's punishment. This was an optimistic list considering the garments had to last eight months of wear and washing in sea water before they were worn in the colony. Cleanliness was a mandate, mitigating the spread of infection and disease on board the transportation ships through disinfecting bodies and boiling clothing (Damousi 1997). Often the supplied clothing was inadequate in quantity, material and manufacture.

The convicts were metaphorically tainted by their criminal records, and physically marked by wearing stained, frayed and ragged clothing. By the time convicts celebrated their disembarkation, even the spit and polish of the supervising marines had vanished (Hughes 1987). The resupply of food and clothing to the settlement was unpredictable. The delayed arrival of the Second Fleet caused starvation and near nakedness for two bleak years. Dress was the key signifier of status in this frontier environment, but this wore thin physically and conceptually due to harsh climatic conditions and the social distress that lack of clothing caused.

Consequently, the boundaries between jailers (or red coats, as the military were known) and convicts began to blur, especially as convicts traded goods or services for clothing. There are very few descriptions or images of the convicts by the British at this time. The Spanish artist Juan Ravenet, however, travelling on the Spanish Scientific Expedition of Alessandra Malaspina (1789–94) depicted a convict couple dressed in simpler versions of civilian clothing worn by free settlers, thus highlighting the potential dissimulation between the free and convicted (Figure 3.2).

Clothing quickly became a currency in New South Wales and Tasmania. Wearable, decent dress was highly valued and sought. Many convicts had been unemployed workers from textile and clothing-related industries in the United Kingdom and a good number of their convictions for transportation were based on the theft of these items (Elliott 1988; Daniels 1998; Hughes 1987). In the colony, although convicts legitimately traded clothing, theft of dress was a problem. Once the colony at Sydney was established, the administrator Governor Phillip, ordered clothing for the convicts to restore social order and decency. Initially, general civilian working clothing, or what were known as slops, were worn until Phillip later introduced uniforms in 1810 to distinguish convicts from free settlers (Maynard 1994). Convict clothing thus included civilian dress, slops and uniforms. By the nineteenth century, convict uniforms lost economic value as the colony matured with clothing shops and textile trade. Ex-convicts became intent on distancing themselves from their past. Who would keep clothing with such negative associations in prosperous times?

Power structures were delineated through dress. For men, uniforms clearly distinguished the military and convicts. Red coats contrasted with those dressed in what are known as magpie and canary suits made of coarse wool. These names indicate the division within the penal system which roughly divided the convicts into four groups (Maynard 1994; Young 1988). The lowest group carried out hard labour in gangs and wore the black and yellow magpie suits. The colours were juxtaposed like harlequin or jester outfits, and were not only denigrating to the

FIGURE 3.2 Juan Ravenet, 'Convictos en la Neuva Olanda' [Convicts of New Holland], 1793, wash drawing, DGD 2/5. Courtesy of State Library of New South Wales.

men, but like all convict uniforms, assisted jailers in surveillance. They served to identify them if caught after escaping and was considered a severe punishment. The next tier up wore the all-yellow canary suits. In 1833, in Port Arthur and Macquarie Harbour, Tasmania, the standing order was that all male convicts on arrival wear the standard yellow suit. Good behaviour entitled the next and largest group to wear clothing of white/grey duck (untwilled cotton). Educated convicts were allowed grey dress, as were prisoners on probation for good conduct. Some of these convicts wore their own clothes when uniforms were not available. Female convicts outside of workhouses wore civilian dress, making their status as convicts less conspicuous than men.

Despite numerous and large orders of convict uniforms, few have survived. By the twentieth century, the only places for convict clothing were contemporary 'cabinets of curiosities' that promoted 'dark tourism' (Lennon and Foley 2000). In 1994, this mode of display inspired the exhibition *Possession*, at the Mitchell

Library in Sydney, which included a magpie suit from its collection. Similarly, prior to the 1980s, the Port Arthur Historic Site (PAHS) in Tasmania, the largest preserved convict site, relished in presenting the horrors of the convict system by displaying canary suits. Linda Clark et al. (2012) note that fewer than 100 convict uniforms and associated dress objects are held in public collections. Most are thought to have a Tasmanian provenance, either linked to a place of incarceration or collected by Tasmanian private collectors. Photographer J. W. Beattie's private museum, which included convict uniforms, was purchased by the Queen Victoria Museum and Art Gallery in Launceston in 1927. It remains a significant holding of convict dress, complementing the collections at PAHS, the Tasmanian Museum and Art Gallery and the National Trust of Australia (Tasmania). The paucity of convict clothing in museum collections materially reflects the historiographical avoidance of the convict past, yet the number of convict uniforms and the large ex-convict population suggests that ex-convict dress is likely to be present in Tasmanian dress collections.

Negotiating colonial identities

Social mobility in the Australian colonies in the nineteenth century was expressed through the consumption of dress. In colonial Australia, fashion consumption fulfilled hedonistic pursuits, social emulation and manifested class identity and agency (Elliott 1988; Maynard 1994). Even female convicts 'always found means to dress better' (Tardif 1990: 21). How they achieved this is ripe for questioning. In Tasmania, convicts formed the majority of what was a class-conscious population. For example, in 1853, convicts accounted for 77 per cent of the island's population of 65,000 (Alexander 2010). Colonial newspapers reveal how certain contemporaries found it difficult to distinguish some convict women from free female settlers through appearance alone. For example, Hobart's police – intent on capturing absconding female convict servants – had difficulty distinguishing between convict and free women (likely including prostitutes) while on duty at night ('Convict Constabulary' 1839). As in Britain, class ambiguity was a prominent concern in mid-nineteenth-century Hobart. A female servant wearing her mistress's clothing, if not a gift, was a punishable offence entailing incarceration at the Female Factory workhouse and probably time at the washtub (Robson 1965). Those wearing their mistress's cast-offs aggravated the problem. When the anonymous 'Concerned Mother of a Family' wrote to a local Hobart newspaper, she suggested that a uniform for female servants could counteract the 'evil . . . attributed to [their] gay dressing' ('Convict Constabulary' 1839: 4). This law and the example of this article show how those with social and political power considered prostitution and class ambiguity to be social evils which threatened the stability of free society.

Convict uniforms followed gendered forms of social control within the colonies. For males, they indicated punishment and reform. Female convict bodies were less obviously inscribed as criminal, although head-shaving was common (Damousi 1997). Women adopted strategies to conceal their marks of punishment including wigs and fashionable dress. Their concealment contributed to the culture in which convict pasts were obscured. Without uniforms, female convicts arguably transgressed social boundaries more easily than male convicts, making it difficult to trace their mobility, both physically and socially. Alexander (2010: 140–1) describes how the 'convict look' (being physically or mentally scarred by trauma, or old, poor, weather-beaten or dishevelled) was discernible in men, but less so in women. Likewise, those employed who could afford decent clothing and took care of their appearance avoided this discrimination.

As noted, convict women, until about thirty years ago, were largely excluded from the histories of convictism in the Australian colonies. Their experiences and characters as prostitutes or drunks were thought to be uniform (Tardif 1990). However, scholarship has revealed the breadth of their experiences, individual hardships and successes as convicts and emancipists, in order to reclaim the diversity of female convict experience and identity (Daniels 1998). The dress of female ex-convicts who achieved financial security and social respectability may thus be included in Narryna's collection. Convict clothing, like convict experience, lacks uniformity.

The historical emphases on the apparently homogeneous (male) convict and ex-convict experience operated within a larger scheme of erasure of the convict stain. Now that history has reclaimed the female convict, it is the prerogative of dress history to follow suit. However, this is a difficult task when surviving material does not easily support her existence, let alone her unique identity. Where history has the benefit of official colonial and British government documents, inventories, censuses, correspondence or personal letters and diaries, object-based dress history relies on few extant examples of male convict uniforms and working dress, as well as textual or graphic evidence, to understand and act as a counterpart to female convict dress. These sources largely portray only the period of punishment in a convict's life, not the pecuniary and social success many enjoyed as emancipists, which was often displayed through fashionable dress such as that worn in a portrait of ex-convict Maria Davis (Figure 3.3). In 1842, aged seventeen, Davis was transported to Hobart for receiving stolen spoons. She worked as a housemaid and despite serving three months' hard labour – likely at a wash tub – at a Female Factory, became free by servitude in 1849. Davis married well, first to a free police officer and later to a ship's captain. Her aspirations to gentility are captured in her reflective pose and fashionable dress including a trimmed bonnet and white cap which was worn by many respectable women. Although it is difficult to gauge how representative Maria Davis' life was of the female convict experience, her adornment in fashionable clothing was typical of successful ex-convicts. This image

FIGURE 3.3 Studio portrait of ex-convict Maria Davis (1825–96), W. Burrows & Co. Photographers (Launceston, Tasmania). Courtesy of Female Convicts Research Centre and Joanne Cranstoun.

is an example from the small but revealing collection of digitized photographs of ex-convict women in the Female Convicts in Van Diemen's Land database.

Narryna Heritage Museum

As noted earlier, Narryna was established as a folk museum, its purpose to educate present and future generations in the social history of the island and past way of life (Mercer 2002; Petrow 2009). The folk represented by Narryna's dress collection were primarily wealthy urban and rural pioneers. Since then, interpretations of Australian pioneer experience now include many Aboriginal, multicultural and convict voices that were previously marginalized. This collecting of dress of the upper classes followed the prevailing mode of collecting dress in the 1950s in dress collections more broadly (Taylor 2004). The omission of convicts, who principally comprised Tasmanian folk culture, was not considered significant by the museum, particularly while penal and Aboriginal material was collected by TMAG.

The museum was nonetheless shaped by the enduring metaphor of the convict stain. Narryna's original committee sought to downplay Tasmania's origins as a penal colony in favour of a grand free settler narrative that excluded convicts and indigenous Tasmanians (Petrow 2009). The Chair of the committee was Dr W. L. Crowther and other members were drawn from the upper-class suburb of Battery Point, Hobart where Narryna is located. Their initial aim was to honour the pioneers of Van Diemen's Land from British settlement in 1803 to 1856 when the colony became self-governing, many of whom were elite landowners. From 1998 to 2012, the museum was marketed as a grand house museum shaped around the original owner, the merchant-gentleman Captain Andrew Haig, narrated mostly through possessions representative of the middle and upper class, as well as depicting domestic labour in the kitchen and laundry. As part of TMAG, Narryna's early vision of folk life is now reframed according to the larger public institution's postcolonial and inclusive account of the past.

Until it was subsumed under TMAG in 2012, Narryna housed the largest private collection of nineteenth-century dress in Australia. The two histories of the museum (Mercer 2002; Petrow 2009) recognize, but do not explore, the significance of the dress collection. The prevailing attitude of fashion as frivolous and solely of interest to women has meant that the collection itself has been neglected, attitudes Taylor challenged in *The Study of Dress History* (2002). As well, only a few dress history texts mention Narryna's collection, using examples to show the breadth of colonial Australian dress (Fletcher 1984; Isaacs 1987; Reade 2010). This is relatively impressive considering the limited body of colonial Australian fashion history in the context of Western fashion research (e.g. Maynard 1994; Joel 1998). More recently, Narryna's dress collection has been the focus of graduate academic research, where Petra Mosmann (2010) studied a dress belonging to a free settler and Jess Nossiter (2011) surveyed colonial-era men's waistcoats. Even so, the full value and potential of the dress collection is little known outside Tasmania, indeed Australia.

From the late 1950s, the museum committee minute books indicate that the descendants of Tasmanian pioneer families and other wealthy Hobart citizens were approached for gifts and donations of objects to establish the collection (VDLFM 1972). Acquisition was based on the antique or historic value of objects (Petrow 2009). Narryna's selectivity was typical. Reade (2010) describes how, from the 1950s to the 1970s, Australian colonial dress collections favoured high-quality colonial- and European-made garments over mass-produced or home-made clothing, similar to British collections (Taylor 2004). The early collecting policy foregrounds the importance of genealogy and family histories in perpetuating the dominant pioneer story and establishing provenance within the collection. For example, Narryna holds clothing associated with the Meredith family, important agricultural pioneers on Tasmania's east coast, as well as the saddlery used by Quaker missionary and notable Hobart philanthropist George Washington Walker, who resided at Narryna in the early 1850s. The convict stain thus influenced the acquisition of items at the museum and the perceived value of items by their owners. Some families' origins were considered stainless; others perhaps were conveniently concealed by the later social respectability and wealth of ex-convicts and their descendants.

When Narryna was established as a museum, the convict stain was prominent in national sentiment, and was thus influential in the museum's agenda (Petrow 2009). House museums are heritage sites that construct, maintain, legitimize and reinforce a range of identities, including national identity (Crouch and Parker 2003; Young 2011). At Narryna, this was supposedly a stain-free identity. Heritage scholar Laurajane Smith (2006: 68) argues that visitors to house museums and heritage sites engage in 'sustained cultural performances in which certain cultural values and identities are continually rehearsed and thus preserved'. The objects of the rooms act as props, the interpretation material as script and the audience as actors. Taylor (2004: 271) criticizes the romanticized role of dress in early folk museums in promulgating 'a comfortable vision of the past which denies economic tensions and political struggles'. This is precisely what happened at Narryna. In the past, Australian folk museums were intent on mood, tradition and a feel-good notion of heritage rather than authenticity and accuracy. Material studies scholar Howard Marshall (1997: 392) notes that 'folk museums have often projected an image that visitors take to be democratic and representative but which are generally full of biases reflecting attitudes and stereotypes of noble pioneers and valiant migrants'. At Narryna, scant labelling contributed to the museum's original agenda of silencing the convict past.

Such silencing of convict history can be explained by the social stigma of the stain, but also by historical museum methods. Collections interpretation is difficult when faced with a lack of factual records. In this case, the Narryna minute books of committee meetings indicate that there was a tacit knowledge of objects, events, people; perhaps the entries (or lack thereof) in the acquisition books signal this. Characteristically for the period, object records were completed often to a bare minimum, merely stating the donor, date of donation and often a vague description of a previous owner along the lines of 'worn by Mrs Smith'. Although scant acquisition records related to clothing objects were typical of many museums at this time, at Narryna, such vague recording – deliberately or otherwise – contributed to the pervading cultural amnesia. The image of respectability built on wealth and prestige created by the museum functioned to erase the stain. The lack of museum documentation resulted in further historical silences and family secrets typical of mid-twentieth-century Tasmanian popular belief.

Despite the overt exclusion of convict and non-elite clothing in Narryna's collection, the lack of clear provenance of objects within the collection allows for many alternative interpretations of the clothing today. The power of garments to provide alternative accounts of the past challenges the museum narratives around the objects, and may bring closer the identities of the original wearers (Lambert 2010). Consider the potential of comparing photographs like that of Maria Davis to the dress collection at Narryna, or the potential impact of exhibiting them together. Promisingly, the acquisition register includes a wedding veil associated with the granddaughter of successful Sydney ex-convict Mary Reibey (Narryna Heritage Museum 2011) who was transported for stealing a horse. Reibey became a prosperous businesswoman, landowner and favourite of Governor Lachlan Macquarie. Yet, ex-convict lineage is not recorded on the acquisition register, due either to pragmatic record systems or silencing of the convict past.

New technologies, such as the digitizing of records, employed by both archives and family history researchers, are valuable additions to the tools already available to dress historians. The FCVDL database makes available online biographical information of female convicts based on descendant research and convict records including their sentence, appearance, conduct and marriage. Significantly, descendants can upload photographs of their convict ancestors to this database. The few available photographs portray the women as respectable and fashionably dressed. Of course, photographs may not always have been preserved and convict and ex-convict women may not have had the opportunity to be photographed at all. Margaret Gray and Elizabeth White were convict servants who worked at Narryna for George Washington Walker, however, photographs of these women are not available. Their convict records reveal they were at times punished for absconding and drunkenness, but little is known of their experiences as ex-convicts. Silences remain. However, the available photographs on this database and digitized colonial newspapers reinforce the fact that in some cases during and most definitely after their sentences, female convicts wore similar clothing to their class peers. For example, Ann Harris, convicted for stealing a shawl from a shop arrived in VDL in 1834, had no colonial offences, married a man of convict origins in 1837 and became free by servitude in 1841 (Figure 3.4). Harris' wide crinoline, decorated bonnet, bag and shawl expressed her claims to respectability. Similar items of dress are held in the Narryna collection. The ability to record such an appearance for posterity in a photograph asserts Harris' improved circumstances. That images of successful female ex-convicts exist in greater number than images of those serving their sentences is telling of the importance of the studio portrait in distancing oneself from a convict past.

Conclusion

Attention given to male convict uniforms has overshadowed enquiry into the dress of female convicts. Ex-convict dress histories might yet be possible despite the difficulty of identifying their dress in museums. Collections offer only a limited range of dress worn by convicts and ex-convicts, and for the study of

FIGURE 3.4 Studio portrait of ex-convict Ann Harris (c.1817–68). Courtesy of Female Convicts Research Centre and the Robotham family.

women especially, the information offered by digitized newspapers and archival material, particularly photographs, reveals a more complete picture of ex-convict dress. A great deal more work is to be done on convict and ex-convict clothing. If, as Giorgio Riello and Peter McNeil (2010: 2) suggest, 'fashion can be used as a lens to consider change – sometimes dramatic – as it embodies and materialises the "interruptions" and "discontinuities" of history' so too can the Narryna dress collection, as a unique assemblage of fashion, be viewed as a further refining aperture to discuss the use of extant dress collections to exhibit filtered versions of the past. Dress researchers can attempt to flesh out limited provenance of dress objects by comparing museum acquisition records to professional and family history biographies and photographs, by investigating gaps and silences, and by reading historical archives against the grain.

The intention of this chapter was to investigate why there is little extant convict clothing in the Narryna Heritage Museum and to highlight the challenge that the convict stain poses to object-based dress research. Acknowledging the broader social, cultural, economic and political contexts gives a fuller account of clothes worn in the past, particularly in the case of Australian convict and ex-convict clothing and its associated metaphoric stain. The selective agenda of former museum collecting cultures have obscured the full picture of historic life in Tasmania. The stain may appear to have been removed at Narryna, but its remnants linger. Questioning historical biases and using a broader repertoire of methods will enable dress historians to uncover the hidden successes of convict women.

References

Alexander, A. (2010), *Tasmania's Convicts: How Felons Built a Free Society*, Crows Nest, N.S.W.: Allen and Unwin.

Ash, J. (2010), *Dress Behind Bars: Prison Clothing as Criminality*, London and New York: I.B. Taurus.

Clark, L. et al. (2012), 'More than Magpies: Tasmanian Convict Clothing in Public Collections', *Historic Environment*, 24 (3): 50–7.

'The Convict Constabulary' (1839), *Colonial Times*, 19 February: 4.

Crouch, D. and Parker, G. (2003), '"Digging-up" Utopia? Space, Practice and Landuse Heritage', *Geoform*, 34 (3): 395–408.

Damousi, J. (1997), *Depraved and Disorderly: Female Convicts, Sexuality and Gender in Colonial Australia*, Cambridge: Cambridge University Press.

Daniels, K. (1998), *Convict Women*, St Leonards, N.S.W.: Allen and Unwin.

Elliott, J. (1988), *The Colony Clothed*, PhD Thesis, University of Adelaide, Australia.

Fletcher, M. (1984), *Costume in Australia 1788–1901*, Melbourne: Oxford University Press.

Griffiths, T. (1994), 'Past Silences: Aborigines and Convicts in Our History-making', in P. Russell and R. White (eds), *Pastiche I: Reflections on Nineteenth-century Australia*, St Leonards, N.S.W.: Allen and Unwin.

Hughes, R. (1987), *The Fatal Shore*, London: Harvill Press.

Isaacs, J. (1987), *The Gentle Arts: 200 Years of Australian Women's Domestic and Decorative Arts*, Sydney: Lansdowne.

Joel, A. (1998), *Parade: The Story of Fashion in Australia*, Sydney: HarperCollins.

Lambert, M. (2010), 'Fashion in the Museum: The Material Culture of Artefacts', in G. Riello and P. McNeil (eds), *The Fashion History Reader*, Oxford and New York: Berg.

Lennon, J. and Foley, M. (2000), *Dark Tourism: The Attraction of Death and Disaster*, London: Continuum.

Liston, C. (2008), *Women Transported: Life in Australia's Convict Female Factories*, Parramatta: Parramatta Heritage Centre.

Marshall, H. W. (1977), 'Folklife and the Rise of American Folk Museums', *Journal of American Folklore*, 90 (358): 391–413.

Maynard, M. (1994), *Fashioned from Penury: Dress as Cultural Practice in Colonial Australia*, Melbourne: Cambridge University Press.

Mercer, P. (2002), *Built for a Merchant: The History of a Colonial Gentleman's Residence*, Hobart: Narryna Heritage Museum Trustees.

Mosmann, P. (2010), 'Sarah Butler's Dress: Women, Fashion, Family and Remembering Van Diemen's Land', Honours Thesis, University of Tasmania, Australia.

Narryna Heritage Museum (2011), Catalogue, Hobart.

Nossiter, J. (2011), 'The Men Who Wore the Narryna Heritage Museum Waistcoats: Wild Colonial Boys?', honours thesis, University of Tasmania, Australia.

Petrow, S. (2009), 'Sanitising or Celebrating the Past? The Van Diemen's Land Memorial Folk Museum 1957–2007', *reCollections*, 4 (2), http://recollections.nma.gov.au/issues/vol_4_no_2/papers/sanitising_or_celebrating_the_past, accessed 20 March 2011.

Preston, M. H. (2004), *Charitable Words: Women, Philanthropy, and the Language of Charity in Nineteenth-century Dublin*, Westport: Praeger Publishers.

Reade, C. (2010), 'Resources: Collections of Colonial Dress and Fashion in Australia' in J. B. Eicher (ed.), *Berg Encyclopedia of World Dress and Fashion*, Oxford and New York: Berg.

Riello, G. and McNeil, P. (2010), 'Introduction: The Fashion History Reader: Global Perspectives', in G. Riello and P. McNeil (eds), *The Fashion History Reader*, Oxford and New York: Berg.

Robson, L. L. (1965), *The Convict Settlers of Australia: An Enquiry into the Origin and Character of the Convicts Transported to New South Wales and Van Diemen's Land 1787–1852*, Carlton: Melbourne University Press.

Smith, B. (2008), *Australia's Birthstain: The Startling Legacy of the Convict Era*, Crows Nest, N.S.W.: Allen and Unwin.

Smith, L. (2006), *Uses of Heritage*, Oxon: Routledge.

Sorkin, J. (2012), 'Stain: On Cloth, Stigma, and Shame', in C. Harper (ed.), *Textiles: Critical and Primary Sources: Identity*, London and New York: Berg.

Tardif, P. (1990), *Notorious Strumpets and Dangerous Girls: Convict Women in Van Diemen's Land, 1803–1829*, North Ryde: Angus and Robertson.

Taylor, L. (1998), 'Doing the Laundry? A Reassessment of Object-Based Dress History', *Fashion Theory*, 2 (4): 337–58.

Taylor, L. (2002), *The Study of Dress History*, Manchester and New York: Manchester University Press.

Taylor, L. (2004), *Establishing Dress History*, Manchester and New York: Manchester University Press.

Van Diemen's Land Folk Museum (VDLFM) (1972), Museum Committee reports, 14 November, Narryna Heritage Museum, Hobart.

Young, L. (1988), 'The Experience of Convictism: Five Pieces of Convict Clothing from Western Australia', *Costume*, 22: 70–84.

Young, L. (2011), 'Why Are There So Many Writers' House Museums in England?', *Museums Australia Magazine*, 19 (4): 26–30.

4 *TRAJE DE CRIOULA*: REPRESENTING NINETEENTH-CENTURY AFRO-BRAZILIAN DRESS

Aline T. Monteiro Damgaard

During the nineteenth century, Brazil underwent a series of political and economic transformations that stimulated its transition from Portuguese colony at the beginning of the century to independent republic by its final decade. Despite extensive social changes, however, slavery remained a legal and widespread practice until its formal abolition in 1888. Many travellers and foreigners who visited Brazil during the nineteenth century depicted slaves' everyday lives in the public sphere. Among these images, the majority of female slaves were represented in a set of garments that has come to be known as the *traje de crioula*.

The term *traje de crioula* can be translated as 'creole clothing', and it is used to classify a specific set of garments that African and Afro-Brazilian women, slaves or not, would commonly wear. Today, this specific combination of clothing is often referred to as 'Bahian dress', or the *traje da baiana*, and is primarily used by women who follow the Candomblé religion and work in the street markets of Bahia, a state located in the northeast of Brazil. While in a modern context the colours, shapes and materials of the clothes can represent a range of meanings, the specific combination of garments and their visual appearance are directly influenced by the *traje de crioula* of the nineteenth century.

Methods and context

This chapter examines representations of Afro-Brazilian dress from nineteenth-century Brazil with the aim of examining the *traje de crioula*'s origin, formation and influence. The research includes comparative analysis of a broad range of nineteenth-century visual representations and written descriptions alongside analysis of surviving garments currently held in museum collections, and their subsequent interpretation and display. To present a case study for this chapter, a sample of four images is utilized. While these were made by different travellers and in different decades throughout the nineteenth century, the examples represent the different types of visual media commonly seen in Brazil during the period, enabling the selection to speak to a broader range of contemporary imagery available in the region. The chapter seeks to explain how the garments and their representations were used to affirm and reaffirm core visual characteristics about the dress of Afro-Brazilians in the eyes of foreigners. It also explores how such representations have informed later understandings of garments in Brazilian museums. In juxtaposing nineteenth-century images with surviving garments, this study illuminates the complex relationship between dress as worn, dress in visual depictions and dress in museum interpretation.

The dress history methodologies suggested by Lou Taylor (2002) have been essential to this research. Studying dress through historical visual representations can add immensely to the knowledge of styles, fashion, materials, and shapes, and it can also assist in elucidating the meaning of clothing. Taylor points out, however, that while clothes portrayed in visual sources can provide information on 'style, quality of fabrics and garments, cut, hair-styles, body stance, accessories and exactly how these were worn', no visual representation will be 'free from the personal preferences and prejudices of its creator nor free from the etiquettes, politics and prejudices of its day' (2002: 115). By examining both objects and images of nineteenth-century creole clothing, this chapter explores these tensions.

This research is informed by a range of dress historical studies of Brazilian garments, but draws in particular upon the work of two important Brazilian dress historians. Teresa Cristina Toledo de Paula (2004) has provided a valuable survey of Brazilian dress history, and has highlighted the gaps apparent in this field of study. She notes, for example, that national studies that use surviving textile artefacts in their analyses are very rare. Rita Andrade (2008) has written the social biography of a dress that survives in the collection of the Museu Paulista in São Paulo, tracing its story from its creation to its entry into the museum; a similar trajectory and object-focused approach underpins the research undertaken here. Research about Brazilian dress and textile history published in English also underpins this study. An early example is Stanley Stein's book (1957), which analyses archival records from different cotton manufacturers in Brazil; more recently and most closely connected to the research in this chapter is the work of Kelly Mohs Gage (2013). Aside from Gage's recent work, there is very little scholarship on the subject of Afro-Brazilian slave dress; notable exceptions include the two articles by historian Silvia Hunold Lara (1997, 2002). Gage acknowledges the important contribution of Lara's articles to the subject, but highlights that 'they do not address what slave women actually wore' (2013: 112). Her own research into Afro-Brazilian dress descriptions as found in runaway slaves advertisements provides an innovative and detailed, but highly specific, account of women's slave dress as worn in Rio de Janeiro in 1861; the research for this chapter addresses a broader period and a different region. Gage also states that '[p]hysical evidence related to the dress of this segment of the colonial Brazilian population is virtually non-existent" (2013: 113); this research draws on some of the few surviving examples.

This chapter forms part of a larger research project that analysed nineteenth-century so-called creole skirts (Plates 3 and 4) from the Museu do Traje e do Têxtil da Fundação Instituto Feminina da Bahia in Salvador (Monteiro 2012). This study examined the quality of imported fabrics, the use of printed cottons and the diversity of identities that a woman dressed in the *traje de crioula* could communicate. The analyses of museum skirts indicated that they were made of good-quality fabric, probably imported from England. Such imported fabrics carried a higher price than the coarser local fabrics that slaves usually were given. This suggests that printed fabric of different origins and qualities were circulating in Brazil, and that both types were used by African and Afro-Brazilian women.

The Museu do Traje e do Têxtil de Salvador houses one of Brazil's most important textile collections, which is composed mainly of nineteenth- and twentieth-century clothes and accessories. The collection was started by D. Henriqueta Martins Catharino, the founder of the institute to which the museum belongs. Catharino's original impetus, in 1933, was to create a collection that would represent the history of Bahian women and in 1946 she donated the first creole skirts to the museum. The skirts were bought at auction from a local church and had previously belonged to Florinda Anna do Nascimento, an Afro-Brazilian woman who had worked as a servant at a farm in the area of Bahia (Peixoto 2003).

According to museum registers, of the fourteen skirts identified as creole clothing, twelve belonged to Nascimento. Three are on permanent display at the museum along with other garments that have also been labelled by the museum as creole clothes. As one of the objectives of the original research was to study printed fabrics from the period, only the skirts were analysed. Two were chosen, based on their printed pattern; one featured floral designs (Plate 3) and the other was geometric (Plate 4). The selection was also informed by the former ownership of the garments; one was among the skirts that had belonged to Nascimento (Plate 4), the other belonged to D. Felicidade (Plate 3), an Afro-Brazilian woman who lived close to Salvador and, according to the museum registers, was born in 1848 (Monteiro 2012).

These skirts, along with the others displayed at the museum, feature very similar patterns and construction. The skirts are full, long and formed of upper, middle and lower sections. Most of the pieces were sewn by hand and the two skirts that were analysed in detail were of very similar size, around 80 centimetres in length and around 400 centimetres in width. The majority of these skirts were made of fabric printed with stripes, flowers or geometric motifs, and often included with embroidery at the hem.

Since the three skirts were displayed by the museum as part of a predefined creole ensemble, and the other skirts in the collection were also designated as creole skirts, it was important to investigate the reasons behind and meanings of these classifications. The skirts had not been part of a set of clothes at the point of donation; the ensemble was thus fabricated to represent a particular category of clothing and a group identity. The questions that underpinned the original research thus overlap with the enquiries of this chapter: why were long, full and printed skirts labelled creole skirts? What did and does the term 'creole' mean when classifying clothes? Were the skirts worn separately from the other component parts of creole dress? How is our understanding of the *traje de crioula* shaped by nineteenth-century visual representations and how accurate are such depictions? And how do museum displays contribute to the contemporary symbolic importance and understanding of historic *traje de crioula*?

In Brazil, slaves were mostly Africans. By the early nineteenth century, African populations in Brazil were sizeable, and black populations may have nearly doubled those of white Europeans and Brazilians in many areas (Gage 2013: 114). African individuals, born and raised in Brazil as slaves or as descendants of slaves, as Kátia Mattoso notes (1997), were often called 'creoles' or *mulatos*. In this chapter, when referring to the descendents of Africans born in Brazil, the term 'Afro-Brazilian' is used in preference to the outdated and now pejorative term creole. 'Creole clothing', however, has been retained as a literal translation of the Portuguese expression *traje de crioula*. Even though the term creole clothing might suggest garments only worn by creoles, that is, by persons of mixed race and by Afro-Brazilians in particular, the visual representations and studies of this topic suggest a broader circulation. For example, Afro-Brazilian slaves tended to be better integrated into society than Africans and therefore usually worked in domestic settings (Monteiro, Ferreira and Freitas 2005). This is notable because creole clothing was usually represented in visual imagery as the occupational clothing of slaves working in the street market. The style of dress was also used in depictions of slaves as well as in depictions of African and Afro-Brazilian free women (i.e. women who were freed by a letter of emancipation received as a present or purchased after years of hard extra work). All these possibilities suggest that the *traje de crioula*, despite its name, was a set of clothing not limited to a specific group, but instead used in different contexts.

Travellers and their representations

An investigation of the visual characteristics of creole dress in pictorial representations throughout the nineteenth century complements the object analysis of the surviving skirts. The majority of existing visual sources that depict slaves' clothing were made by travellers and foreigners who visited Brazil during the nineteenth century. These included, for example, the artists Carlos Julião and Joaquim Guillobel from Portugal, Johann Moritz Rugendas from Germany, and Henri Chamberlain and Maria, Lady Callcott, both from England. Later in the century the photographers Christiano Junior from Portugal and Albert Henschel from Germany also worked in Brazil, as did Brazilian-born photographer Marc Ferrez, son of the French sculptor Zepherin Ferrez. Artists, travellers and photographers left a large collection of visual sources. Letters, journals and reports also assist in comprehending and contextualizing nineteenth-century dress in Brazil.

Among the best-known visual representations of this period are the drawings, lithographs and watercolours of Jean-Baptiste Debret, a French painter who arrived in Brazil in 1816 together with other artists in an expedition that has become known as the French Artistic Mission (Schwarcz 1993). His works are compiled in three volumes entitled *Voyage pittoresque et historique au Brésil* which were first published in 1834 and 1839 in Paris (Debret 1834). The historian Eneida Maria Sela (2008) has analysed these alongside several other visual works by artists and travellers which represented the everyday life of slaves in Brazil. Sela compared depictions by Guillobel with those by Chamberlain and Debret, suggesting that these works together provided a visual model of representing slaves; Lara also suggests that artists worked within genres and with 'types', reproducing 'what is already known in advance' (2002: 131). Sela observes the similarity between the settings depicted by different travellers, for example, domestic interiors, Sunday walks and market activities are all common. As will be discussed below, in the samples scrutinized for this study, similarities between the poses of depicted subjects, their clothes and associated objects can also be observed. Art historian Ana Maria de Morais Belluzzo has argued that the circulation of Guillobel's compositions influenced later representations of customs, people and activities in nineteenth-century Brazil. Belluzzo explains, however, that even though there was a model of representation, each artist had his or her own characteristics (2006: 300).

The *carte-de-visite* is another important visual source through which Afro-Brazilian slave dress can be studied. Smaller and more affordable than the daguerreotype and, importantly, reproducible, this type of photograph achieved widespread popularity in the nineteenth century. The practice of photographing the client's whole body and not just the face was also more common in this medium. Art historian Annateresa Fabris (2004) explains that Brazilian studio portrait photographers began to explore scenic elements in order to compose pictures, to create the desired ambiance and to emphasize what she calls the 'theatrical pose'. Manuals were written by experienced studio photographers, and these books contained information on utilizing backdrops, arranging objects and improving lighting conditions (Koutsoukos 2008). Consequently, the formal similarities seen in Brazilian *cartes-de-visite* can be understood as visual conventions carefully designed to enhance the value of a portrait framed by social codes and furnished with symbols of respectability.

The paintings, drawings, engravings and sketches made by travellers in a colonial context may have been inspired by what they perceived as real life, however, their finished products could have been shaped by a range of factors outside the frame of the image. These could have included the prejudices, preferences and political allegiances of the maker, the perceived demands of their intended audience and a range of other shaping influences including the artists' style and the limitations of the medium. As Gage has put it, of the nineteenth-century Brazilian context, 'slave images were often created for propaganda purposes to express anti-slavery sentiments, the impression of a benevolent slave owner, or as curiosity images purchased by tourists' (2013: 113). To read such images as simple repositories of information when they may be idealized, exotized, exaggerated, stylized or downright fictional is a methodological challenge that faces any historian using visual sources; the same challenges apply no less to the dress historian. Taylor suggests throughout her work that the best way to study clothing through image sources is by juxtaposing imagery with other comparative sources such as surviving garments, other types of visual representation and contemporaneous literature (2002); this intertextual method is utilized here.

The *traje de crioula* and market activities

The *traje de crioula* was mainly represented as a set of clothes formed by a full, gathered skirt, a loose shirt, turban, a *pano-da-costa* shawl and ornaments such as necklaces, bracelets and pendants. It is not known when these individual items of clothes first became the ensemble commonly referred to as the *traje de crioula*, but it was during the nineteenth century that it came to represent the main way in which African women and their descendants dressed in Brazil. This tendency is exemplified here by comparing a drawing by Julião from the late eighteenth century (Plate 5), a lithograph made from a drawing by Debret from 1835 (Figure 4.1), a *carte-de-visite* by the photographer Christiano Junior from 1864–6 (Figure 4.2), and a drawing by the Maria, Lady Callcott, probably made during her visits to Brazil in 1821, 1822 and 1823 (Plate 6).

Although there is a marked difference in the style, nature and media of the respective images, all visualize African and Afro-Brazilian women, slaves or not, dressed in elements of the *traje de crioula*. Moreover, the market scene and its related activities and objects (i.e. trade and commodities) were often important constituent parts of the visual context in which the garments are shown, indicating that the *traje de crioula* was commonly depicted as a form of occupational clothing.

IL COLLIER DE FER,
Châtiment des fugitifs.

FIGURE 4.1 Jean-Baptiste Debret (1768–1848), 'Le collier de fer, châtiment de fugitifs' [The iron collar, punishment of fugitives], 1835, lithograph. Courtesy of Fundação Biblioteca Nacional, Brazil.

Julião presents two women selling what seem to be fruits, sugarcane and chickens (Plate 5). In Junior's photograph, a woman is seated alongside trays of fruits and a young boy (Figure 4.2) and in Callcott's drawing, market trade is represented by a box of sweetmeats (Plate 6). Although a depiction of market activity does not seem to be the main purpose of Debret's image, his drawing nevertheless shows a woman selling pineapples and holding a basket on top of her head (Figure 4.1). As indicated by the title of the image, 'The Iron Collar', the intention is to show one of the punishments that slaves could receive at that time. The status of women as traders is nonetheless common to all of these images.

Debret also presents a black woman who is not selling, but buying products. Compared to the slave who sells pineapples, she is shown in different clothes, wearing what appears to be a dress with a longer, patterned skirt and styled hair. Although Debret was clearly influenced by earlier illustrations of slaves' clothing, he also depicted both slaves and free women in clothes that were more consistent with European fashion in the first decades of the nineteenth century. It is not clear from the visual content of Debret's publication why some women would be represented wearing the *traje de crioula* and others in European-style dress. However, it is noticeable in his work that the European way of dressing was represented as more

FIGURE 4.2 Christiano Junior (1832–1902), photograph from the series *Escravos* [Slaves], 1864/66, *carte-de-visite*. Courtesy of Museu Histórico Nacional / IBRAM / Ministério da Cultura.

luxurious, in part due to the details of the fabrics, jewellery and hairstyles. Free women could decide what to wear, but acquiring new European dress was not easy. As mentioned by Koutsoukos, the financial situation of free Afro-Brazilians was critical as they had to face all sorts of prejudices and challenges in order to find work, family and housing (2002: 1). Gage notes, in addition, that slave women could project what she describes as a 'quasi-European appearance'. This was in part because 'the practice of passing old clothing from the women of the house to slaves was common. Similarities in dress between Afro-Brazilians and Euro-Brazilians existed and are evidenced in photographs from this period'. Although it is hard to identify whether European styles were adopted 'by choice or force', 'the incorporation of European dress . . . [was] part of the daily dress of slave women' (2013: 130, 121, 115).

Although certain elements of the *traje de crioula* appear in all the images used in this chapter, the details of the individual clothes vary. One example is the *pano-da-costa*. Literally translated as 'coastal cloth', the term can be used to indicate a specific type of shawl originally imported to Brazil from Africa, but coast can also be used to indicate a range of African geographic, economic, social and cultural spaces (Lody 2003: 20, 14). All the depicted women carry a *pano-da-costa*, but they are worn in different ways. In Julião's drawing, the woman on the left uses the shawl to carry a baby in a method which shows the continuing influence of African cultural practices in Afro-Brazilian dress (Gage 2013: 125). Another wears it draped ornamentally over her shoulders (Plate 5). Debret presents a woman carrying the shawl on her right shoulder, as it is shown in Callcott's drawing (Figure 4.1 and Plate 6), while Junior presents the shawl around the woman's hips in such a way that it is not possible to see her blouse or shirt (Figure 4.2). This shawl, however, seems not to be the type of shawl usually classified as a *pano-da-costa*. In a simple description, Heloisa Torres states that *pano-da-costa* was a rectangular cloth constructed by the junction of several stripes in the longitudinal direction and the edges finished with a simple hem (2004: 419). Even though in many depictions of the *pano-da-costa* these stripes were not represented, the rectangular shape is often evident. The fringed shawl used in Junior's photograph differs from this description and also from the other images mentioned in this chapter, indicating that different types of shawls may have also been worn with this ensemble.

The upper parts of the clothing are similar, but not the same. It is very clear from the visual sources mentioned here that the blouse or shirt could differ in shape, pattern and material. Colour is often difficult to determine since many of these illustrations were painted at a later stage, or were black and white photographs (Torres 2004: 418); indeed, their colouration may have been entirely imaginary. In the four images discussed, each woman wears a different type of blouse. In Julião's image, the woman on the left wears a tighter shirt of what appears to be printed fabric (Plate 5). The second woman wears a looser white shirt with puffed sleeves, and they both have uncovered arms. In Debret's image the female slave wears a simpler model of a loose blouse, sleeveless and with no print or ornamentation (Figure 4.1). In Junior's *carte-de-visite* the woman wears a shirt with sleeves covering only the upper arms. The shirt has what seems to be a printed fabric detail in the collar and in the hem (Figure 4.2). She was probably wearing a long-sleeved shirt with the same pattern of the skirt, but she could have been wearing a dress. In the last image (Plate 6), the woman wears a blouse that reveals not only her arms, but also her shoulders. The blouse has short sleeves and lace decoration at the edges. Even though it is possible that the slaves would wear a looser blouse, closer to what was used as an undershirt by the elite, it is also clear that there is overt sexualization of the subject in many colonial images of slaves, which frequently reveal exposed flesh on arms, shoulders and breasts.

The turban and the full skirt depicted in the great majority of the travellers' representations, and in the sample of images examined here, share some similarities but also show differences in volume, colour and ornamentation. The skirts studied at the museum are very similar to the ones depicted by Callcott (Plate 6) and the one worn by the woman in Junior's photograph (Figure 4.2). This similarity, not only in the printed fabric, but also in the presence of a ruffle at the lower edge of the skirts indicates that the nineteenth-century visual representations and the skirts from the museum are very closely related. The regular inclusion of a skirt in visual imagery also attests to their typicality within slave clothing. Gage has demonstrated the prevalence of the skirt (*saia*) in descriptions of Brazilian dress in advertisements for runaway slaves; of her sample of 118 examples, 96 per cent include reference 'to a form of lower body covering similar to a long skirt' (2013: 119). The turban headdress, with its dual utilitarian and aesthetic function, was also a core aspect of Brazilian slave dress. Originally inspired by Muslim men's dress of the desert regions of Africa and the Middle East, its expressive and protective capacity made it popular as African women's dress throughout the Caribbean and Americas in the nineteenth century. More locally, Gage has argued that 'there was not an area of Brazil where this was not in use' (2013: 123).

In Junior's photograph, it is interesting to note that the market woman shows a closer connection to the imagery of earlier travellers' illustrations than to styles known from comparative Brazilian *cartes-de-visite* of the same era. Even though Junior's images were created about thirty years after the first publication of Debret and Rugendas, and forty years after the first publication of Guillobel, they reveal a similar style of representing the *traje de crioula*, showing that these representational models passed over time from drawn depictions to photographs (Leite 2002). In Junior's photograph, popular studio objects such as bags, umbrellas, fans and books were replaced by a tray of fruits; European-inspired dresses were replaced by the *traje de crioula*, and the positioning of arms and body resembles the positions a woman would have assumed while working in the street. As a conventional *carte-de-visite*, the picture was taken in a studio and not in the street market, evidencing the theatricality of this kind of composition. According to Koutsoukos (2002), throughout the nineteenth century in Brazil many African and Afro-Brazilian women and men tried to escape the stigma and horror of slavery. To do this, it was not enough to be free, one also needed to *look* free. In this way, wearing European-inspired dresses and accessories, and being photographed in these garments could be an important way of affirming their identity as free individuals in an otherwise highly prejudiced and hierarchal society. In addition, as Gage has argued, the forced crossing of African slaves to Brazil resulted in 'an amalgamation of European and African dress attributes . . . European dress components crossed economic, social, and cultural boundaries from white owner to black slave' (2013: 130).

If *cartes-de-visite* in general served a symbolic function and displayed the social distinction of the sitters, the pictures by Junior are an example whereby the initiative and stylistic choices came primarily from the photographer rather than from the individuals who were photographed. Junior's studio advertised photographs of black woman for sale to European visitors (Koutsoukos 2002). This suggests that the role of the *traje de crioula* in the photograph was to provide an attractive souvenir designed to appeal to the tastes and meet the expectations of foreign consumers. In such representations, the sitter might appear as a type rather than an individual, as a 'typical' representation of black women and/or slaves. In these cases it is particularly problematic to read the clothing of the sitter as indicative of her daily wear. As Taylor points out about commercial, souvenir studio photography more broadly, 'some of these images were . . . entirely faked' (2002: 166). The standard *carte-de-visite* composition involved scenery, props, clothing and pose. Junior used each of these elements to emphasize and commercialize the exotic visual appeal of Afro-Brazilians and African slaves to European travellers. For all of the realism of photography, as in the drawings and paintings, these types of images were imbued with social and cultural beliefs, reflecting the expectations of the time and the influence of the photographers (Taylor 2002).

Slaves, ostentation and dress

The province of Bahia was densely populated and large number of slaves lived there. Although in the nineteenth century it was known for its opulence and ostentation, historian Kátia Mattoso explains that social inequalities also characterized this region, but that such differences were often hidden by a common practice to signal wealth and social status by means of opulent public dressing. This mode of visual communication was so entrenched that it was not unusual for families to 'dress up' beyond their true financial capacities (1997: 147).

This display of opulence was not only related to urban contexts, but also was common in rural areas where the wealthiest farmers were concentrated. The writer and anthropologist Gilberto Freyre describes the luxurious everyday life of farmers and their families in this region before the nineteenth century, and notes the presence of Asian products such as fine china, silver, silks and precious stones (2003: 342). Mattoso (1997) adds that even with the drop in the export of sugar in the nineteenth century and the concomitant decrease in power of these farmers, many continued to live beyond their financial means, indicating a society that valued the outward expression of wealth and power.

Luís dos Santos Vilhena, a Portuguese professor who lived in Bahia in the beginning of the nineteenth century, wrote that the excessive display of luxurious commodities would also be part of the house slaves' dress in some of the families of Salvador, the capital of Bahia. According to Vilhena, it was noticeable that those slaves had certain privileges in comparison with other slaves, whose work was heavier or in the fields. The house slaves could, for example, be better dressed and were sometimes even adorned with jewellery. In fact, Vilhena explains that many women would dress their slaves with such ostentation that the jewellery they wore could have bought two or three other slaves (1969: 54). The journalist Laurentino Gomes, who published research about the Portuguese royal family's arrival in Brazil in the nineteenth century, also observes that slaves' symbolic social value became so important that some families who did not have many would rent them for public walks (2007: 158).

The drawings attributed to Maria, Lady Callcott by the National Library of Brazil (Fundação Biblioteca Nacional) present a detailed portrayal of the clothes and fabric prints used in the *traje de crioula* by women in Bahia. Callcott travelled to Brazil in 1821, 1822 and in 1823 after her first husband died in Chile. Calcott published her travel journal in 1824 in London as Maria Graham, her name from her first marriage (Graham 1824). As in the other representations of the 'market woman' in Rio de Janeiro (Plate 5 and Figures 4.1 and 4.2), Callcott's drawing (Plate 6) also presents the *traje de crioula* as being used for market activities. Callcott often emphasized the printed fabric in her drawings, and in this example with the white blouse and turban, and the black *pano-da-costa,* the red skirt dominates the image. The woman wears jewellery, including a necklace, bracelets, pendant and earrings, and she is carrying the products she sells on her head and what seems to be a lamp in her hand. The golden jewellery and the colourful fabric could symbolize luxury in dress meant for market activities, however, in other drawings by Callcott, holiday dresses – that is a festive dress or a dress not meant for workwear – are represented with laces and finer fabrics.

Although Vilhena (1969), Mattoso (1997) and Freyre (2003) refer to the opulence of the slaves of Salvador, this rarely appears in the visual sources from Bahia that depict the *traje de crioula*. Luxury dressing is, for example, presented in many photographs by Marc Ferrez, a famous Brazilian photographer who worked in the late nineteenth century and beginning of the twentieth century (Ferrez 2005). In some of his photographs he showed Afro-Brazilian women adorned with large amounts of jewellery and dressed in outfits similar to the *traje de crioula,* but which were black in colour and constructed from finer fabrics. These luxury clothes are known as the *traje de beca* (tunic/uniform clothing) and were worn by women who were part of an Afro-Brazilian religious sisterhood formed by women over forty-five years of age and called *Imandade de Nossa Senhora da Boa Morte,* or the Sisterhood of Our Lady of Good Death. According to Raul Lody (2003), the sisterhood connects the Afro-Brazilian religion Candomblé to Roman Catholicism; it still exists in the city of Cachoeira in Bahia. These women have preserved the use of the *traje de beca* that continues to be worn, although now only during the festivals of the religion. While similar to the *traje de crioula*, the *traje de beca* was a very specific set of garments with its own peculiarities and history. The exclusivity of the *traje de beca* not only played its role in religious life, but also in the society at large and especially among other Afro-Brazilian women who could not wear such luxurious dress (Monteiro, Ferreira and Freitas 2005). The *traje de beca* is described by Lody (2003) as being composed of a voluminous, black pleated skirt, a white embroidered shirt, a turban and a black *pano-da-costa* lined in red. Lody explains that the ensemble also includes a large amount of gold jewellery, with big chains, bracelets, bangles, rings, pendants and amulets. Therefore, while this is an important example of dress used in the nineteenth century, it should not be considered representative of everyday luxury of that time.

Conclusion

The *traje de crioula* was often represented as everyday dress by the travellers, artists and photographers cited in this chapter. Signalling a distinctive set of clothes most closely related to slaves and free black women and associated with market activities, it was comprised of an interconnected set of visual motifs and component parts which together make up a characteristic local ensemble. Lody has noted that despite its hybrid make-up of African, Islamic and European influences, the *traje de crioula* is nonetheless very Brazilian (2003: 15). The luxury found in literary descriptions and studies that mention female urban slaves may not easily be found in their contemporaneous visual representations, however, if compared with the clothes worn by other slaves in the nineteenth century – for example those doing hard physical labour in the city or those in the plantations and mines – the *traje de crioula* was undoubtedly a remarkable way of dressing. It certainly caught the eye of many travellers and commercial image-makers who sought to record national distinctiveness and promote exotic appearances. There are many reasons for the broad consistency and lack of modification in the visual representation of the dress form over many decades; artistic standards, foreigners' views and economic reasons all contributed to the development of enduring models of visual representation for these garments.

The meanings of this dress today are different; however, they also varied in the nineteenth century. Despite the consistency of motifs in visual representations, codes of clothing were in constant flux and this was no different with the set of clothes that formed the *traje de crioula*. During the twentieth century the ensemble formed of a turban, blouse, long skirt, *pano-da-costa* and different types of jewellery gradually became a form of regional dress of Bahia, being used in various cultural activities and events. In 1939, the singer Carmen Miranda wore a stylized version of the *traje da baiana* for the first time. Tânia Garcia explains that Miranda not only popularized the figure of the *baiana* abroad, but also in Brazil. In the years that followed, the outfit then established as the *traje da baiana* also became the type of clothing that was used to represent Brazil in Miss Universe competitions. Marta

Rocha in 1954 and Adalgisa Colombo in 1957 were among the first contestants to use the *traje da baiana* as a national costume of their country (Garcia 2004). In addition to the beauty competitions, the costume was, and still is, frequently present in national magazine editorials, poems, songs and fashion.

Studying the historic visual representations of the *traje de crioula* alongside surviving garments allows a better understanding of the dynamics of how one set of clothing can be used to represent a variety of subtle meanings and messages. Many of the images created by travellers in Brazil had the purpose of journal illustration or were created as images for a commercial market. Consequently, they should not be seen as depictions of a consistent reality but as products of particular viewpoints. While the skirts from the museum and the ones represented by Callcott and Junior are very similar in shape, pattern and material, when compared with other sources such as importation archives, artist's sketches, photographs and other descriptive texts from that time, the *traje de crioula* is clearly a flexible and adaptable way of dressing, which resists the static conceptualization suggested by the majority of visual sources.

When defining and studying the *traje de crioula*, if one only examined the most famous visual sources (e.g. Debret or Rugendas), it would be tempting to perceive the use of printed fabric in clothes as very rare in nineteenth-century Brazil. The drawings of Julião and Callcott, the *cartes-de-visite* of Junior, and, indeed, the skirts themselves, challenge this and add new perspectives to the understanding of slaves' dress and living conditions. Gage has also noticed that printed fabric calico was mentioned in the majority of the descriptions of female slaves in runaway advertisements (2013: 123). These reflections reinforce the need for studying clothes through varied types of sources in order to avoid misinterpretations (Taylor 2002).

The display of three *trajes de crioula* in the Museu do Traje e do Têxtil de Salvador follows the same pattern of visual representation that is seen throughout depictions of Afro-Brazilian dress during the nineteenth century. Indeed, there is a strong relation between these nineteenth-century images and how the *traje de crioula* is perceived and represented today. This chapter began by explaining that the analysis of the museum garment classifications and display precipitated this research on the representation of the *traje de crioula*. In querying and challenging fixed classifications and fabricated ensembles the study did not mean to point out mistakes in museum interpretation, but instead to provide a more nuanced account and to demonstrate that clothes are not static artefacts; they can acquire different meanings in different contexts, societies and over time (Taylor 2004: 201). Often these other possibilities are overlooked when displaying so-called traditional outfits.

The component elements that form this dress and are today part of the museum's collection may have been used as part of the *traje de crioula* by their original owners, and this would then be in accordance with the way the museum has chosen to register and display them (Peixoto 2003). The definition, however, of what the *traje de crioula* was, as well as why and how it was used is much more complex and elastic. By studying its visual representations and descriptions, it becomes clear that its seemingly simple formation is opposed by the multifaceted contexts, meanings and identities that this dress can encapsulate, where it can variously encompass dress of the enslaved and freed, occupational and religious clothing, as well as everyday and luxurious attire. In its multiple uses and visualizations, the *traje de crioula* can represent dress-as-worn and dress-as-imagined; it can be read as the particular garments of a named person but can also function as a category of clothing that can represent a larger population. Ultimately, and above all, the *traje de crioula* provides a visual synthesis of female Afro-Brazilian identities in the nineteenth century in Brazil; such identities influence Brazilian society to this day.

References

Andrade, R. M. (2008), *Bouè Souers RG 7091: a biografia cultural de um vestido*, PhD thesis, São Paulo: Universidade Pontifía Católica de São Paulo.

Belluzzo, A. M. et al. (2006), *Coleção Brasiliana/Fundação Estudar*, São Paulo: Via impressa edições de arte.

Debret, J. B. (1834), *Voyage pittoresque et historique au Brésil*, Paris: Firmin Didot Frères.

Fabris, A. (2004), *Identidades virtuais: uma leitura dos retratos fotográficos*, Belo Horizonte: UFMG.

Ferrez, M. (2005), *O Brasil de Marc Ferrez*, Rio de Janeiro: Instituto Moreira Salles.

Freyre, G. (2003), *Casa-grande & senzala: formação da família brasileira sob o regime da economia patriarcal*, 48th edition, São Paulo: Global.

Gage, K. M. (2013), 'Forced Crossing: The Dress of African Slave Women in Rio de Janeiro, Brazil, 1861', *Dress*, 39 (2): 111–33.

Garcia, T. C. (2004), *O 'it verde e amarelo': 1930–1946*, São Paulo: Annablume/Fapesp.

Gomes, L. (2007), *1808: como uma rainha louca, um príncipe medroso, e uma corte corrupta enganaram Napoleão e mudaram a história de Portugal e do Brasil*, São Paulo: Planeta.

Graham, M. (1824), *Journal of a Voyage to Brazil and Residence There during Part of the Years 1821, 1822, 1823*, London: Longman, Hurst, Rees, Orme, Brown, and Green, and J. Murray.

Koutsoukos, S. S. M. (2002), 'No estúdio do fotógrafo: Um estudo da (auto) representação de negros livres e escravos no Brasil da segunda metade do século XIX', *Revista Studium*, 9, http://www.studium.iar.unicamp.br/nove/index.html, accessed on 26 August 2014.

Koutsoukos, S. S. M. (2008), 'O aprendizado da técnica fotográfica por meio dos periódicos e manuais: segunda metade do século XIX', *Revista de História e Estudos Culturais*, 5 (3): 1–18, www.revistafenix.pro.br, accessed on 26 August 2014.

Lara, S. N. (1997), 'The Signs of Color: Women's Dress and Racial Relations in Salvador and Rio de Janerio, ca. 1750–1815', *Colonial Latin American Review*, 6 (2): 205–25.

Lara, S. N. (2002), 'Customs and Costumes: Carlos Julião and the Image of Black Slaves in Late Eighteenth-century Brazil', *Slavery and Abolition*, 23 (2): 125–46.

Leite, M. E. (2002), 'Os múltiplos olhares de Christiano Junior', *Revista Studium*, Campinas/Unicamp, 10, http://www.studium.iar.unicamp.br/10/6.html, accessed 19 September 2014.

Lody, R. (2003), *O que que a baiana tem: pano-da-costa, roupa de baiana*, Rio de Janeiro: Funarte, CNFCP.

Mattoso, K. M. Q. (1997), 'A opulência na província da Bahia', in F. Novais and L. F. Alencastro (eds), *História da vida privada no Brasil*, vol. 2, São Paulo: Companhia das Letras.

Monteiro, A. O. T. (2012), *Para além do traje de crioula: um estudo sobre materialidade e visualidade em saias estampadas da Bahia oitocentista*, MA thesis, Goiânia, Brazil: Faculdade de Artes Visuais/Programa de Pós-Graduação em Cultura Visual/ Universidade Federal de Goiás.

Monteiro, J., Ferreira, L. and Freitas, J. (2005), 'As roupas de crioula no século XIX e o traje de beca na contemporaneidade: símbolos de identidade e memória', *Mneme-Revista de Humanidades*, 7 (18): 382–403.

Paula, T. C. T. (2004), *Tecidos no Brasil: um hiato*, PhD thesis, São Paulo: Escola e Comunicações e Artes/ Universidade de São Paulo.

Peixoto, A. L. U. (2003), *Museu do Traje e do Têxtil*, Salvador: Fundação Instituto Feminino da Bahia.

Schwarcz, L. M. (1993), *O Espetáculo das Raças – cientistas, instituições e questão racial no Brasil 1870–1930*, São Paulo: Companhia das Letras.

Sela, E. M. M. (2008), *Modos de ser, modos de ver: viajantes europeus e escravos africanos no Rio de Janeiro (1808–1850)*, Campinas: UNICAMP.

Stein, S. J. (1957), *The Brazilian Cotton Manufacture: Textile Enterprise in an Underdeveloped Area, 1850–1950*, Cambridge: Harvard University Press.

Taylor, L. (2002), *The Study of Dress History*, Manchester: Manchester University Press.

Torres, H. A. (2004), 'Alguns aspectos da indumentária da crioula baiana', *Cadernos Pagu*, 23: 413–67.

5 THE EMPRESS'S OLD CLOTHES: BIOGRAPHIES OF AFRICAN DRESS AT THE VICTORIA AND ALBERT MUSEUM

Nicola Stylianou

As recently as 2009 the Victoria and Albert Museum (V&A) explicitly excluded historic artefacts from most of Africa. The *V&A Collections Management Policy* defined the geographical boundaries of the collection thus: 'Objects are collected from all major artistic traditions of Europe and Asia. The museum does not normally collect pre-European settlement material from the Americas and Australasia. The Museum does not collect historic material from Africa South of the Sahara' (V&A 2010). Despite this apparent exclusion, however, the V&A has a small but significant collection of African textiles. Included in this are three items of clothing that belonged to Queen Woyzaro Terunesh (also known as Tiruwork Wube), the wife of Emperor Tewodros II of Abyssinia (present-day Ethiopia).

Cultural anthropologist Igor Kopytoff has argued that objects have cultural biographies that change throughout their lives. They should not be understood as unchanging entities, but rather in relation to the culture and society that is using them and how they are valued (Kopytoff 1986). This chapter will explore how these Ethiopian objects came to be in the V&A and how they were regarded in the nineteenth century, as well as the apparent change in their perceived worth in the 1930s and how they are considered today. By following the biography of these objects through detailed archival research, studying written accounts and by close study of the clothes themselves it is possible to trace the V&A's changing attitude to Africa in the context of British imperial history. Echoing John and Jean Comaroffs' (1997) exploration of the movement of European dress into colonial Africa in their chapter, 'Fashioning the Colonial Subject: The Empire's

Old Clothes', this chapter explores the changing status of African royal dress in colonial Britain.

This research has drawn heavily on the archives of the V&A to trace their arrival in the museum and how they were treated afterwards. I have also used the records of the India Office and nineteenth-century accounts of the battle of Mäqdäla. Crucially, I have been able to study the garments themselves. Although some scholars address sub-Saharan African textiles and dress in their work (Picton and Mack 1989; Picton 1995; Spring 1997; Eicher and Ross 2010), and much interesting work has begun on Ethiopian dress in the nineteenth century there remains little English-language research published. With this lack of scholarly context, an object-focused approach is a particularly suitable way to tackle this under-researched area of dress history.

Queen Terunesh's clothes

On 20 April 1869 the V&A accessioned a number of objects from Ethiopia including clothes and jewellery that were listed in the museum register as having been given to the museum by the 'Secretary of State for India' and 'belonging formerly to the Queen of Abyssinia' (V&A 1869). At this time the V&A had not yet been divided into departments with objects being accepted for inclusion in the museum on the grounds of design excellence or as demonstrations of particular techniques. Included in this gift were eighteen pieces of jewellery (which are still in the V&A's metalwork collection) and seven items of clothing, three of which are still in the V&A. Two are now in the Museum of Archaeology and Anthropology, Cambridge (MAA) and two are missing.

The pieces that remain in the V&A are two *kamis* (cotton dresses) and a *shamma* (cotton shawl). Both *kamis* (accession numbers V&A: 399–1869 and V&A: 400–1869) are made from two layers of soft cotton probably produced in Manchester and are heavily decorated with embroidery around the neckline and on the cuffs (Plate 7 and Figure 5.1). In the middle of the nineteenth century Manchester calico was preferred to locally produced cotton in Ethiopia. This was due to the fact that machine-manufactured cottons had a very even weave which provided a better base for detailed embroidery (Spring and Hudson 1995: 125).

The *kamis* are decorated with embroidery on the front and the back. The embroidery is worked in silk which could not have been produced in Ethiopia. Silk thread for embroidery could be obtained by unravelling imported silk cloth, although some raw silk was bought from China and then spun and dyed locally (Spring and Hudson 1995: 123, 128). The embroidery patterns are quite different. At the base of the neck decoration and on the back of one of the *kamis* (V&A: 399–1969) are embroidered crosses reflecting Ethiopia's Christian culture and the queen's Christian identity.

FIGURE 5.1 *Kamis* [dress] belonging to Queen Terunesh, Ethiopia, mid-nineteenth century, cotton embroidered with silk, accession no. 400–1869. Courtesy of the Victoria and Albert Museum, London.

The third piece of clothing that was said to belong to the queen and is still in the V&A collection is a *shamma* (V&A: 401–1869), a wraparound shawl worn by both men and women in Ethiopia. The *shamma* is made up of two layers of soft cotton sewn together which, unlike the *kamis* appears to have been hand woven. There are three main types of *shamma*: the *natala*, the *kutta* and the *buluko* (Spring and Hudson 1995: 122). The example in the V&A is a *natala*, the lightest form of *shamma* and worn by women with a *kamis*. The *natala* is decorated with a band of coloured stripes, predominantly red, and this is known as a *tibeb* (Figure 5.2). Towards the end of the nineteenth century the *tibeb* became more elaborate with greater variety in pattern and colours. However in the mid-nineteenth century it was unusual to have any pattern on a *shamma* and the fact that this one had a *tibeb* of red and yellow reflected the queen's high status. As Chris Spring and Julie Hudson, curators in the Africa Department at the British Museum, state, 'In the mid-nineteenth century only a very few were permitted to wear . . . a type of *shamma* that boasted a decorative band (*tibeb*) with supplementary weft patterns in red, yellow and blue silk' (Spring and Hudson 2002: 13).

FIGURE 5.2 Detail of *shamma* [shawl] belonging to Queen Terunesh, cotton with a silk *tibeb* [border], Ethiopia, mid-nineteenth century, accession no. 401–1869. Courtesy of the Victoria and Albert Museum, London.

In addition to the three pieces in the V&A there are two other pieces of clothing that belonged to Queen Terunesh at the MAA in Cambridge, quite different garments from those described above. The first is a blue silk *kabba* (cloak) (MAA: Z19188, previously V&A: 396–1869). It would form a roughly semicircular shape laid out flat, but has been folded in to create a pointed hood. There is a neck band creating a neck opening and a tassel is attached to the point of the hood. The *kabba* is decorated around the opening with a band of scallop shapes cut out of yellow, red and blue silk and appliquéd on. There are triangles of similar decoration at the base of the robe.

The second item of Queen Terunesh's clothing in the MAA is also a dark blue silk *kabba* lined with a contrasting silk, this time in a floral pattern. It is of similar construction to the other cloak and also has a scalloped border (MAA: Z19184, previously V&A: 395–1869). This example, however, is heavily decorated with pierced and beaten silver gilt bosses. A censer hangs from a chain attached to the tip of the cloak. The chain has bugle-shaped metal pieces hanging from it, which continue around the edge of the dress and would fall into the face if the hood is up. These shapes are repeated in Queen Terunesh's jewellery in the V&A collection. The fastening across the neck is a large, metal buckle attached to the cloth with three arms and decorated with filigree. During the nineteenth century *kabbas* were worn by the wives of high-ranking Ethiopian noblemen on ceremonial occasions (Plankensteiner 2005: 29). However, the level of work on the cloak and expensive material denoted high status and its weight, along with the way in which the decorations would have obscured the wearer's vision, suggest it would only have been suitable for ceremonial use.

The queen's possession of the clothes is one stage of their cultural biography. Different stages can leave traces on an object and clothes that have been worn are peculiarly intimate objects, revealing things about their wearers. They reveal, for example, the queen's size. The wrist openings of one of the *kamis* (V&A: 399–1869) has a fourteen-centimetre circumference and the neck opening, which is fastened with a single blue button, has a twenty-seven-centimetre circumference. The woman who wore this was small and slender. We can also tell she was not very tall from the length of the garments. Although all of her clothes were clearly high-quality items when they were made, by the time they reached the museum they were all in poor condition. For example, the two *kamis* and the *shamma* are very dirty and the bottoms of the dresses are beginning to fray. Many of the silver bosses on the dark blue *kabba* are damaged, although this may have happened while the garments were in transit. The tassel on the plainer *kabba* has burrs caught in it suggesting the clothes were frequently worn, not cared for, or both. The clothes may reflect the practical challenges experienced by Queen Terunesh as she travelled around Ethiopia with Tewodros II as he began to lose control of the territory he had previously unified.

The battle of Mäqdäla and its aftermath

As a national museum, the V&A collection inevitably reflects the history of Britain, including the story of its engagement with Africa. The queen's clothes arrived in the V&A as a direct result of the battle of Mäqdäla fought in April 1868, at the culmination of the Abyssinian Expedition. The aim of the expedition was to free British diplomats, missionaries and other Europeans being held hostage by the Ethiopian Emperor Tewodros II. By this time Ethiopia had a long history of Christianity and as a Christian Emperor Tewodros had hoped to receive assistance, in particular relating to the development of military technology, from Christian Europeans in his struggles with Ottoman Egypt. When this help was not forthcoming he captured a number of European diplomats and missionaries working in Ethiopia in 1862. In 1868 the British Government decided to use force to free the prisoners (Marsden 2008).

The government decided to launch the expedition from India under the Royal Indian Army with Sir Richard Napier in command. Tewodros, in the face of internal unrest, had by this time retreated to the hilltop fortress of Mäqdäla. The battle took place on Friday 10 April 1868 and over the following two days Tewodros released his European prisoners (Rubenson 1966). On 13 April the fortress of Mäqdäla was stormed by the British forces and Tewodros shot himself just before their arrival (Marsden 2008).

The queen and her son Prince Alemayou were taken into the care of the British military who planned to escort them from the country. Unfortunately the queen died before they left Ethiopia and her child was brought to Britain where he lived until his death in 1879. Roger Acton, a journalist travelling with the expedition, described Queen Terunesh's death for the *Illustrated London News*:

> When the head-quarters' camp reached Aikhullet, on May 15, this poor lady died . . . Her funeral took place next morning in the great church at Chelicut, three miles distant from our camp. The women of her household, showing her robe, her ornaments, her slippers and her drinking cup, beat their breasts, tore their hair, and scratched their cheeks, shedding tears of real grief as they bewailed her death in a sorrowful chant prolonged for two hours. (Acton 1868: 76)

It is possible that the robe, ornaments, slippers and drinking cup mentioned were the objects that ended up in the V&A collection. Whether or not these are the exact clothes that were later deposited in the V&A, this description shows how the function of clothes can change from worn objects to potent symbols of the wearer.

A document in the India Office files traces the journey of the queen's clothes to Britain following her death. The queen's possessions passed into the ownership of the British military following her death. Not technically war booty, but clearly in the possession of the British as a result of military action, the clothes have an ambiguous status. On 20 February 1868 a message was sent from Aden in Yemen to the Secretary of State for India in London:

> My Lord, I have the honour to inform your lordship that I propose handing over . . . on about the 24th just one case containing the dress and ornaments of H.H. the late Queen of Abyssinia for transmission to your lordship.

> Set of articles of the deceased Queen of Abyssinia

> 1 royal robe with silver ornament, 1 Red silk cloak, 1 silk cloak, 1 pair silk pyjamas, 2 worked cotton and silk (mixed) robes, 1 cotton sheet (silk border), 1 pair slippers silver, 1 pair bracelets silver, 2 small metal chains, 6 rings gold or brass, 6 rings silver or lead, 1 bundle of small rings, 1 chain with 2 copper rings attached, 1 silver pin, 1 bundle of small bells on copper wire, 1 silver

neck ornament chain, 2 charm necklace amber leather and silver, 1 silver neck ornament chain, 1 pair bracelets silver, 1 pair bracelets silver (IOR).

On 18 March 1868 it was confirmed that the queen's possessions had been sent from Aden to the Secretary of State for India in England. The jewellery and clothes listed match what he later deposited in the V&A. The three items of clothing that remain in the collection are listed as '2 worked cotton and silk (mixed) robes' (V&A: 399–1869 and V&A: 400–1869) and '1 cotton sheet (silk border) (V&A: 401–1869)'. The two objects now in the MAA are listed as '1 Royal robe with silver ornament' and '1 silk cloak'.

Although this expedition was not motivated by a desire to acquire territory on the part of the British, these objects are in the V&A as a direct result of British military action and their acquisition was part of an imperial culture. James R. Ryan, in his work on photography and the British Empire, uses the Abyssinian Expedition as a case study and points out:

[I]mperialism involved not only territorial acquisition, political ambition and economic interests but also cultural formations, attitudes, beliefs and practices. In particular . . . imperialism [can be seen] as a pervasive and persistent set of cultural attitudes towards the rest of the world informed to varying degrees by militarism, patriotism, a belief in racial superiority and loyalty to a 'civilising mission'. (Ryan 1997: 12)

Seen like this, the battle of Mäqdäla was not only the result of imperial culture but was also used to consolidate it. By collecting and displaying objects associated with Mäqdäla, the V&A was complicit in this process.

It is worth noting the position of dress in the museum at the time these objects were acquired. Dress historian Lou Taylor has noted that during the nineteenth century, British museums in general, and the V&A in particular, were not systematically collecting examples of dress due to a perception that an interest in clothes was feminine and frivolous (Taylor 2004: 2). She goes on to point out that examples of dress existed in the collection, but that they were collected and valued only as examples of craft or technique (Taylor 2004: 110). This context, together with the items' provenance, originating in a royal wardrobe and associated with a famous episode in British military history explains why the museum was originally interested in the queen's clothes.

The queen's clothes in the V&A

In 1868 the V&A put on its first exhibition devoted to material from Africa. It was entitled *Abyssinian Objects from the Emperor Theodore. Lent by the Queen, the Admiralty and Others* (James 1997: 520). Queen Terunesh's clothes could not have been included in this exhibition because, as the India Office papers reveal, in February 1869 officials were still arranging to have them sent from Aden.

However, at least one of the robes was included in an exhibition held the following year in Manchester and sponsored by a missionary group. Such groups used displays and exhibitions of artefacts to promote their work and raise money for overseas missions (Taylor 2004: 73). The use of the queen's clothes in this context is ironic to modern eyes as it was partly the role of European missionaries in Ethiopia that had triggered the conflict between Tewodros II and the British. Henry Cole (the first Director of the South Kensington Museum, as the V&A was then known) gave a speech at the missionary exhibition entitled 'Abyssinian Art especially, as well as upon the Art of Savage Nations and People considered Uncivilised'. A review of Cole's talk stated, 'He referred to a blue dress in the collection the ornament on which is somewhat similar to that on St Patrick's bell' (*Journal of the Society of Arts* 1870: 183). The blue dress is likely to be the *kabba* now in the MAA and the similarity to St Patrick's bell a reference to the large metal clasp around the neck.

The report of the speech in the *Journal of the Society of Arts* showed Cole praising the art of 'savage' nations, often comparing it favourably to European works. He was reported as saying:

> principles of decorative Art exist in all art, however uncivilised the producers of it may be . . . The present exhibition showed visitors to it the invariable rule that the art works of savage peoples are based upon some system of principles. In main points their art is perfect . . . Instinctively savages never sin against the nature of things. (183)

This attitude is not particularly surprising from Cole, who believed that British makers had lost sight of the basic principles of good art and design. Indeed it was coterminous with a range of nineteenth-century viewpoints that praised art and design outside Europe and America, while frequently essentializing its characteristics as primitive and natural (Mackenzie 1995). Cole frequently championed the art and design of foreign countries and wanted British makers to learn what he considered to be true principles of good design by looking at examples. This was one of the driving forces behind the museum, which had spent most of its original budget acquiring items from overseas, in particular India (Burton 1999). What is different about this speech is that he talks specifically about Africa. Cole gives examples from Turkey, India, Persia and West Africa but the main focus of his talk was Ethiopia. He was reported as saying:

> With respect to Abyssinian art, the specimens exhibited that evening ought to interest those present, from the mere fact that the cost and difficulty of collecting

them exceeded by a long way, the cost and difficulty in obtaining any other similar curiosities ever brought to this country. Never have there been such costly curiosities. The Kohinoor [Indian diamond] cost nothing compared to Theodore's crown which was obtained from Magdala [*sic*] by a Prussian attaché and graciously sent by the King of Prussia to this country. (*Journal of the Society of Arts* 1870: 183)

The fact that Mäqdäla is referenced directly shows the extent to which this event continued to live in the public imagination. Equally this direct reference reveals that some of the objects on display, such as the crown, had come to Britain as a direct result of the battle and were therefore war booty.

Cole made other specific comments about Ethiopian art, presenting it as unchanged during the previous 300 years. This confirmed the Orientalist view that beyond Europe and North America, the world was a place of unchanging tradition rather than development and progress. However, to Cole this timelessness was a virtue because he believed that it allowed objects to remain true to basic design principles. A substantial proportion of the V&A's budget when it was founded in 1852 was spent on objects from India for this very reason (Burton 1999). Cole also saw links in the Ethiopian objects to other places and earlier times further emphasizing that they met with what he regarded as universal principles of good design. The report of his speech explains:

Abyssinian art has some distinctive types of its own, but much has been borrowed from other countries . . . He found in the Abyssinian objects a certain propriety of ornament and proceeded to point out the merits of the workmanship in the crown, which is of the Byzantine type of ornamental work. The armlet seemed to him to have been inspired by Greek, Genoese, and Maltese motives. (*Journal of the Society of Arts* 1870: 183)

Cole was good at promoting the V&A and the aim of this speech was to win support for the museum, so he was likely to talk positively about objects in the museum collection. However, Cole's enthusiasm appears genuine and he often displayed what Andrew Burton has called 'eager open-mindedness' (Burton 1999: 80). It would not have been out of character either in terms of aesthetic beliefs or personality for Cole to be genuinely enthusiastic about the Ethiopian objects.

It appears that during the 1860s and 1870s, then, the V&A was keenly interested in objects from Ethiopia. As well as staging the exhibitions described above and the support offered by Cole's positive comments, the V&A continued to buy artefacts that originated in Ethiopia. These were mostly metalwork but also comprised additional textiles, including in 1870 a religious vestment (V&A: 1424–1870) and in 1873 a set of saddlery (V&A: 921–1873 – V&A: 931–1873). Most, if not all, of these textiles had fallen into European hands following the looting at Mäqdäla. However, by the 1930s the V&A's enthusiasm for Ethiopian art specifically and African art more generally had waned and a new chapter was about to start in the biography of some of the queen's clothes.

Disposal during the 1930s

In 1933 a process was begun that would lead, by the end of the decade, to the permanent removal of thirty-eight African objects held in the textile department from the V&A's collection. At this time the V&A had only accessioned seventy-one textiles from sub-Saharan Africa so these removed objects account for more than half of the collection at that time (Stylianou 2013). The de-accessioning of items from the V&A was not a process that was undertaken lightly. The process for removing items from the collection was (and still is) called a Board of Survey. In the 1920s, the process for conducting such a board had been outlined, refined and discussed in detail. Briefly, the department that wanted to remove objects from its collection would compile a list of the items they wished to deaccession. The Board of Survey, which was 'composed of at least three Officers of the Museum nominated by the Director', then had the responsibility of going through the list and making recommendations about what should be done with each object. If possible the object would be transferred to another department or donated to another museum; if no institution could be found to take them they would be offered for sale at auction. The board's decisions were signed off by the museum's Director, the Board of Education and ultimately the Treasury (V&A Museum Decisions No. 30).

The issue of how and if to remove items from the V&A was clearly a pressing problem and a source of some anxiety at this time (V&A 1933). It seems storage space was becoming an issue and the museum had to think much more carefully and systematically about what it wanted to collect. The museum was also under pressure from the Board of Education to remove objects no longer felt to be relevant in a museum of art and design (V&A Boards of Survey). No official collection policy existed at this time, so it is difficult to know exactly how objects were evaluated in terms of potential deaccessioning. However, the papers in the V&A archives sometimes provide reasons for acquiring or removing specific objects.

In its report the Board of Survey stated that it had looked at 440 objects, mostly artefacts that had been made in Japan, Persia and Hungary during the nineteenth century; they argued that the museum had accepted these items in far greater quantity than it should have done (V&A 1933). The committee recommended about 110 things for sale, twenty for use as material in the museum's Art Room and the rest to be either given to other museums or destroyed. Included in the

440 objects were forty-eight from Africa. Fifteen of these were from Ethiopia, and four had belonged to Queen Terunesh. On the lists a reason for removal has to be given and four of the Ethiopian items are deemed 'Unsuitable for Exhibition or reference, deteriorated or lacking in artistic merit' (V&A 1933).

This is a tricky catch-all category which means we cannot know which objects were actually damaged in some way and which merely deemed to be lacking in artistic merit. Included in this category were one of the queen's robes and a pair of silk drawers which it has not been possible to locate. Although many of the queen's clothes were dirty and somewhat tattered, this does not appear to have affected which were kept and which were removed. All the other Ethiopian items were classified as 'No longer required in the textiles department'; this includes the two *kabba* previously discussed. According to V&A records, seven pieces of dress from Ethiopia were sent to the MAA (V&A 1933).

Initially the only evidence that these textiles were sent to Cambridge was a memo to the V&A transit room dated 24 August 1934 asking them to 'pack and despatch the objects in the attached list' (V&A 1933). The objects listed are the Ethiopian textiles, three Chinese textiles, some Russian silk, an artefact from the South Seas and a Hawaiian cape.

It is impossible to tell from the records kept in the MAA how the museum decided which pieces it wanted for its collection and when or if they viewed the textiles before accepting them. It is also unclear whether they approached or were approached by the V&A because there is no written record of these objects arriving at the MAA. The acquisitions list in the annual report for the year 1934 only lists the arrival of one object from the V&A 'Victoria and Albert Museum: Feather cloak formerly belonging to Kamehameha I, King of the Sandwich Islands (34.1159)'. However, a note in the annual report warns that the acquisition list is incomplete (MAA 1934).

As discussed above, during the 1920s and 1930s the Textile Department was having to think more carefully about what it collected at this time, but why did this lead to the exclusion of African dress specifically? By this time European dress was being actively and systematically collected by the V&A. Julia Petrov has argued that an institutional interest in European dress was established by 1910 and that between 1910 and 1914 the V&A was making 'unprecedented efforts to acquire collections of historical dress from private donors' (2008: 237). This, however, did not apply to African dress which was viewed as ethnography rather than dress history.

At this time the world was being divided into those objects and cultures that were suitable for study using an ethnographic approach and those that were not. The development of anthropology as an academic discipline and ethnography as a museum category went hand in hand with the development of British Empire in Africa. Ethnographers' desires to stake out an area for themselves in museums and academia led them to emphasize the need for a different, 'scientific' approach to the material cultures of people judged by them to be savage (Coombes 1994). This so-called scientific approach was only deemed suitable to the understanding of people who were seen as other and had been judged in some way inferior to those studying them; hence it was not used to understand the material cultures of Britain or Europe. Although this process began in the late nineteenth century, it is not until the 1920s and 1930s that we start to see references in the V&A files about which objects should be classed as ethnographic (V&A Black Hawkins). This is because it was not until this time that ethnography and anthropology were firmly established as disciplines in their own right. For example, it was only from the 1920s onwards that anthropology could rely on state funding (Coombes 1994: 4). The V&A, as a museum of art and design, was not interested in ethnographic objects. In line with these evolving disciplinary categories the Ethiopian artefacts were transferred to a museum specializing in ethnography.

At the same time the V&A was keen not to duplicate the work of the British Museum and ethnography was seen as their province. There was particular concern about this issue during the late 1920s and the 1930s which led to the production of a memorandum entitled 'Line of Demarcation to be Drawn Between Collections of the V&A and the British Museum' (V&A 1926). This document dealt mainly with the division between art and archaeology, however, it also mentioned briefly the division between art and ethnography: 'The whole question of the overlapping between the Museum and the British Museum, and more particularly with the two Departments of British and Medieval art and Ceramics and Ethnography . . . is unquestionably a difficult one' (V&A 1926). This pattern of African dress objects being viewed as ethnographic and therefore not of relevance to the V&A Textiles Department, despite the inclusion of European dress, would persist until the twenty-first century, with the V&A only accessioning a small number of African dress and textile objects and continuing to transfer those they already had to ethnographic collections in other museums (Stylianou 2013).

A change in attitude

There has been a change in the V&A's attitude towards Africa since 2000. Crucially, the current *V&A Collections and Development Policy* contains a section called 'Africa Collecting Strategy' (V&A 2010: 66). The collecting strategy addresses both historic and contemporary African objects:

> We will develop our existing historical collections primarily through gallery-, publication- and web-based projects rather than through collecting . . . For [sub-Saharan] Africa, for the African diaspora and for the African impact on non-African art and design, we will concentrate collecting activity in twentieth-century and contemporary design, graphic arts, photography, performance

arts and other fields for which the V&A holds a nationally recognized remit. (V&A 2010: 67)

This change at the V&A came about as a result of a Heritage Lottery Funded (HLF) project addressing Cultural Ownership and Capacity Building, which ran from 2005 to 2009 and included a Research Fellow post devoted to researching African objects in the collection. The V&A also recently attempted to address some of its complex history in relation to collecting African material in a two-room display entitled *V&A Africa: Exploring Hidden Histories* which ran from November 2012 until February 2013 curated by Zoe Whitley (V&A 2012). Substantially informed by my PhD research, the display sought to showcase the V&A's little known collection of African artefacts and also to understand why and when the V&A was acquiring objects from Africa. A case containing Queen Terunesh's *kamis* alongside her jewellery and other artefacts relating to the battle of Mäqdäla formed a core part of this display. The most recent stage of the cultural biography of the queen's clothes has thus been to enhance understanding of the V&A's attitude to African dress.

The display of the queen's dress and jewellery was part of an institutional process whereby the V&A has begun to reconsider its attitude towards Africa and reassess the historic African artefacts within its collection. This cultural shift can be seen as part of a new understanding of museums and material culture. It developed first in academia and then made its way to the gallery floors. Towards the end of the 1980s and during the 1990s the study of museums became both more widespread and more diverse in the topics that it examined. For example, systems of classification were studied in relation to the kinds of understanding they generated (Hooper-Greenhill 1992) and interest grew in what museums chose *not* to collect (Kavanagh 1996).

The rapid expansion of museum studies during the 1990s and up to the present was also partly a response to an academic shift in which researchers and curators sought to apply the theories of postmodernism and postcolonialism to our understanding of museums and to their own practices. The V&A was not immune to these developments and the V&A's role in displaying the spoils of empire in India, China and Japan and the Middle East has been studied in some depth (Barringer 1998), but very little has been written about the African objects in the V&A. Craig Clunas and Partha Mittar, for example, who have studied the V&A's Asian collections, have argued: 'A national institution such as the Victoria and Albert Museum was an important adjunct of the empire, classifying and displaying the art of non-European nations in an assertion of political control over them' (1997: 230). The anthropologist James Clifford argued that although the power relationship between the colonized and the colonizer is inherently unequal in a museum the museum is still able to act as a 'contact zone', a dynamic space allowing interaction and dialogue (Clifford

1997). The V&A's recent increasing engagement with its African collections in general and these Ethiopian objects in particular are part of an effort to address the inequalities of the past and create new ways of understanding and presenting these collections.

A further role for these objects, however, may be to illustrate the contested role of imperial trophies in cultural institutions more directly. The presence of material taken after the battle of Mäqdäla in many British museums remains controversial, and an organization called the Association for the Return of the Mäqdäla Ethiopian Treasures (AFROMET) is actively seeking the return of looted treasures to Ethiopia, with the support of the Ethiopian Government. They produced a Memorandum on the Loot from Maqdala (Ethiopia) addressed to the Culture, Media and Sport Committee of the United Kingdom Parliament which stated:

> We feel that the injustice committed by the British at Maqdala, like other injustices of the past, must be repaired; and that this can be effected only by full restitution to Ethiopia of all cultural objects unjustly looted from the country. We feel, in the words of a British lover of justice, that nothing is truly settled until it is settled justly. (AFROMET)

Although the queen's clothes were not technically looted after the battle, like the objects the memorandum notes, their presence in the V&A is a direct result of the battle. The cultural biography of Queen Terunesh's clothes remains unfinished, for they may yet feature in AFROMET's repatriation campaign.

Conclusion

Queen Terunesh's old clothes have had a long and complicated cultural life; they have been perceived and made use of differently by a variety of people in a range of contexts. As Kopytoff wrote, 'A culturally informed . . . biography of an object would look at it as a culturally constructed entity, endowed with culturally specific meanings, and classified and reclassified into culturally constituted categories' (Kopytoff 1986: 68). This process of classification and reclassification is evident in the case of Queen Terunesh's ceremonial and travelling clothes. These objects have been symbols of her lost life to her grieving compatriots, useful display items for a missionary society's reformist agendas, and aesthetic objects of admiration for Henry Cole. After their initial acquisition, some of them were devalued enough to be deaccessioned. More recently, they have been substantially reconsidered, playing a significant role in an institutional and governmental programme to redress historical neglect. They have been variously categorized as examples of technique, of dress and as ethnographic artefacts. They have been variously valued and rejected, scrutinized and ignored, celebrated and contested.

Collecting and displaying art and artefacts of empire and displaying them at the metropolitan centre was crucial to the imperial project and it has been impossible to ignore how deeply implicated the V&A was in this process. By examining this small group of Ethiopian garments it is possible to begin to see how Britain's changing attitudes towards Africa are represented in the V&A collection.

References

Acton, R. (1868), *The Abyssinian Expedition and the Life and Reign of King Theodore*, London: Illustrated London News.

Appadurai, A. (ed.) (1986), *The Social Life of Things: Commodities in Cultural Perspective*, Cambridge and New York: Cambridge University Press.

Association for the Return of the Magdala Ethiopian Treasures (AFROMET), 'Memorandum on the Loot from Magdala', www.ethioembassy.org.uk, accessed 30 July 2014.

Baker, M. and Richardson, B. (eds) (1997), *A Grand Design: The Art of the Victoria and Albert Museum*, London: V&A Publishing.

Barrringer, T. (1998), 'The South Kensington Museum and the Colonial Project', in T. Barringer and T. Flynn (eds), *Colonialism and the Object: Empire, Material Culture and the Museum*, London and New York: Routledge.

Burton, A. (1999), *Vision and Accident: The Story of the Victoria and Albert Museum*, London: V&A Publications.

Clifford, J. (1997), *Routes: Travel and Translation in the Late Twentieth Century*, Cambridge and London: Harvard University Press.

Clunas, C. and Mittar, P. (1997), 'The Empire of Things: Engagement with the Orient', in M. Baker and B. Richardson (eds), *A Grand Design: The Art of the Victoria and Albert Museum*, London: V&A Publications.

Comaroff, J. and J. (1997), *Of Revelation and Revolution (Vol. 2): The Dialectics of Modernity in a South African Frontier*, Chicago: University of Chicago Press.

Coombes, A. E. (1994), *Reinventing Africa: Museums, Material Culture and Popular Imagination in Late Victorian and Edwardian England*, New Haven and London: Yale University Press.

Eicher, J. B. and Ross, D. H. (2010), *Berg Encyclopedia of World Dress and Fashion, Vol. 1, Africa*, Oxford: Berg.

Hooper-Greenhill, E. (1992), *Museums and the Shaping of Knowledge*, London and New York: Routledge.

India Office Records (IOR), Abyssinia Original Correspondence, vol. 3, IOR/L/PS/9/205.

James, E. (1997), *The Victoria and Albert Museum: A Bibliography and Exhibition Chronology 1852–1996*, London: V&A Publications.

Journal of the Society of Arts (1870), 21 January: 183.

Kavanagh, G. (ed.) (1996), *Making Histories in Museums*, Leicester: University of Leicester Press.

Kopytoff, I. (1986), 'The Cultural Biography of Things: Commoditization as Process', in A. Appadurai (ed.), *The Social Life of Things: Commodities in Cultural Perspective*, Cambridge and New York: Cambridge University Press.

Mackenzie, J. (1995), *Orientalism: History, Theory, and the Arts*, Manchester: Manchester University Press.

Marsden, P. (2007), *The Barefoot Emperor: An Ethiopian Tragedy*, London: Harper Perennial.

Museum of Archaeology and Anthropology, Manchester (MAA) (1934), Annual Report.

Petrov, J. (2008), '"The Habit of Their Age": English Genre Painters, Dress Collecting, and Museums, 1910–1914', *Journal of the History of Collections*, 20 (2): 237–51.

Picton, J. (1995), *The Art of African Textiles: Technology, Tradition, and Lurex*, London: Lund Humphries.

Picton, J. and Mack, J. (1989), *African Textiles*, London: The British Museum.

Plankensteiner, B. (2005), 'African Art at the Museum für Volkerkunde in Vienna', *African Arts*, 38 (2): 12–37.

Rubenson, S. (1966), *King of Kings: Tēwedros of Ethiopia*, Addis Abeba: Haile Sallasie I University; Nairobi:Oxford University Press.

Ryan, J. R. (1997), *Picturing Empire: Photography and the Visualization of the British Empire*, Chicago: University of Chicago Press.

Simpson, W. ([1868] 2002), *Diary of a Journey to Abyssinia, 1868*, R. Pankhurst (ed.), Hollywood, CA: Tsehai Publishers and Distributors.

Spring, C. (1997), *African Textiles*, London: British Museum.

Spring, C. and Hudson, J. (1995), *North African Textiles*, London: British Museum.

Spring, C. and Hudson, J. (2002), *Silk in Africa*, London: British Museum.

Stylianou, N. (2013), *Producing and Collecting for Empire: African Textiles at the V&A, 1852-2000*, PhD thesis, London: University of the Arts.

Taylor, L. (2004), *Establishing Dress History*, Manchester: Manchester University Press.

Vergo, P. (ed.) (1989), *The New Museology*, London: Reaktion Books.

Victoria and Albert Museum, London (V&A), Boards of Survey, 1932–1956, Museum Archive ED/84/433 on VA/60/ED/84.

Victoria and Albert Museum, London (V&A), 'Memorandum on the Constitution and Procedure of Boards of Survey for the Guidance of Officers Serving Thereon', Museum Archive, Museum Decisions No. 30.

Victoria and Albert Museum, London (V&A), Nominal File: 'Black Hawkins, Mary (Mrs)', Museum Archive MA/1/B1545.

Victoria and Albert Museum, London (V&A) (1869), Central Inventory.

Victoria and Albert Museum, London (V&A) (1926), 'Memorandum Re Line of Demarcation to be Drawn between Collections of the V&A and The British Museum', Museum Archive ED/84/116.

Victoria and Albert Museum, London (V&A) (1933), 'Textiles Board of Survey', Museum Archive RP/1933/584.

Victoria and Albert Museum, London (V&A) (2010), 'V&A Collections and Development Policy', http://media.vam.ac.uk/media/documents/about-us/2010/v&a-collections-development-policy.pdf, accessed 15 January 2014.

Victoria and Albert Museum, London (V&A) (2012), 'V&A and Africa', http://www.vam.ac.uk/content/articles/v/v-and-a-in-africa/, accessed 1 October 2014.

6 PICTURING THE MATERIAL/MANIFESTING THE VISUAL: AESTHETIC DRESS IN LATE-NINETEENTH-CENTURY BRITISH CULTURE

Kimberly Wahl

Reconciling historical representations of fashionable clothing with the lived reality of dress in practice presents an ongoing challenge for scholars of dress history. In my work, I have been fascinated by the myriad and complex sartorial expressions of nineteenth-century British Aestheticism. Intriguing gaps, even ruptures, exist between the visual representation and literary framing of 'artistic' dress and how these forms of clothing were actually acquired, adapted and worn on the body, only partially traceable through their material remains. The development of my methods and approach to dealing with these seemingly disparate narratives and histories has been foregrounded and enhanced by several prominent scholars in the field of dress history. In the late 1990s, Lou Taylor argued that there remained a divide between 'object-centered methods of the curator/collector' and 'social/economic history and cultural theory approaches' practiced by university academics (1998: 338). With the rise of fashion studies and a range of emerging methods utilizing both object-based and visual/text-based approaches, as well as a self-conscious degree of interdisciplinarity, the gap between academic and curatorial approaches is narrowing. For Taylor, the most productive work fuses artefact-based approaches with theory and she has surmised that future debates might investigate distinctions between 'processes of "leading out" from the object into theory, or working back from theory to object . . .' (2002: 85). In a similar vein, Alexandra Palmer has argued that an interdisciplinary approach which includes a material culture analysis allows scholars to 'contextualize artefacts and documents in a multi-layered fashion' (1997: 302). John Styles has asserted that the application of theoretical models in tandem with solid empirical study has increased the interdisciplinarity of dress history underpinning its 'new prominence, nay respectability' (1998: 388). More recently, Adrienne Hood has written that if objects are 'our driving force and the questions asked of them interdisciplinary, our research will be nuanced, complex and historically valid' (2009:193).

Unlike disciplines such as archaeology and anthropology wherein artefacts are often the only source of cultural information about the past, historians have traditionally relied primarily on written documentation. Greater integration of sources and methods across fields has eroded disciplinary boundaries, and increasingly, scholars emphasize the 'power of objects to open up new avenues of historical thinking and to provide insights into the past not possible with documents alone' (Hood 2009: 176–7). Giorgio Riello has explored the relationship between history and objects in some depth, drawing subtle distinctions between approaches which examine the history *of* things themselves, the relationship between history *and* things and the study of history *from* things. In other words, the way in which object-based approaches can inform the study of history itself is both complex and open-ended, and much relies on the kinds of questions asked. Riello draws attention to the cross-referencing of sources in historical studies which might include artefacts and visual representations, ultimately concluding that the 'strict boundaries by which historians read documents in dusty archives, while art historians analyse paintings, and museum curators and archaeologists deal with objects have now been superseded' (2009: 29).

For scholars working in the area of visual studies in relation to dress history, the importance of fashion imagery as a form of both representation and material culture is crucial. Irit Rogoff has insisted that the 'contingent, the subjective and the constantly reproduced state of meanings in the visual field' has the potential to 'evacuate' objects of study from 'disciplinary and other forms of knowledge territorialization'. Celebrating the 'free play of the Signifier' Rogoff references Roland Barthes's description of interdisciplinarity as constituting a 'new object of knowledge' (1998: 15). While a straight visual culture approach may be limiting in some ways, and certainly cannot illuminate dress as an embodied practice, it pushes the discipline of dress history to consider the importance of the visual in new ways. Outlining a range of cultural studies approaches, Christopher Breward has noted that the 'power of the sign, together with film theory, revels in the ambiguity of fashion and its shifting signifiers, which moves the discipline away from earlier reductive or moralistic approaches' (1998: 308).

The role of the visual in the study of material culture has important ramifications for understanding tensions between the study of dress history and the emerging field of fashion studies. Giorgio Riello has argued that material culture is 'not the object itself . . . but neither is it a theoretical form . . . Material culture is instead about the modalities and dynamics through which objects take on meaning (and one of these is that of fashion) in human lives' (2011: 6). As a mobile and performative form of culture, clothing should be understood as historically contingent; Caroline Evans has observed that fashion is '. . . an embodied, four-dimensional practice that exists in both space and time and, therefore, that it is an important, if often overlooked, part of the history of sensibilities as well as of commerce and culture' (2013: 1).

Aesthetic dress

The complex relationship between material forms of clothing and visual/literary representations of 'fashion' is nowhere more clearly articulated than in the dress practices of nineteenth-century Aestheticism. From the 1870s to the 1890s, Aesthetic dress in Britain was characterized by its comfort, elegance and adherence to classical and medieval dress-ideals. Initially based on earlier Pre-Raphaelite models, Aesthetic dress was eclectic and historicist, merging Antique or medieval models with picturesque elements drawn from later periods: smocking, a high or natural waist, puffed sleeves, squared off necklines from the Renaissance and more often than not, the inclusion of a 'Watteau' panel inspired by the sacque-back styles of the eighteenth century. Loose-fitting and intended to be worn without a corset, it was often viewed as an artistic variant of dress reform (Wilson 1996: 21–2). It occasionally included features drawn from Orientalism in complex, and at times, problematic ways (Wahl 2011: 58–67). At the height of its popularity during the 1880s, bohemians and intellectuals argued that artistic forms of dress provided an elegant and refined alternative to the more ubiquitous and restrictive aspects of mainstream fashion (Cunningham 2003: 103). Despite a sustained interest in dress reform and artistic clothing in the late nineteenth century, few scholars have investigated the gap between Aesthetic dress as it was actually worn on the body and its existence as an idealized sartorial trope in the print culture of the period.

My research into the development and popularization of Aesthetic dress in late Victorian culture has been enabled and enhanced by emerging scholars advocating culture approaches to the study of dress (Wahl 2013). A full understanding of Aesthetic dress considers its idealizing tendencies at the level of image/concept, as well as several facets of its reception as an embodied practice. Evidence for these two contexts exists in the print and visual cultures of the period, but also resides in the material remnants of Aesthetic clothing, most notably in the form of 'artistic' tea gowns. Although few examples survive from the 1860s, early physical evidence is suggested in photographs of artistic women such as Jane Morris and the Pattle sisters, and several extant garments dating from the late 1870s onwards can found in dress collections in the United Kingdom, United States and Canada (Ehrman 2011: 206). In *Dressed as in a Painting, Women and British Aestheticism in an Age of Reform*, I argued that a rupture between the visual discourses of artistic dress and its material dimensions provides insights into the important role of clothing in the literary, visual and material expressions of Aesthetic culture. I also proposed the tea gown as the requisite Aesthetic garment, viewing it as an embodied and expressive mode of engagement with the artistic culture of late-nineteenth-century Victorian Britain (Wahl 2011, 2013).

In this chapter I expand on this earlier work by examining two previously unpublished case studies of Aesthetic dress, a house dress/tea gown in the Royal Ontario Museum in Toronto, Canada (Plates 8 and 9), and a tea gown held by the Royal Pavilion and Museums, Brighton and Hove, in the United Kingdom (Plates 10 and 11). I approach these garments as artefacts/objects, but also as manifestations of Aesthetic culture; there is a constant (and productive) tension between the material reality of these garments, and their connection to the visual cultures of Aestheticism. Across a range of media, the tea gown was presented as a mode of dress which embraced diversity, creativity and comfort. Its changeability was heralded as a route to sartorial freedom, an embodied artform which might question mainstream fashionable practices and conventions. In practice Aesthetic dressing did not always function as a form of cultural critique, particularly as it became progressively popularized and produced in a variety of settings: domestic, artistic and commercial. Tracing its material record through extant garments is therefore challenging, but necessary. This approach articulates the ideological ramifications of fashion as part of a contested visual culture sometimes at odds with the material facts of dressing. Ultimately, Aesthetic dress emerges as a complex social practice with both material and visual manifestations.

Textual/visual sources

The presence of Aesthetic dress in the print culture of the nineteenth century is rich, varied and ubiquitous. There are references not only in fashion journals of the day, but in fictional works, press coverage of social events, and cultural and literary essays. Visual sources include paintings, commercial illustrations, fashion plates, cartoons and even photography. With the exception of exhibition catalogues which feature extant artistic dresses held in specific dress collections, the typical approach to studying Aesthetic dress has been to access this extensive visual and literary archive. The cross-referencing and inclusive use of a range of text-based and visual sources have established the significance of Aesthetic dress in the symbolic imaginary of the art culture of the period. Descriptions and illustrations of Aesthetic dress frequently appear in popular fashion journals such the *Queen, Lady's Pictorial* and *Woman's World*, as well as specialty art publications like *The Artist and Journal of Home Culture* and the *Magazine of Art*. More tellingly, the timely rise of various dress reform organizations including the Healthy and Artistic Dress Union (mainly comprised of an elite group of artists and intellectuals), reveal the growing awareness of, and interest in, artistic forms of dressing.

Stella Mary Newton was one of the first dress historians to provide a full account of artistic culture in the context of dress reform. Though descriptively rich, and well-researched in terms of primary visual and written sources, she did not examine garments, nor did she cite key examples held in dress collections. Despite this, Newton's work represents a ground-breaking effort to convey the complex cultural dimensions of Aesthetic dress through the print culture of the fashion literature and art world; emphasizing the ephemeral and perishable nature of clothing, she argued that the immediacy of clothing allowed it to respond more quickly to changing social requirements and standards (1974: 2). This was certainly true of the shifting preferences of artists, bohemians, and intellectuals who viewed Aesthetic styles as artistically advanced, elegant, comfortable and creative. Advocates also viewed Aesthetic dress as an antidote to modern fashions, which they denounced as excessive, arbitrary and without substance. As a consequence, many design reformers looked to the past for sartorial inspiration. Specific reform principles were set out in select publications by designers and writers such as Eliza Haweis (1878), Lucy Crane (1882), Henry Holiday (1893) and Walter Crane (1894). Favourable views on 'artistic' forms of clothing were also promoted more broadly by several high-profile artists, designers and cultural critics of the period, namely William Morris, E. W. Godwin, G. F. Watts and Oscar Wilde (Stern 2004: 5–10). Although the rhetorical framing of Aesthetic dress rejected the rapid turnover of styles within mainstream fashion, it too was constantly in flux, subject to the evolving tastes of art audiences who craved innovation and sartorial change. For this reason, Aesthetic dress itself was expressive of key aspects of modernity despite its obvious links with past styles. This modernist aspect of Aestheticism was most clearly authorized and articulated in the paintings of James McNeil Whistler and Edward Burne Jones (Galassi 2003: 95; Wahl 2013: 83–4).

While the symbolic role of fashion in painting can be situated within the discourses of the art world, the visual significance of the Aesthetic body in popular print culture speaks to a more contested terrain—one that was impacted by the commercial aspects of popular Aestheticism. In this context, understanding the important role of different audiences helps frame and contextualize the visual meanings of Aesthetic dress. Within the Aesthetic movement, although stylistic markers were shared and socially formed, subjective responses to art were celebrated, rather than judgements based on social consensus or academic tradition. Not surprisingly, the visual representations of Artistic forms of dress

NEW TEA-GOWNS.

FIGURE 6.1 Illustration: 'New tea-gowns', *Woman's World*, 1890: 76. Courtesy of Toronto Public Library.

were varied and eclectic. *Woman's World*, a progressive publication briefly edited by Oscar Wilde, included thought-provoking articles on a range of topics intended to be of interest to artistic and educated readers. An illustration in the 1890 volume depicts three very different tea gowns, and celebrates the creativity and individuality implied by this type of garment (Figure 6.1). By the 1890s, the tea gown was firmly linked with notions of fantasy and female leisure, suggestive of sartorial experimentation and empowerment for artistically inclined women.

The popular framing of the tea gown in a range of fashion and art publications of the 1880s and 1890s reveals its perceived comfort, mobility and up-to-date fashionableness. All descriptions emphasize ease and looseness through the waist – particularly through the front of garments – in a way that seemingly rejects rigid or constricting underclothing. In the *Queen*: 'Many tea gowns . . . are Princesse shape at the back, and loose in front' (1881: 675). The *Lady's Pictorial* describes the front of a new tea gown from Liberty's: 'A scarf of grey-green silk is loosely knotted across the gauze, slightly on one side, and prettily finished with tassels and small balls of silk cord in the same colour' (1887: 353). Similarly, the *Artist and Journal of Home Culture* outlines another gown: 'The underdress, or front, merely consisted of plain folds of cashmere falling from the neck to the feet and just kept in to the figure by means of two narrow straps of embroidery crossing diagonally from the shoulder to the waist on either side' (1890: 29). Most tellingly, a writer for *Woman's World* marvels in the continued demand for comfortable tea gowns, and delights in describing a featured gown as 'just the kind of dress which could be worn without stays, as tea gowns all originally were' (Johnstone 1888: 186).

Beyond simple comfort, the tea gown is positioned as a cipher of female leisure and creativity, particularly in specific settings: 'The loose unconventional robe is not influenced by the last decree in fashion, and the wearer's personality seems to have scope for freer expression in this picturesque garment' (*Woman's World* 1890: 185). Tea-time itself was progressively viewed as a space of feminine sociability, ideal for receiving close friends and acquaintances in the home and belaying notions of domestic seclusion: 'It is so much the fashion for young ladies to meet in their rooms, after they have seemingly retired to rest, that very smart dressing-gowns are brought into requisition, and flannel is forsaken for more dressy materials' (*Queen* 1881: 675). Such gatherings dispute the categorization of the tea gown as a form of undress. There is even the suggestion that such gowns might be daringly worn outside conventional tea-time occasions: 'Artistic dressing gains ground . . . Tea gowns have come to be the accepted style of dress for home dinner wear, and these are often made up with the Watteau plate' (*Cassell's Family Magazine* 1880: 441–2).

Some conservative critics expressed concern over the proper use and function of tea gowns. In *Woman's World*, a regular columnist commented that 'In London they are the fashion for home dinner wear, and probably this is why they are made at all events to appear to fit more closely than they originally did. It is not considered that they are in good style if in any way they suggest a dressing-gown or wrapper . . .' (Johnstone 1888: 186). Thus, freedom of expression through Aesthetic dress was not universally praised and even within the more elite artistic coteries there were differing positions on what constituted tasteful 'artistic' dress. The diaries of Jeannette Marshall reveal varying levels of commitment to, or perhaps tolerance for, extreme forms of artistic dress. Citing a particular Pre-Raphaelite 'at-home' event held by the Ford Madox Browns, she wrote 'The flood of "artistics" in everything hideous in the way of costume was appalling.' For a different gathering at the home of Holman Hunt, she referred to the dress of Jane Morris as 'sloppy' (as cited in Cunningham 2003: 115). Yet Patricia Cunningham has pointed out that Miss Marshall herself was known to wear a subdued version of Aesthetic dress, and often favoured amber beads and 'artistic' fabrics such as those found at Liberty's (2003: 115).

The contested and at times contradictory writings on artistic dress signal its discursive and rhetorical power as a destabilizing form of clothing with regard to gender roles and notions of appropriate dress. In the late 1890s the preeminence of the tea gown in the literary imagination of fashionable women was still under discussion, its transcendent nature marked by its suitability, creativity and ephemerality. In *The Ascent of Woman*, Roy Devereaux concluded that 'The dominant glory of the tea gown is that it enables the wearer to discover new perspectives of life, and infinity of untried attitudes which the presence of a corset utterly defeats' (1896: 92–3). Thus, while visual sources alone can tell an intriguing story about the relationship between art and dress within the Aesthetic movement, such images are animated and inflected by the language, pacing and poetry of the tea gown's literary existence in writing. Only in writing can the rejection of the corset become explicit, articulating a growing interest in comfort and mobility among women who might categorize themselves as both artistic *and* progressive.

Dress reform was often presented as a form of female emancipation, but debates arose as to how this might be accomplished without violating artistic principles as well as notions of health and beauty (which were often conflated at the time). A crucial form of print culture which helped define the boundaries of Aesthetic dress can be found in the publications, events, and activities of organized groups and associations. Formed in 1890, The Healthy and Artistic Dress Union brought together artists, designers and socialites in order to promote an artistic approach to dress reform (Cunningham 2003: 124). Members of the Union included prominent artists of the period, such as Louise Jopling, Hamo Thornycroft and G. F. Watts. The artist Henry Holiday was president of the Union and advocated Aesthetic dress not only on the basis of dress reform, but on creative grounds as well, objecting to what he perceived as the monotony and vulgarity of mainstream Victorian dress. In an article dealing more generally with the state of the decorative arts in Britain, Holiday wrote: 'Let us now look at dress. Here, surely, there will be more freedom. Cannot the individual assert his personality here? . . . Gloom, and the total absence of individuality are the characteristics of our system' (1890: 64).

The Union's meetings, talks, exhibitions and events encouraged the adoption of Aesthetic dress through both education and persuasion, and provide clear examples of the exploration, dissemination and at times, implementation of Aesthetic standards of dress in practice. One of the highly successful events organized by the Union was a series of 'living pictures' arranged and performed at St George's Hall in May of 1896 (Holiday 1914: 408). Most of this event was photographed, and the resulting images document a range of tableaux such as 'Pastoral Scene,' 'Dress of the Future' and 'Aglaia'. These images invoke the performative and dynamic aspects of Aesthetic dress impossible to trace through more traditional means. In 'Aglaia' (Figure 6.2), by inhabiting an illustration by Walter Crane for the cover of the journal *AGLAIA: The Journal of the Healthy & Artistic Dress Union*, members drew on their belief in the artistic and moral superiority of the classical age as fundamental to the process of design and dress reform. Bringing together art, theatre and education, these staged scenes demonstrate the interrelation of various modes of representation where

FIGURE 6.2 Photograph: 'Aglaia', 1896. Courtesy of Whitworth Art Gallery, The University of Manchester.

discourses of the body and fashion are interwoven with social activism and dress reform. Photographs of such events document isolated moments in history, and yet simultaneously serve as a form of material culture in and of themselves and are thus imbricated with the visual cultures to which they refer. While there might appear to be an obvious division between the 'representation' of dress in visual culture and the reality of dress as a series of artefacts/objects, in truth some forms of material/visual culture, such as photographs, complicate these seemingly discrete realms.

Extant examples of Aesthetic dress

The production of fashion artefacts should be contextualized as an embodied practice by their makers and wearers – in essence, animating various forms of material culture and providing clues to the social relevance of particular objects. Despite a sustained and active role for Aesthetic dress in the art and print culture of the period, extant examples of Aesthetic garments are relatively rare. Here I discuss several examples, but of these, few can be considered true models as they do not follow the principles of Aesthetic dress as defined in artistic and dress reform literature of the period: relaxed/loose fit, ease of mobility and a natural/uncorsetted waist. Thus, contrary to text-based and visual representations of Aesthetic dress in the primary literature which are often posited as nearly revolutionary in conception if not construction, most examples of Aesthetic dress in the form of extant garments do not cohere with the rhetorical dictates of design reform. Instead, they are often more structured and tend to conform to the predominant stylistic features of mainstream fashionable dress. Many of the surviving gowns classified as 'Aesthetic' or 'artistic' in museum-based clothing collections in Britain and North America are stylistic hybrids rather than radical examples of alternative dress as called for in the art and reform literature of the day. These extant examples challenge the categorical distinction between fashionable and Aesthetic dressing, and make explicit the adaptive nature of Aesthetic dressing as an embodied practice. They also confirm the importance of object-based approaches in the study of dress history.

Case study 1: tea gown/house dress at the Royal Ontario Museum

A tea gown/house dress held by the Royal Ontario Museum represents a rare extant example of an Aesthetic dress which conforms to design and construction principles as defined within artistic communities and through the associated literature on Aestheticism and dress reform (Plates 8 and 9). Dated between 1894 and 1897, and held in a Canadian collection, the gown was made in England and therefore produced in the context of British Aestheticism. By this date, many features of Aesthetic dress had been absorbed by mainstream fashion culture, which may explain the greater number of tea gowns held in collections from the mid-1880s to late-1890s. Made from olive green velvet and trimmed with matching satin and knitted lace, the dress is princess cut through the back with 3/4 inch puffed sleeves, shirred and puffed at the seams. The front of the gown is loose, with a side closure down the left, ending below the hips. A Watteau panel is briefly detached at the centre of the back, but merges with the body of the gown above the hips, ending in a small train. The Watteau panel extends from the back of the neck where it is marked by a satin rosette – an artistic detail which may reference eighteenth-century styles. There is knitted lace trim around the capes, cuffs and down the side panel of the front closure; according to museum records the lace trim was likely added later. There is no inner boning, nor would the dress have been constricting in any way.

The Watteau panel and several other historical features such as its use of olive green velvet, puffed sleeves, and the rustic addition of lace trim, all serve to identify this garment as essentially 'artistic'. Although puffed sleeves were fashionable in the mid-1890s, other features serve to reinforce a historicist reading of the garment. The square neckline, broad/voluminous silhouette through the shoulders and deep divided collar overhanging the shoulders and upper back of the gown are also reminiscent of Renaissance and later seventeenth-century styles. The shirring across the front neckline and articulating the cuffs is reminiscent of smocking techniques used widely in artistic circles at this time. Most importantly, this gown is unstructured through the waist, although it is more tailored through the back, the use of goring providing support and enhancing the overall silhouette and drape of the loose fabric across the front of the garment. Unboned, but lined with cotton for comfort and perhaps reinforcement, it was likely worn without a corset. As a garment worn indoors, this dress would have been extremely loose and comfortable, if perhaps a bit heavy.

The ROM dress bears some resemblance to a Liberty tea gown produced around 1894, and on display in the British Galleries in the Victoria and Albert Museum (acc# T.56–1976). Although slightly different, particularly in the way the bodice is constructed and in the details of the neckline, the two garments share some notable features. Both have puffed sleeves and both are made of green velvet – a textile/colour combination found in many descriptions of Aesthetic dress. Importantly, although both appear to fit high and loose through the waist, the Liberty dress has a boned under bodice. Unlike many home-sewn or locally produced examples of Aesthetic dress which are less structured, boning can be observed in most of the Liberty gowns found at the V&A, as well as several artistically inspired gowns produced by commercial dress-makers held by the Gallery of Costume in Manchester as well as the Museum of London (Ehrman 2014). Based on late-fifteenth-century styles, the tea dress at the V&A resembles an illustrated design by Walter Crane, for the journal *AGLAIA* (1894: 6). While the Crane design suggests a lighter-weight garment that might drape in a more classical manner, the V&A gown is closer to earlier Pre-Raphaelite examples, with a heaviness more reminiscent of late medieval/early Renaissance modes.

The V&A also holds an earlier well-known example of Aesthetic dress (acc# T.171–1973); made from Liberty textiles in 1885, it was designed and constructed by Hamo Thornycroft and his wife Agatha, members of the Healthy and Artistic Dress Union. Unlike the examples given above, this dress is not a tea gown and is based on early-nineteenth-century styles evoking a pastoral English ideal. Lighter-weight textiles (silk lined with cotton), the high natural but defined waist, slightly puffed sleeves, and use of smocking on the bodice and the sleeves all conform to design principles outlined by Aesthetic reformers. One feature does appear to be influenced by contemporary fashions of the period: a gentle bustle is suggested through the use of gathers, folds, tapes, and bunching of the fabric in the upper part of the back of the overskirt. It could also be said however, that this feature is referencing the Polonaise style for skirts in the eighteenth century. It is also reasonable to assume that this voluminous gathering of fabric was not supported by an actual internal bustle, as it was intended to fit a 'good, natural, uncorsetted figure' (Rothstein 1984: 139). Thus, the ROM tea gown, the V&A Thornycroft dress, and to a slightly lesser extent the V&A Liberty tea gown, can all be classified as rare extant examples of Aesthetic dress which exemplify reform principles in terms of their basic construction; these garments were likely intended to enhance the comfort and mobility of the wearer while still accommodating creativity and innovation.

Case study 2: Farebrother tea gown at the Royal Pavilion and Museums, Brighton and Hove

While the ROM dress and two V&A dresses discussed above were clearly impacted by design and reform principles, in the majority of artistic garments I have examined, Aesthetic details such as smocking or choice of fabric, have been adapted without significantly altering conventional, and at times, constrictive construction techniques typical of mainstream fashion. In the Royal Pavilion and Museums, Brighton and Hove Farebrother collection in the United Kingdom, there is an example of this – an Aesthetic gown dated to 1895, that is 'artistic' in appearance, but in actuality, particularly in terms of its construction through the waist, follows the dictates of mainstream fashion (Plates 10 and 11). Made of brown silk taffeta, the princess line dress has a Watteau panel in the form of a double box pleat falling from the back of the neck, free from the bodice, and joining with the skirt at the small of the back. This feature it shares with the ROM example, however the Farebrother tea gown is more structured with a fan-style back which although suggestive of volume, uses ties underneath to keep the skirt compact. A printed yellow silk fabric ornaments the standing collar and is also used for the full length puffed sleeves, supported with starched muslin and are fitted towards the wrist. The same patterned fabric cascades down the front of the gown in a loose panel. Brown machine-embroidered net lace covers the standing collar and falls over the shoulders. Over the lace, but marking the top of the Watteau panel at the back of the neck is a large decorative bow made of the same patterned yellow silk fabric used for the sleeves and front panel. The Watteau panel, deep lace collar and muted, but decorative patterned silk fabric all suggest historical references, primarily to the eighteenth century.

In keeping with many descriptions and illustrations of tea gowns in the fashion journals of the period, the gown's princess-cut is fitted through the back, but the front of the gown is loose and presents an unbroken line to the hem. Its up-to-date fashionability is also marked through its emphasis on internal structure, which places it squarely in the nineteenth century. Although on first glance the dress appears to feature a flowing and loose underdress, in actuality the garment features an internal cuirass bodice, which although unboned, closes with ten buttons, fitting snugly underneath the looser front panel. Interestingly, original museum records initially classified this gown as a maternity garment, indicating that Aesthetic dress in its material and visual manifestations has been stylistically unstable. The variability and eclectic hybridization of historical and artistic attributes in many tea gowns (squared off or ruffed necklines, Watteau panels, loose empire styles, smocking) with more fashionable features (close-fitting princess line construction and in particular, during the 1890s, puffed sleeves) may have made this kind of garment difficult to isolate, or even identify, as a coherent category of dress.

Unlike the ROM example, the Farebrother gown has biographical information provided and some context for the original wearer can be ascertained. The most notable aspect of the gown is its inner fitted cuirass bodice (29 inches at the smallest point) as well as an inside brown tape fastened at the centre back, which would have encircled the waist, most likely over a corset. Museum records show that the gown was worn by Mrs Katherine Sophia Farebrother of 'Leehurst' Salisbury between 1895 and 1910 – this late date likely explains the numerous fashionable features and distinguishes it from earlier, more eclectic examples of Aesthetic dress. Early accession records state that it was likely worn by Mrs Farebrother during her time of 'confinement', however, later examination and research undertaken by the museum reveals that the gown was probably made by a local dressmaker, machine stitched with the lining hand-finished, and is not adjustable. More importantly, it does not appear to have ever been altered, a point which negates its functional use as a maternity dress. In addition, a newer catalogue entry notes that it was unlikely Mrs Farebrother was pregnant in the mid-1890s when the dress was worn (museum records, acc# C003352).

In the past, I have drawn a distinction between examples of Aesthetic dress which follow artistic and reform principles and more conventional gowns subject to the hegemonic forces of fashion which use artistic features or surface effects for decorative purposes only (Wahl 2013: 117–21). The best example of this is a tea gown made by Chipperfield and Butler in 1885, held by the Museum of London and featured in the exhibition *The Cult of Beauty* at the V&A in 2011. The overall tailoring of the gown conforms to mainstream fashionable precepts: princess line construction, cut close to the body and very tight-fitting, the bodice boned and reinforced. The skirt is also quite narrow; internal ties used to maintain its narrow shape and keep its train in place would have encumbered the wearer. In contrast, the type of the fabric used, a sprig print silk of a kind popular in the eighteenth century, the addition of a Watteau panel in the back, and the use smocking, all point towards Aesthetic dress. However, these artistic features deviate from purist conceptions of Aesthetic dress. The use of smocking is patched on and decorative rather than essential to its shape or construction, extending across the back of the shoulders in a broad flat panel and circling the bottom of the skirt in repetitive rows; it is merely a visual indicator of difference in texture, echoing a fascination with complicated trimming typical of fashions of the period. This is an arbitrary and playful inversion of Aesthetic methods of construction where smocking on bodices or sleeves actually sculpts the fabric in a functional way. In the Farebrother gown and other such hybrids of fashionable and artistic dress, Aestheticism is a whimsical pastiche of ideas and details rather than a set of underlying and unified artistic principles guiding how garments might be constructed and worn on the body.

'Seeing' the materiality of dress

Closely examining the material record for Aesthetic dress and cross-referencing it with the text-based and visual dimensions of Aestheticism in terms of fashion, gender, and evolving narratives of modernism provides revealing clues. In terms of the object-based evidence for Aesthetic dress, its instability and changeable nature as an identifiable category of clothing in the late nineteenth century may have caused extant examples to be misattributed or misclassified. Also, the fact that the material record for Aesthetic dress seems incomplete and largely shaped by the fashionable dictates of the day indicates that in practice Aesthetic dress in its most radical form was not widely worn by a broader public. In contrast, the rhetorical and visual dimensions of Aesthetic dress in print culture, combined with its frequency and popularity across a wide variety of art and fashion publications reaffirm that the value and function of Aesthetic dress were largely symbolic. Elizabeth Wilson has argued that like other forms of aesthetic production, fashion can be understood as having an ideological function, where social contradiction and conflict can be resolved on a formal and imaginary level (1985: 9). This may be the case with Aesthetic dress which allowed women to internalize and creatively explore the values and principles of dress reform through a range of visual and text-based sources. Few, however, embodied these values; the physical evidence for Aesthetic dress is not as ubiquitous, nor as stylistically radical as its discursive presence in the literature and seems far more mediated by hegemonic practices in the production and consumption of fashion as a means of circumscribing and reinforcing existing gender norms. In addition, while the roots and influences of Aesthetic dress were seen as primarily historical, its cultural function and practice were both disruptive and suggestive of modernist tropes of progress and innovation. Ilya Parkins has explored the interrelation of text-based and visual sources in order to articulate the complex role of gender in modern culture, stating that fashion 'makes visible some overlooked aspects of gendered modernity, precisely because of the ways that it juxtaposes ephemeral time with the dominant appearance of femininity'

(2012: 16). Therefore, the placement and significance of Aesthetic and alternative forms of dress in the late nineteenth century can and should be understood as indicative of the shifting and negotiated nature of modern culture itself, which was intimately tied with the picturing of the female body as a fashioned object.

A material culture approach which includes object-based methods in combination with text/visual analysis investigates how these symbolic aspects of Aesthetic culture were actually received and embodied through dress practices. It also reveals how the material dimensions of dress undergo radical revision when rendered through forms of representation such as painting, illustration and photography, each of which is subject to internal narratives carved out through tradition and convention. Observing the gaps between Aesthetic dress as a literary and visual trope and its material record through extant garments reveals the complex relations between fashion and dress across a wide array of mediated cultural forms and how these manifest at the level of the body, where other discursive constraints are implicated. Caroline Evans has suggested that fashion is a 'situated, embodied and spatial practice as much as it is an image, object, design or artefact' (2013: 7) Ultimately, modes of inquiry which examine the materiality of history through a range of sources, including object-based, visual, and textual, offer the best chance to understand fashion as simultaneously embedded in a temporal context while constantly in flux – a form of embodied production and consumption which exceeds the boundaries of any one discrete and mediated category of culture.

References

The Artist and Journal of Home Culture (1890), 11 (122): 29.

Breward, C. (1998), 'Cultures, Identities, Histories: Fashioning a Cultural Approach to Dress', *Fashion Theory*, 2 (4): 301–14.

Cassell's Family Magazine (1880): 441–2.

Crane, L. (1882), *Art and the Formation of Taste: Six Lectures*, London: Macmillan.

Crane, W. (1894), 'On the Progress of Taste in Dress, in Relation to Art Education', *AGLAIA: The Journal of the Healthy and Artistic Dress Union*, 3: 6–14.

Cunningham, P. A. (2003), *Reforming Women's Fashion, 1850–1920: Politics, Health and Art*, Kent, OH and London: Kent State University Press.

Devereux, R. (1896), *The Ascent of Woman*, London: John Lane.

Ehrman, E. (2011), 'Women's Dress', in S. Calloway and L. F. Orr (eds), *The Cult of Beauty: The Aesthetic Movement 1860–1900*, London: V&A Publishing.

Ehrman, E. (2014), e-mail correspondence, 22 April.

Evans, C. (2013), *The Mechanical Smile: Modernism and the First Fashion Shows in France and America, 1900–1929*, New Haven and London: Yale University Press.

Galassi, S. G. (2003), 'Whistler and Aesthetic Dress: Mrs. Frances Leyland', in M. F. MacDonald et al. (eds), *Whistler, Women, and Fashion*, New Haven and London: The Frick Collection in association with Yale University Press.

Haweis, E. ([1878, 1879] 1978), 'The Art of Beauty; The Art of Dress', in *The Art of Beauty and the Art of Dress*, New York and London: Garland.

Holiday, H. (1890), 'The Artistic Aspects of Edward Bellamy's "Looking Backward"', in C. R. Ashbee (ed.), *Transactions of the Guild and School of Handicraft*, vol. 1, London: Guild & School of Handicraft.

Holiday, H. (1893), 'The Artistic Aspect of Dress', *AGLAIA: The Journal of the Healthy and Artistic Dress Union*, 1: 13–30.

Holiday, H. (1914), *Reminiscences of my Life*, London: William Heinemann.

Hood, A. (2009), 'Material Culture: The Object', in S. Barber and C. Peniston-Bird (eds), *History Beyond the Text: A Student's Guide to Approaching Alternative Sources*, London and New York: Routledge.

Johnstone, Mrs (1888), 'February Fashions', *Woman's World*: 186.

Jones, A. (ed.) (2003), *The Feminism and Visual Culture Reader*, London: Routledge.

Lady's Pictorial (1887), 14: 353.

Newton, S. M. (1974), *Health, Art and Reason: Dress Reformers of the 19th Century*, London: John Murray.

Palmer, A. (1997), 'New Directions: Fashion History Studies and Research in North America and England', *Fashion Theory*, 1 (3): 297–312.

'Paris Fashions' (1890), *Woman's World*, 185.

Parkins, I. (2012), *Poiret, Dior and Schiaparelli: Fashion, Femininity and Modernity*, London: Berg.

The Queen (1881), 70: 675.

Riello, G. (2009), 'Things that Shape History: Material Culture and Historical Narratives', in K. Harvey (ed.), *History and Material Culture*, London: Routledge.

Riello, G. (2011), 'The Object of Fashion: Methodological Approaches to the Study of Fashion', *Journal of Aesthetics and Culture*, 3 (1): 1–9.

Rogoff, I. (1998), 'Studying Visual Culture', in N. Mirzoeff (ed.), *The Visual Culture Reader*, London: Routledge.

Rothstein, N. (ed.) (1985), *Four Hundred Years of Fashion*, London: V&A Publications.

Stern, R. (2004), *Against Fashion: Clothing as Art, 1850–1930*, Cambridge: MIT Press.

Styles, J. (1998), 'Dress in History: Reflections on a Contested Terrain', *Fashion Theory*, 2 (4): 383–90.

Taylor, L. (1998), 'Doing the Laundry? A Reassessment of Object-based Dress History', *Fashion Theory*, 2 (4): 337–58.

Taylor, L. (2002), *The Study of Dress History*, Manchester and New York: Manchester University Press.

Wahl, K. (2011), 'A Domesticated Exoticism: Fashioning Gender in Nineteenth-Century British Tea Gowns', in I. Parkins and E. M. Sheehan (eds), *Cultures of Femininity in Modern Fashion*, Durham: University of New Hampshire Press.

Wahl, K. (2013), *Dressed as in a Painting: Women and British Aestheticism in an Age of Reform*, Durham: University of New Hampshire Press.

Wilson, E. (1985), *Adorned in Dreams: Fashion and Modernity*, Berkeley: University of California Press.

Wilson, S. (1996), 'Away with the Corsets, on with the Shifts', in S. Wilson and J. Benington (eds), *Simply Stunning: The Pre-Raphaelite Art of Dressing*, Cheltenham: Cheltenham Art Gallery and Museums (reprint edition).

7 DRESS, SELF-FASHIONING AND DISPLAY AT THE ISABELLA STEWART GARDNER MUSEUM

Christine M. E. Guth

When the American art collector Isabella Stewart Gardner began planning her museum, popularly known during her lifetime as Fenway Court, she chose a site on the marshy fens. This location was far from the Museum of Fine Arts, an institution then located in Boston's fashionable Copley Square whose board of directors had excluded her from membership. The foundation of a private museum offered the opportunity to command an entire canvas, as it were, on which to project her singular aesthetic vision and, following her husband's death in 1898, she actively developed the museum in her own likeness. She personally supervised every detail of the three-storey building, demanding that its interior walls be vetted with a stone facade in the manner of a Venetian palazzo and open onto a flower-filled courtyard. She also designed the galleries where her collection, comprising by the time of her death in 1924 more than 2,500 paintings, sculptures, tapestries, furniture, manuscripts, rare books and decorative arts from around the world, was displayed (Chong, Lingner and Zahn 2003). In so doing she created an enduring aesthetic environment for and material representation of her identity both as a woman and a collector.

Isabella Stewart Gardner was the most eminent of a handful of American women collectors and philanthropists who rose to national prominence between the 1880s and 1920s, an era that saw the formation of museums in cities large and small across the United States (McCarthy 1991; van Hook 1996; Corn 1997). One of many manifestations of the transformation brought about by the rise of an industrial capitalist society and the erosion of social frameworks of community and religion that attended it, these institutions were at the centre of new economic, social, and cultural orders that were dominated by male 'cultural entrepreneurs', wealthy benefactors who saw these as a means of consolidating American cultural identity and improving public taste in an increasingly pluralistic society (DiMaggio 1982). At a time when women were effectively barred from active roles within the museum, pioneering female collectors created, in art historian Wanda Corn's resonant term, 'a distinctive style of matronage'. These included Louisine Havemeyer, who formed notable collections of Impressionist painting and Japanese art, which she donated to the Metropolitan Museum of Art, and Jane Stanford, the founder of the Stanford University Art Museum, as well as Gardner (Corn 1997: 11). Gender played a role in the way public and private converged in their activities, but the decisions each brought to the formation, installation, and disposal of her collection reveal highly individualistic styles of feminine modernity. Women collectors did not and do not all behave in the same way simply because they are women; practical considerations, such as financial means and the availability of space, age, geography, social and moral values, as well as psychology, are significant factors.

This chapter seeks to extend and complicate existing scholarship on gender and collecting by focusing on the role that body and dress played in the way that Isabella Stewart Gardner designed her museum. It builds on my own research on American collectors' engagement with Asia (Guth 2004, 2009, 2014), drawing on the work of scholars in the fields of museology, American studies, interior design and dress history. Notable among the latter is Lou Taylor's *Establishing Dress History*, a foundational text for understanding the development of museum collections of dress and the particular approaches brought to their formation and interpretation (Taylor 2004).

Much has been written about collecting as an extension of self with respect to the selection and use of objects. As museologist Susan Pearce has observed, this notion accounts for the way we use metaphors such as 'the body' or 'corpus' of the collection to refer to those pieces that are central to its meaning. If collections are the extended self, it follows, she argues, that these also have the capacity to take on a masculine or feminine identity (Pearce 1993: 56–7). Such museological studies emphasize the museum as a projection of the gendered self through the selection and display of objects, but they have not given sufficient attention to the way that textiles and dress may contribute to the aestheticization of such spaces. Gardner, for instance, collected textiles related to forms of clothing from many parts of the world including French lace accessories, Italian ecclesiastical garments and Japanese Noh robes. Textiles from Asia figured especially prominently in her design of Fenway Court, but she deployed all of them, irrespective of date or national origin, to frame paintings and other forms of decorative art and to soften spatial contours as part of a design vocabulary that unsettled the boundaries between interiority and exteriority, East and West. The manner in which Gardner chose to dress for portraits strategically installed in her galleries extended this use of textiles and clothing while also making her a permanent physical presence within the museum. For her, the museum was not simply a passive container or protective enclosure of masterpieces, but rather a dynamic environment in which she, along with the viewers who moved through it, were encouraged to think 'outside the box', by taking into account the works of celebrated male artists as well as the female creativity brought to their manner of display. In this respect, Gardner's 'dressing of Fenway Court' may be seen at the intersection of museum and gender studies as well as dress history.

The work of two scholars, Beverley Gordon and Penny Sparke, has been especially helpful in situating Gardner's use of dress within the particularities of the North-American context. Gordon, a cultural historian, has written in richly textured detail on the conceptual conflation of women and interiors in America from about 1875 until 1925 with particular attention to the way that choices made about the display of art may blur the boundaries between subjectivities and spaces. She highlights the fact that exclusion from the political power structures of their day led American women to define the domestic world as their own. Their connection with their houses was so strong, she argues, that it helped to shape the perception of both: 'The woman was seen as the embodiment of the home and, in turn the home was seen as an extension of her – an extension of both her corporeal and spiritual self' (Gordon 1996: 282). This discourse permeates metaphorical language, prescriptive literature, popular imagery, and, especially the way the interior was decorated. Rooms were personified as 'animated' through women's 'vital spark', and were 'dressed up' for special occasions (Gordon 1996: 287, 288). Yet as Gordon cautions: 'There is nothing inherently or implicitly biological in the term – the *Oxford English Dictionary* defines the verb "to dress" as "to make right, set up, array, tend or arrange" – but the association with the body seems to lie deep in our psyches' (Gordon 1996: 288). Gordon focuses on middle-class female consumption of domestic furnishings, but her arguments may be aligned with the collecting and display practices of their more affluent counterparts.

Design historian Penny Sparke's study of Elsie de Wolfe's evolution from 'clothes horse' to professional interior decorator has further contributed to my interpretation of the links between fashionable dress and fashionable interiors in Gardner's times (Sparke 2010). De Wolfe was a contemporary of Gardner's, but was not born to wealth. Until she married into British royalty late in life, she moved in very different New York-based, nouveau riche social circles where she developed a professional career as a model, advice columnist and interior decorator. Nonetheless, the two women shared a sense of the theatrical, as well as an awareness of the importance of the media in promoting themselves and their activities. Photographs of her fashionable attire and interior décor were essential in securing de Wolfe's celebrity; similarly, photographs and portraits by well-known artists were crucial to the reputation and representation of Fenway Court and the woman who designed it. The two women also shared an awareness of the synergies between their clothing and surroundings. As Sparke observed, 'dressing in fashionable clothes and selecting the decoration of their private surroundings not only permitted modern women to express their personalities to others, but also, more importantly, to themselves' (Sparke 2010: 206). In what follows, I want to discuss the mediating role of textiles and dress in the design and installation of the galleries of Fenway Court in terms of similar physical processes of intense psychological identification between the female body and space. The space examined here, however, is the museum, and the focus is Gardner's mobilization of textiles and dress to dissolve rigid art historical hierarchies and escape the spatio-temporal dislocations of such institutions.

Isabella Stewart Gardner's Asian travels

Isabella Stewart Gardner negotiated a prominent public position for herself in Boston through the establishment of a museum that promoted a different attitude towards art than those founded with the aim of educating the public. She assembled her collection as an individual, producing a competing, but equally ideologically motivated account of what she regarded as art. Her collection embraced the cultures of Europe and Asia, but also gave recognition to products of female craft such as lace. While she was concerned with artistic authenticity, and paid dearly for the professional advice that guaranteed it, she located this authenticity both in individual works of art and in the total phenomenological experience of the aesthetic environment in which they were displayed. The intensive and extensive experiences of cultural difference engendered by her travels in Asia between 1883 and 1884 were crucial to her personal and cultural investment in such bodily experience, and the religious practices and beliefs she discovered there helped to validate it (Guth 2014).

When she set off with her husband on their world tour she had not yet begun to collect art and she made few references to the Japanese scrolls, screens and woodblock prints or the other kinds of art her Boston friend William Sturgis Bigelow was enthusiastically purchasing. Her journals and letters instead reveal how taken she was by Asian textiles and fashions. This was, of course, conventional gendered taste at the time. Textiles and dress were key constituents of late-nineteenth-century Euro-American constructs of Asia: admiring descriptions of the exotic fabrics and styles of Asian dress figured prominently in most travel accounts and, in response to touristic interest, were subjects well documented in commercial photography as well. Portraits of women surrounded by fashionable silks and other *objets d'art* from China and Japan by James Whistler and other artists also speak to the perceived homology between the formation of feminine sensibilities and artistic taste and Asian textiles (Wilson 1999; Yoshihara 2003; Guth 2009; Cheang 2010).

Gardner's letters and diaries, however, reveal that her appreciation of Asian textiles and dress was inseparable from the bodies – both male and female – that wore them. The photographs of women dressed in kimono, sari, and sarongs artfully pasted into her travel albums speak to her fascination with female fashions, and the way that, unlike the corseted costume of her own culture, woven and patterned silks were artistically draped to clothe the body. In India, she commented on the way that cashmere shawls, muslins and silks were loosely wound around the body (Chong, Lingner and Murai 2009: 303). Unlike many of her compatriots, Gardner was also quite open to Euro-American adoption of local dress styles. As noted below, she was, for instance, sympathetic to Bigelow's donning of Japanese kimono, a garment that in American eyes had strong feminine connotations.

The activities in which she participated (often without her husband, who found little of interest in Asia) suggest the degree to which she was willing to flout social rules and expectations and the openly sensual pleasure she derived from male (un)dress. On one occasion while in Japan, she attended a sumo wrestling match where she sat next to a Japanese man, 'a great swell . . . [whose] beautiful clothes were carefully laid aside on account of the heat and there he sat, smoking a most beautiful pipe with nothing on but a waist cloth and a European straw hat'. But, she continued quite happily, 'We didn't even notice his want of clothes, as everybody is almost always in that undress' (Chong, Lingner and Murai 2009: 155).

Other letters from Japan further reveal not only her enjoyment of lifestyles that broke with her own but a sexualized acknowledgement of non-Western men: 'We have tiffined and dined together in every conceivable place and style; and I should say that we have drunk gallons of canary colored tea out of their dear little cups and have eaten pounds of sweets, as we three have sprawled about on the soft, clean mats, in the funny little shops, looking at curios. If the Japanese were only handsomer, they would be perfect. Such charming manners, so gentle . . . and their clothes are delicious, so soft in colour and fabric. Bigelow wears the Japanese garment always when in his house, and shoes are such an unheard of thing on the pretty mats that I kick mine off on every occasion' (Chong, Lingner and Murai 2009: 123). While it may offend by its stereotyping, by the same token, it is striking to find a middle-aged Victorian woman (she was forty-three at the time) so openly discussing the allure of Japanese men in the same terms used with regard to men of her own race and class. These sentiments challenge stereotypes of Victorian sexual repression.

The aesthetic attractions of Japanese and Chinese male dress, and especially the sensuousness of the materials from which it was made, had significant bearing on her judgements. In Shanghai she visited a silk merchant and, after choosing some silks for herself, watched him tend to a 'handsome creature' who was 'as excited over his clothes as a young girl over her first ball dress'. He took forever to decide 'whether he would have the drawers of a light yellow green, the under long flowing robe of the tenderest "blue-after-a-rain", and the short coat of mauve', but in the end 'seized a superb ruby red and began a new combination that at last contented him' (Chong, Lingner and Murai 2009: 211).

While Gardner was prepared to 'kick off her shoes' and lounge about on the tatami mats of private homes and curio shops in Japan, there is no photographic evidence that she ever donned a kimono, as did so many of her friends. By all accounts a rather plain woman, Gardner was, former Gardner Museum curator Alan Chong has observed, 'always very controlling of her image', and she seems to have disliked having herself photographed, preferring the idealizing touch of the portrait painter (Chong, Lingner and Murai 2009: 20). Dressing up in Japanese kimono apparently was not to her taste, but she actively adapted exotic textiles and styles of dress to suit her own purposes. The various forms of self-fashioning Gardner engaged in following her return from Asia reveal the degree to which her psychological, sexual, and creative desires were imaginatively wrapped up in textiles and fashion.

Dressing the galleries

Her Asian experiences aroused in Gardner a new recognition of the way textiles could be wrapped and draped rather than cut and tailored and as materials to be celebrated aesthetically in their own right. Over the years she developed styles of hanging, draping, and even cutting textiles to bring colour, fantasy and surprise into the appreciation and interpretation of her galleries. This approach challenged the growing tendency in museums at the turn of the century to hang paintings against a neutral backdrop to dramatize their masterpiece status, thus distancing them from domestic display practices (Guth 2009). Public museums were designed as impersonal and professional places, but Gardner was not willing to submerge her personality in this way. In her design of Fenway Court, she self-consciously collapsed the boundaries between museum and house by her playful and often subversive refusal of conventionally ascribed meanings. This is not to say that Fenway Court was a 'house museum', a gendered term implying that it was initially a lived space. It was intended from the start as a museum, and Gardner's personal living space was confined to the uppermost floor.

While Gardner rejected many aspects of contemporary museum practice, there was a clear logic underlying the galleries' design. She made conscious decisions about each room in order to make statements about period, style or regional artistic importance. At the same time the galleries brought into aesthetic dialogue works of many countries and media from East and West. Masterpieces by artists including Titian, Botticelli, Vermeer and Velasquez, as well as European furnishings, were commingled with Asian *objets d'art* ranging from Japanese screen paintings and Asian textiles to Buddhist sculpture. She also dressed Fenway

Court by deploying luxurious silks, velvets and damasks throughout the galleries, using them to frame paintings, and create unexpected visual juxtapositions that complicate the readings of classical masterpieces. In the Gothic Room, for instance, a fresco of Hercules by Piero della Francesca was displayed between two startling flame-stitched embroidered panels (Plate 13) and in the Titian Room and a chasuble hung below two secular male portraits, visual and material conjunctions that arouse quite different responses than if each were shown in splendid isolation.

Her decoration of the Titian Room reveals a startlingly sexualized dialectic between her private and public life. The room gets its name from one of the greatest treasures in the Museum: Titian's painting of *The Rape of Europa* in which Jupiter, in the form of a white bull, carries off the terrified Europa on his back. Gardner displayed beneath this celebrated masterwork a length of shimmering gold silk satin with a tassel pattern cut from the skirt of a dress designed for her by Worth, transforming the sensuous materiality of the patterned silk and absent body into a gloss on the erotic drama of the painting above it (Plate 12). According to Alan Chong, the museum only become aware that this silk panel was cut from one of Gardner's own gowns in the course of preparing a catalogue of her textile collection in 1986. That visitors were unaware of this dramatization of her own 'ravishment', was perhaps part of the mischievous, secret pleasure she derived from this juxtaposition (Chong 2007: 213–14). By this creative self-referential use of a garment that had been in physical contact with her body to extend the significance of Titian's painting, Gardner not only demonstrated the porousness of the boundaries between herself, her collection, and her museum, but also asserted her identity as a sexual being.

Naming is one of the tools that curators and collectors alike use to circumscribe the objects in their possession and insert them into museum time. Gardner used this strategy to create personal narratives that evolved in keeping with the growth of her collection and her own preoccupations. In addition to the Gothic and Titian Rooms, she created rooms that mapped the exotic geographies evoked in her art works. Her first Chinese Room (1903) was an eclectic space where Chinese embroidered silk panels were hung on the walls alongside Japanese folding screens and wooden architectural transoms. A Japanese theatre robe dresses a nearby table (Figure 7.1). Gardner herself is woven into the space by a portrait by Andreas Zorn showing her with arms outstretched as if welcoming invisible guests, and by extension the viewers of the photograph recording the appearance of the room. Dressed in a white robe that stands out against the dark surroundings, this portrait further underlines the carefully constructed and multi-layered physical and spatial relationships that Gardner sought to evoke.

In 1915 she dismantled this Chinese Room and created a new semi-private space that came to be known as the Buddha Room which brought together her by

FIGURE 7.1 Photograph of the Chinese Room, 1903. Courtesy of Isabella Stewart Gardner Museum, Boston.

then extensive collection of Asian art. This later relocation of the space where her Asian collection was concentrated coincided with a growing preoccupation with Buddhism. This new room presented a more cohesive ensemble dominated by Buddhist statues, complete with altar tables covered with silk clothes, candlesticks, an incense burner and pierced metal temple hangings suspended from the ceiling. This arrangement creatively displaced to Boston the multi-sensorial aura of the Buddhist temples she had found so affecting during her travels to Japan. Entered only at her invitation, this intimate ritualized space was not intended to create a visual impression, but to move, a figure of speech that captures the corporeal effect that she sought.

Performative portraits

Gardner invested subjective emotions and expectations in her museum in many material forms. Known for her wardrobe as well as her theatricality, she used the display of portraits of herself in fashionable dress strategically to assert her presence and way of seeing in the museum. By conveying her appearance at different moments in time and in very different attires, these also extend and complicate the temporal-spatial experience of the collection. The Zorn portrait on view next to the hearth in the Chinese Room performs the welcoming role she might have assumed herself. As the scholar Wayne Koestenbaum has observed of this painting:

> She stands in our way as if to say: look at me, not at the more traditionally exciting spectacle outside. She distracts us and puts forward her own glamour as art – not an intervention in the cause of art, but as a worthy spectacle in its own right. She reminds us, in other words, to listen to the complexities of female performance, and not to take it as subordinate to works of artifice such as painting. (Cited in Chong, Lingner and Zahn 2003: 215)

An earlier portrait by John Singer Sargent, completed in 1888, four years after Gardner's return from her world tour, fulfils this performativity more explicitly. It is an unusual full-length frontal likeness showing her standing, dressed in a clinging black gown with a deep décolletage standing before an ornate Venetian or Middle Eastern textile, the pattern of which forms a halo-like effect behind her (Ormond and Kilmurray 1998: vol. 1, 210–11) (Plate 14). Gardner's pose, with her hands clasped before her, and use of an exotic textile as backdrop, invite comparison with two portraits of the young Princess Mary Stuart of England, painted by Anthony Van Dyck around 1640 when he was court painter to Charles I, works now in Hampton Court and the Museum of Fine Arts that Gardner or Sargent may have seen during visits to Britain. Isabella Stewart Gardner liked to claim descent from the royal Stuarts, had relics including silk and lace, purportedly parts of a dress once worn by Mary Stuart, and for Christmas eve mass she is even said to have adopted costume influenced by a portrait of the Queen (Carter 1972: 3–4). The collaborative nature of Sargent's painting is further suggested by the story, possibly apocryphal, that when the painter declared his wish to use a piece of Venetian brocade on the wall of his London studio as background, Gardner replied that she had the other half in her collection. Sargent shared Gardner's enthusiasm for Oriental silks and clothing and used these as studio props in other paintings (Ormond and Kilmurray 1998: vol. 1, 210). Whatever the velvet's source, it is clear that both artist and sitter understood the iconic power of exotic textiles.

The portrait's daring combination of sensuality and spirituality caused a sensation in Boston. On the one hand, viewers saw in it an allusion to Sargent's notorious portrait of the fashionable Madame X painted four years earlier in Paris. The model for that painting, Virginie Amélie Gautreau, was one of the great beauties of the time, an association that Gardner may have welcomed. In the original version, Sargent showed one of the straps of her dress slipping suggestively off the shoulder, but this caused such a scandal that he later altered the painting (Fairbrother 2000: 72–81). On the other hand, her unusually hieratic pose, the mandorla-like textile and, especially, the seemingly ritual position of her hands suggested identification with Buddhist icons of the kind she had seen in China and Japan and would later collect herself. During Gardner's lifetime, one Boston viewer called its subject a 'Byzantine Madonna with a halo' while another imagined her as a devotee of some 'fashionable Hindoo cult'. William Bigelow, an enthusiastic collector of Japanese Buddhist art, was perhaps closest to the mark when he observed: 'It was not a bad idea to have yourself painted as Kwannon [Kannon] the benign and omnipotent Providence' (cited in Chong, Lingner and Murai 2009: 27).

During his lifetime, her conservative husband would not allow the painting to be shown. When the museum opened in 1903, however, Gardner installed it in the Gothic Room (a room of limited public access during her lifetime because it served often as Sargent's studio), where it still reigns, 'a luminous and audacious presence' (Chong, Lingner and Zahn 2003: 17). Displayed in the corner at an angle, the portrait performs a kind of curatorial oversight. Even the modern viewer who enters and walks through Fenway Court cannot fail to feel Isabella Stewart Gardner's regal presence and be guided by her eye.

A second, radically different watercolour portrait that Sargent painted two years before Gardner's death in 1924, gives further expression to the way she, in collusion with Sargent, used sartorial strategies not simply to adorn her body, but to express her deeply felt religious ideals. Gardner is again portrayed in an iconic frontal pose, but instead of the tailored European black dress of the earlier portrait, she is draped, head to toe, in a loose, pure white garment, the ample folds of which form a kind of protective cocoon around her frail body (Plate 15). The Sargent scholar Richard Ormond has suggested that this portrait alludes to the draped figure in Sargent's 1888 Orientalist painting 'Incensing the Veil' of which Gardner owned a sketch, but it is more likely that it is multi-referential (Ormond and Kilmurray 1998: vol. 3, 252). The shroud-like draperies simultaneously evoke classical Greco-Roman dress, medieval monastic robes and, especially, the flowing white garment worn by Kannon, one of the most popular religious figures in Chinese and Japanese religious art. Painted at a time when Gardner was facing her own mortality, this portrait is strikingly similar to that of the enigmatic bronze statue Augustus St. Gaudens had created in 1891 as a memorial for Henry Adams's wife, a work that both Sargent and Gardner would have known. This celebrated bronze statue of a mysteriously draped figure, evoking classical, Christian and Buddhist aesthetic traditions, embodies a complex, cosmopolitan religious symbolism that resonated closely with Gardner's own. A deliberate reference to Kannon is also likely as this Buddhist deity occupied a special place in the imagination of Boston Japanophiles, who regarded the figure as the embodiment of an eternal feminine that transcended East and West (Guth 1995; Murai 2009: 83–9).

Conclusion

Gardner's activities should be seen within the nineteenth-century geopolitical relocations and reconfigurations of art, as temples and shrines in China and Japan were divested of their treasures and old collections were dissolved and transferred from European private houses to American public ones. Most of the actors in this drama were male, but with a spending power matched by only a few of her peers in Boston, she had both the financial means and the drive to subvert their more conventional approaches. Gardner has been popularly characterized as an imperious and flamboyant eccentric, but her so-called eccentricity contained within it a critique of Victorian norms and, as Wanda Corn has argued, was part of a strategy to develop a performative style of cultural leadership that was in sharp contrast to that of her male counterparts (Corn 1997: 13).

For Gardner, the Museum constituted a kind of social performance, a narrative, explicitly and implicitly designed to materialize her presence. Her recognition of the active power of dress textiles led her to mobilize them to clothe the walls and furnishings of the museum. The language Gardner developed to express herself was dependent on conventional museological practice in as much as she sought out certified masterpieces, such as Titian's *Rape of Europa*, to display on its walls, but it was also shaped by the displacement of her own psychic life to its interior spaces. She relied on the professional advice of art historians and dealers such as Bernard Berenson in the acquisition of masterpieces, but once acquired, she often undermined their accepted meanings by showing them in unexpected juxtapositions of her own design that involved the use of textiles or other unusual framing devices.

Gardner articulated her museological vision under conditions of affluence and choice, but also constraints that stifled female creativity. Public museums served to explain and locate within a particular civilizational context the objects within them. If they were understood to involve cosmopolitan engagement with other parts of the world, it was selective, and this was in order to create a sense of what constituted American culture. Their didactic goal also included promoting, in the name of civility, their own, masculine, codes of public behaviour. The feminist theorist Gaby Porter has argued that 'the differences between the histories of men and women as represented in the museum lie at much deeper levels [than simple representation] . . . the whole structure of museums – abstract knowledge as well as concrete manifestations of buildings, exhibitions, and collections – was built upon categories and boundaries which embodied ascriptions about men and women, masculine and feminine . . . At the crux of this difference', she continues 'is the tension between abstract theoretical concepts and the material physical body' (Porter 2004: 105).

Gardner, exceptionally, was able simultaneously to mobilize and transcend these ascribed gender categories and boundaries to assert her personal aesthetic vision. For her, 'dressing' was inseparable from collecting. In her design choices she endeavoured to create a cosmopolitan physical environment in which painting, sculpture, furniture and textiles were part of a complete aesthetic environment of the type that might be fairly characterized as a *gesamskunstwerk*. Like the collection itself, the museum was a dynamic, living space that changed over her lifetime as she altered the galleries in keeping with her changing vision and emotional needs. The display of her portraits materialized her corporeal presence, underscoring her intention that the museum be a site of artistic interpretation coextensive with her life. This is underlined by the terms of her bequest. When she left the museum to the city of Boston, she declared that nothing in the rooms was to be changed or altered and no works of art were to be added or subtracted; if they were, the museum was to be dissolved, the works of art sold in Paris and the proceeds given to Harvard College (Corn 1997: 22). Even today visitors who move through her galleries do so in collaboration with her.

Acknowledgements

My thanks to Verity Wilson for her helpful comments on an earlier draft of this chapter.

References

Carter, M. (1972), *Isabella Stewart Gardner and Fenway Court*, Boston: Isabella Stewart Gardner Museum.

Cheang, S. (2010), 'Chinese Robes in Western Interiors: Transitionality and Transformation', in A. Myzelev and J. Potvin (eds), *Fashion, Interior Design and the Contours of Modern Identity*, London: Ashgate.

Chong, A. (2007), 'Mrs. Gardner's Museum of Myth', *Res*, 52 (Autumn): 213–20.

Chong, A., Lingner, R. and Murai, N. (eds) (2009), *Journeys East: Isabella Stewart Gardner and Asia*, Boston: Isabella Stewart Gardner Museum.

Chong, A., Lingner, R. and Zahn, C. (eds) (2003), *Eye of the Beholder: Masterpieces from the Isabella Stewart Gardner Museum*, Boston: Isabella Stewart Gardner Museum.

Corn, W. (1997), 'Art Matronage in Post-Victorian America', *Fenway Court Volume XXVII; Cultural Leadership in America: Art Matronage and Patronage*, Boston: Isabella Stewart Museum.

DiMaggio, P. (1982), 'Cultural Entrepreneurship in Nineteenth-Century Boston: The Creation of an Organizational Base for High Culture in America', *Media, Culture and Society*, 4: 33–50.

Fairbrother, T. (2000), *John Singer Sargent: The Sensualist*, New Haven: Yale University Press.

Gordon, B. (1996), 'Women's Domestic Body: The Conceptual Conflation of Women and Interiors in the Industrial Age', *Winterthur Portfolio*, 31 (4): 12–41.

Guth, C. (1995), 'The Cult of Kannon among American Japanophiles', *Orientations*, December: 28–34.

Guth, C. (2004), *Longfellow's Tattoos: Tourism, Collecting and Japan*, Seattle and London: University of Washington Press.

Guth, C. (2009), 'Asia by Design: Women and the Collecting and Display of Oriental Art', in A. Chong, R. Lingner and N. Murai (eds), *Journeys East: Isabella Stewart Gardner and Asia*, Boston: Isabella Stewart Gardner Museum.

Guth, C. (2014), 'Multi-sensorial Asia', in N. Murai and A. Chong (eds), *Inventing Asia: American Perspectives around 1900*, Boston: Isabella Stewart Gardner Museum.

McCarthy, K. (1991), *Women's Culture: American Philanthropy and Art, 1830–1930*, Chicago: University of Chicago Press.

Murai, N. (2009), 'Matrons of the East: Okakura Kakuzō and His Female Friends in America', in A. Chong, R. Lingner and N. Murai (eds), *Journeys East: Isabella Stewart Gardner and Asia*.

Ormond, R. and Kilmurray, E. (1998), *John Singer Sargent: Complete Paintings*, 3 vols, New Haven: Yale University Press.

Pearce, S. (1993), *Museums Objects and Collections: A Cultural Study*, Washington, DC: Smithsonian Institution.

Porter, G. (2004), 'Seeing through Solidity: A Feminine Perspective on Museums', in B. M. Carbonell (ed.), *Museum Studies: An Anthology of Contexts*, Oxford: Blackwell.

Sparke, P. (2010), 'Framing the Modern Woman: From Clothes Horse to Interior Decorator', in A. Myzelev and J. Potvin (eds), *Fashion, Interior Design and the Contours of Modern Identity*, London: Ashgate.

Taylor, L. (2004*), Establishing Dress History*, Manchester: University of Manchester Press.

Van Hook, B. (1996), *Angels of Art: Women and Art in American Society, 1876–1914*, University Park: Penn State Press.

Wilson, V. (1999), 'Studio and Soirée: Chinese Textiles in Europe and America, 1850 to the Present', in R. B. Phillips and C. B. Steiner (eds), *Unpacking Cultures: Art and Commodity in Colonial and Postcolonial Worlds*, Berkeley: University of California Press.

Yoshihara, M. (2003), *Embracing the East: White Women and American Orientalism*, Oxford and New York: Oxford University Press.

8 'AT ONCE CLASSICAL AND MODERN': RAYMOND DUNCAN DRESS AND TEXTILES IN THE ROYAL ONTARIO MUSEUM

Alexandra Palmer

Lou Taylor ends her review of John Harvey's book *Men in Black* writing: 'What is this book? Dress History? Literary Criticism? Cultural History? Gender Study? Visual Culture? Who cares! Read it!' (1996: 303). It is the open-minded and multidisciplinary 'who cares' that Taylor has consistently promoted that has expanded the field of dress studies, and indelibly influenced my thinking as a fashion and textile curator at the Royal Ontario Museum (ROM). Museums are unique microcosms where natural and man-made specimens are transformed into precious, numbered, itemized artefacts. Within this socialist world all objects are treated equally, regardless of beauty, age, gender, material or origin. The same amount of work applies to all, no matter how small, beautiful or ordinary, dirty or decaying. For these reasons it is crucial to ask 'who cares?'

A curator has to weigh the value of each potential acquisition and ask this question in multiple ways. Acquiring a new piece through donation or purchase has a long-term impact on the museum purse as it has to be cared for in perpetuity in frequently overstuffed storage rooms. Does the potential acquisition 'fit' within the existing collection or fill a gap? Why and how might it be used in scholarly research now or in the future? Are other museums already caring for a similar piece and, if so, does that make this one more or less significant? What are the conservation concerns? The list goes on and many questions are difficult to predict, but decisions often rely upon information that is published and accessible. What is certain is that each decision to add to the permanent collection sets off a domino effect generating new work for numerous staff members who have to make and file a temporary receipt for the object, legally acquire it, freeze it for pests, register it, catalogue it, safely house it, record its location at all times, research it, conserve it, prepare it for photography, photograph it, and maybe, even install it in an exhibition.

Curators are repeatedly confronted with objects that diverge or are not in the canon, and somehow have to determine the potential relevance of these pieces for the museum's collection. Frequently textiles are anonymous without manufacturers' marks on the selvedge, or fashions without dressmakers' labels, and no provenance or associated history. In these cases the designs are usually contextualized by comparison to similar pieces in terms of style, technique and construction, a valid, but limiting, material culture approach. Only by conducting new research that queries, challenges and locates objects within a broad setting can knowledge be expanded. So how does one contextualize an artefact that has little or no history, and does not 'fit' the written history (Palmer 2013)? The following case study on the research for an acquisition of dress and textiles made by Raymond Duncan (1874–1966) discusses how and why using a multidisciplinary approach is sometimes the only way to construct meaning. The results not only open the canon of dress history, but suggest new, unforeseen avenues of enquiry.

In 2008, New York dealer, Titi Halle of Cora Ginsburg, showed me a group of painted and printed dress and textiles designed by the American, Raymond Duncan. I thought the designs were beautiful and that they could add to the collection of eighteenth- to twentieth-century painted and printed textiles in the ROM. In order to fund the acquisition I had to write a grant that would be peer reviewed and knew that beauty alone was insufficient reason for approval. In order to contextualize the pieces, I first contacted colleagues to determine how the designs compared with other examples of his work. I could find no Duncan textiles in Canada or the United Kingdom, although several museums in France and the United States have his designs, but there was little other information forthcoming about him or provenance. Most surprisingly, there is virtually nothing written on Raymond Duncan.

I began patching together information from traditional archival and library research that incorporated art, design and archaeological history to construct a social, cultural and economic meaning and history of the designs. Object analysis was important to build links to other artefacts in the ROM's decorative arts collection. I compared the proposed acquisitions to the ROM's collection of painted and printed textiles. I also collaborated with my colleague, Anu Liivandi, whose extensive knowledge of the ROM's archaeological textile collection has been vital to unravelling meaning, and underscores the benefits of cross-disciplinary and collaborative work. Collaboration bolstered my argument for acquisition, particularly because I could find out so little about Duncan and his work.

By 2010, I felt I had enough information and submitted the peer review grant. It was approved, and five Raymond Duncan textiles entered the permanent collection of the ROM. In 2011, I expanded the research to consider the history of late-nineteenth and early twentieth-century movement, gymnastics and dance studies, and I sought out autobiographies and biographies of those in Duncan's social circle. Increased access to archival publications online yielded more data. More recently contact with the Duncan family and subsequent oral histories with Raymond's daughter, Ligoa and her children Michel Duncan Merle and Dorée Duncan Seligmann, has been invaluable. Interestingly, the Duncans are repeatedly approached with inquiries about, Isadora Duncan, Raymond's famous sister, whose fame and tragic death have overshadowed his accomplishments. The family were surprised and pleased by my request, commenting that few have previously asked about Raymond. Their oral histories corrected my previous interpretations of his *oeuvre*, underscoring the value of this research method for the dress and textile historian (Taylor 2002: 267). Together, all this research clearly demonstrates the significance of his production, influence, engagement and support of the arts and what emerged is a larger, on-going project on Duncan's life and work. Following is a synthesis of this research.

Who was Raymond Duncan?

I first learned about Raymond Duncan from a lecture on men in togas given by Lou Taylor in the mid-1980s. She showed an astonishing image from the turn of the century of a man walking along the banks of the Seine wearing a draped toga, sandals and pushing an enormous black perambulator. I was flabbergasted, not only by his appearance, but also by the fact that I had not heard nor read about such a colourful character during my years studying art, fashion and textile history. Since seeing his textiles in 2008 I have become more and more intrigued by his philosophies and work, but also very curious as to why so little is known about him and his prodigious output that spans the arts and crafts movement at the turn of the century, Art Deco, modernism and abstraction in Europe and America. Even a book with the promising title, *Utopian Craftsmen: The Arts and Crafts Movement from the Cotswolds to Chicago,* by Lionel Lambourne (1980) does not mention Duncan. There is no scholarly work I could find that discusses him as a philosopher, commune leader, activist, pacifist, dancer and theorist, poet, playwright, actor, musician, musicologist, graphic artist, typographer, gallerist, artist, spinner, weaver, textile artist or fashion designer; yet he worked in all these disciplines. The exception is an illustrated chapter in Sara Bowman and Michel Molinare's book (1985) that contains details that, I assume, were gathered through interviews. Duncan's only biographer, Adela Spindler Roatcap, describes him as 'a self-made man, a self-educated teacher, a self-proclaimed poet and bard, an actor and playwright, an expatriate Californian flower child devoted to handicrafts and plain . . . thinking' (1991: 10). Unfortunately, neither of these sources have footnotes to assist further research.

In his lifetime Raymond Duncan was so 'astute in attracting attention that he was often dismissed as little more than a clever publicity hound' ('Raymond Duncan' 1966: 31). The contemporary media characterized him as an eccentric oddball because he wore a homespun Antique Greek tunic, a *chlamys* or shawl that was usually called a toga, and was barefoot in his famous handmade Raymond Duncan Greek-style sandals (Figure 8.1). He was a larger than life character who

FIGURE 8.1 Raymond Duncan performing the title role in his play *Oidipous* c. 1927, Paris, France. Courtesy of the Royal Ontario Museum, ©ROM. This acquisition was made possible with the generous support of the Louise Hawley Stone Charitable Trust.

was easy to parody, as Kay Boyle did in her 1934 novel *My Next Bride* (1986), which drew from her 1928 experiences living and working at his colony in Paris and Neuilly. After the Second World War he was regarded as an anachronism and even a 'pioneer beatnik' ('Lost Beat Generation' 1962: 2A).

Raymond Duncan was an American expatriate living in France who kept in touch with his roots by intermittently touring the United States with lectures and plays. He was a fixture on the Paris art scene from 1900 until his death in 1966, aged ninety-two. In 1911 he created an artistic gathering place in Paris called the Akademia that was 'a free school in which the arts and crafts work were taught to all who wished to come and learn' (R. Duncan 1929: n.p.). Duncan also taught his own gymnastic system of movement (R. Duncan 1914). The Akademia was not only a school but also a gallery and performance place for many artists, musicians, poets and refugees.

The French considered Duncan a Parisian. He participated in the *Salon des indépendants* showing a controversial painting, *La nativité*, in 1923, and in 1924 *The Flesh* was considered so shocking that it was vandalized ('Painting Slashed' 1924: 6). Duncan also exhibited at the 1925 International exhibition, despite the fact that the United States declined to participate ('Exhibit Lacks Americans' 1925: 23), where he had a 'place of honour at the head of the great stairways . . . on the dividing line between the French and foreign sections' (R. Duncan 1929: n.p.). He was, according to press reports, the only man in Paris who could attend the opera not wearing evening dress ('Duncan's Clothes Catch Eye' 1947: 16).

'Going Greek'

By the late nineteenth century, Greek revival was believed to be preserving the canons of the ancients, when in fact it was a reinterpretation of Renaissance classicism, not archaeological study. Even before the Duncan family left America in 1898, Gertrude Stein noted that they were going 'italian renaissance' before they had 'gone greek' (Stein 1961: 43–4). Duncan's ideas, influences and work operated within this Classical revival at the turn of the century, and he was brought up with American Greek Revival aesthetics that satisfied a 'nation adrift after its heroic revolutionary accomplishments' (Kennedy 2010: 1). Raymond Duncan is an unrecognized artist among a group of acknowledged artists who all worked in a classically inspired idiom. His friends included the well-recognized artist Emile-Antoine Bourdelle, who wrote for Duncan's newspaper ('Raymond Duncan' 1921: n.p.).

Scholarly Greek studies and Greek-inspired architecture, art, design, fashion and dance were identified with a natural balance and symmetry discovered in 'rational' ancient Greek art, crafts, architecture, philosophy and society

(Silver 2010; Fensham 2011). However, Duncan's linear graphic style also shows the influence of drawings by Henry Fuseli, John Flaxman and William Blake as he was familiar with all the classical revivals. His work demonstrates a comfortable understanding of the mathematical proportions and geometry of the Golden Ratio, a symbol of ideal elegance and beauty that has been emulated since the Renaissance and solidified in the art historical canon from Da Vinci's Vitruvian Man to Le Corbusier's Modular Man. It also reflects contemporary and modern classical ideas of Purism and Orphism, and the spiral, circle and quadrants also explored by Thayaht (Fiorentini 2007) and Madeleine Vionnet (Kirke 1998) and popularized in the United States by Canadian-born Jay Hambidge in his books *Dynamic Symmetry: The Greek Vase* (1920) and *The Elements of Dynamic Symmetry* (1926) that post-date Duncan's studies. It is more than likely that Hambidge knew Duncan, read his books and heard him lecture in the United States or when Hambidge was in Paris in 1919–20. Yet, while Hambidge's books are acknowledged as influential on American industrial designers, such as Walter Dorwin Teague, the place of the pioneering work of Duncan has yet to be seriously considered.

When the Duncan family first went to Greece in 1903 they purchased land and, as Isadora Duncan explained, 'set down the rules for our lives to be spent on Kopanos. We did this somewhat on the same plan as Plato in his "Republic"' (1927: 127). The Duncans immersed themselves in the Antique. Raymond oversaw the construction of a house based on Agamemnon's Palace and continued his studies of Greek thought, society, art, sculpture, pottery, music and dress. He published his carefully illustrated book, *Hellenic Vase Painting* (1908) that reproduced key pieces he had sketched in Paris, New York and Berlin museums.

Duncan's first-hand object-based research and experience of turn-of-the-century Greek life were united with his own ideas and artistry that fit within a modernist vocabulary to create his original, eclectic hybrid Greek-inspired culture. His publications and Socratic lectures explained how to apply ancient Greek ideals to make an alternative progressive lifestyle. Duncan advocated the study of Hellenic art, not as a mere occupation for archaeologists or a pastime for amateurs, but as a useful study for the public (Duncan 1908: 1–2). He explained that 'We do not want people to borrow from Greek thought, but to take lessons from Greek ideals so that they have the same basis on which to work as the ancient Greeks – healthy bodies, capable hands and active minds' ('Greek Ideals' 1912: 9).

A healthy body was a central tenant of Duncan's philosophy called Actionalism that countered the contemporary mechanical ideas of scientific management proposed by fellow Americans Frederick Winslow Taylor and Henry Ford. Duncan's Actionalism linked a Ruskinian and Morrisian idealism of craftwork to ideals of American know-how and independence. He believed that man was a natural machine that was kept in good working order by the natural movement of pre-mechanized life. Thus the actions performed in activities such as farming, weaving, making pots, or carpentry (R. Duncan 1914: n.p.) not only worked the body and mind, but also resulted in all the basic food and staples one needed for an autonomous life. The real value of labour was in 'the development of the labourer himself, and not the production of goods' (Gulliver 1952: 44). Recent scholarly studies on the ancient body and the gymnasium demonstrate that Duncan's theories of movement were part of a larger undertaking that was taking place throughout Europe and North America (Hawhee 2004: 109–22). This was internationally demonstrated by the 1896 revival of the Olympic Games in Greece and was continued as part of the 1900 Exhibition in Paris, and the 1904 St Louis Exhibition in the United States. As Isadora Duncan scholar Ann Daly remarks, 'In Duncan's day, the body was more like a meeting ground, where discourses of science, nature, art and metaphysics were happy to find themselves not-so-distant relations' (1995: 4)

Duncan's Greekness was most clearly seen in his adoption of classical male dress that was neither donned for healthful reasons nor to dress up as an ancient Greek. Duncan spun and hand wove his cloth on a loom he invented. He then wore the cloth uncut. His clothes did not need sewing and he deliberately had no need of a tailor (R. Duncan 1912: n.p.). His dress was a clear representation of his political ideas on independence that extended to freedom from industrial clothing production, and freedom of movement by wearing non-constricting garments; undeniably, it was also good marketing ('Raymond Duncan Amazed' 1946: 1).

The Akademia and Raymond Duncan shops

Over the years the Akademia had several locations in Paris, and when it was on the rue du Colisée it even included a theatre. The final setting opened in 1929 in a large building on the rue de Seine. The Akademia was supported by sales of art objects that were handmade by community members in return for free classes, accommodation and vegetarian food. The textiles were block-printed, painted and dyed with Duncan's original designs on silks and cottons for wall hangings, cushions or shawls, or could be made up into dresses. Journalists repeatedly wrote about Duncan's Greek costumes woven on his own looms ('The I.C. M'Keevers Give Unique Reception' 1929: 16) and colony members 'dipping batiks' ('Isadora Duncan girls assailed' 1922: 15). The 'batiks' were in fact not wax resist, but refer to the painted and printed textiles. They were sold by staff who wore Duncan Greek-style dress in the two boutiques decorated with Greek columns, one on the Right Bank, at 26 rue de Faubourg Saint-Honoré, and the other on the Left Bank at 9 rue Boissy d'Anglais (Bowman and Molinare 1985: 100). L'Officiel announced that the shop featured 'a magnificent display of peculiar tones given to materials designed and woven but once to suit a connoisseur's taste. It is pure art allied to the most refined and qualified esthetism' ('Raymond Duncan' 1925: 53). Also sold were Duncan's looms, sandals, carpets, paintings and limited edition books all fabricated by colony members ('Duncan Amazed' 1946: 1).

Although it is not known how many textiles were made, or even survive, production was steady before the Second World War (L. Duncan 2014). Duncan's decorative designs offered something exclusive in the interwar years, at a time when France and Europe's textile industry was devastated, by realizing the demand for 'hand-spun merchandise and work for the human hands' ('New Styles' 1931: 22). Between 1916–18 the cost of wool rose 250 per cent and raw cotton 350 per cent, making any French textiles expensive and exclusive. Even after the war designers had difficulty obtaining high-quality textiles and dyes, an important reason that couturiers used beading, embroidery and handwork to embellish and distinguish their designs (Field 2001: 77–91). Duncan's textiles were highly prized by fashionable tourists. One guidebook suggested that visitors to Paris should 'not fail to see the shop of Raymond Duncan, a brother of the late Isadora. He is still making very lovely hand-blocked pieces, using hand-woven silk, vegetable dyes, and designs at once classical and modern' (Bonney 1929: 96–7).

Kay Boyle wrote that she sold quantities of his handwoven rugs, tunics and draperies (1984: 274) and that Duncan's sister Elizabeth, who ran the Paris School of Duncan Dance, used the artistic settings of the shops as an office where she interviewed prospective students (1984: 294). Isadora Duncan dance students were required to wear the tunics that were made and sold by Raymond because Isadora's style of dance taught 'the freedom of the body of women and the return to the organic and animal movement' ('Toga-togged Exponent of Actionalism' 1948: 12.) The sale of dance tunics provided an important revenue. Boyle claimed they were 'an exorbitant price' with the profits split between the two Duncan siblings (1984: 294). Her critique of the Duncans ignores the fact that the family's dance schools, performances and the Akademia were all artistic projects that had been shared among family members since they were children, and were driven by artistic impetus even though Raymond Duncan had difficulty making ends meet ('Gazette des tribunaux' 1912: 4; 'Raymond Duncan Evicted in Paris' 1924: 13). All the products, including the textiles, were marketed as handcrafted luxury goods and were critical to maintaining the finances of the Akademia.

Production of Raymond Duncan dress and textiles

Duncan's textile production moved seasonally between Nice and Paris. The silk tabby was purchased from Lyon on large rolls. The spongy-looking crepe is in fact a loosely spun cotton in the simplest plain tabby weave, called *crêpon de coton* and although its origins of manufacture are unknown it may have been purchased in

Paris. The silk had to be boiled over a little stove to be de-gummed. The cloth was then dried and cut into lengths (L. Duncan 2014). In the garden at Neuilly (Paris), there were two bathtubs that Boyle noted were used for the preparation of the 'batiks' and the dyeing of the silk scarves (1984: 294). In the summer, the colony moved to Nice for six months and continued textile production. There the dyed textiles were washed in the sea so that the salt water fixed the dyes, then they were carried to a nearby stream to be rinsed and laid out to dry on the rocks, away from the sand (L. Duncan 2014).

The 'primitive' (R. Duncan 1929: n.p.) wooden blocks for printing were designed by Duncan and carved by him or, under his direction, by colony members and his two children, Menalkas and Ligoa. Ligoa recalled the process. She began carving 'as soon as he thought we were old enough to safely handle a chisel. The design was drawn on transparent paper and applied to the block, or sometimes directly onto the block freehand'. The cut lengths of cloth were laid out on a table padded with thick material to absorb the ink. Duncan directed the placement of the woodblocks and would draw the patterns freehand directly on the silk using charcoal he made by burning the end of a pointed stick. It is likely these are the designs that are referred to as batiks. The drawings were combined with combinations of his blocks (L. Duncan 2014).

The lengths were then stretched on frames for painting and dyeing. The frame rested on multipurpose benches that Duncan had designed and built for his theatre on the rue du Colisée (Duncan, Pratl, Splatt 1993: 173). The textile painters could stand or sit to do their work, called brush dyeing, and were instructed on the spot as Ligoa describes; 'I was told to do this one in yellow, this one in red. They were all natural dyes he made'. She said that on average there were twelve to twenty-four women working in the atelier and that many of them were refugees who came from all across Europe (L. Duncan 2014). A photograph of a woman, identified by Ligoa Duncan as Emilie Vial, shows her dry brushing at the Akademia, surrounded by painted textiles draped on easels (Figure 8.2).

Duncan explained that he had

> developed a new school of painting on linen, silk and coton [sic] . . . [that] evolved a new technique in modeling and in tone graduation. Unlike pigments, natural dyes cannot be mixed in order to arrive at the tone or shade designed. Often the graduations of the same color are made from different bases. This necessitates that each tone be painted in separate fields and each color be kept from running into its neighbor. Thus has been formed with this new art its own special technique. It has take a place midway between fresco and tapestry and is much more fitting and nearer related to the requirements of modern architecture. (R. Duncan 1929: n.p.)

Raymond Duncan textiles are clearly masterful and carefully handmade original artefacts designed for modern living, not to recreate the past.

FIGURE 8.2 Emilie Vial drybrush painting Raymond Duncan textiles at the Akademia, Rue de Seine, Paris, c. 1925. Courtesy of the Royal Ontario Museum, ©ROM. This acquisition was made possible with the generous support of the Louise Hawley Stone Charitable Trust.

Raymond Duncan designs: disparate inspirations

Raymond Duncan's hand-printed and painted textiles are inspired by his close study of Antique sources, yet are clearly products of their creation in early-twentieth-century Europe. His designs feature vegetal, floral, animal and human forms seen in classical arts and document his research of Antique vase painting (R. Duncan 1908), and his study of 'correct' movement realized in his gymnastics (R. Duncan 1914). Another influence on the designs is Late Antique textiles.

In the 1890s and 1900s thousands of Early Byzantine textiles and costumes were excavated in Egypt. The site at Antinoë, overseen by French archaeologist Albert Gayet, was particularly prolific and very well publicized. Commencing in 1898, Gayet exhibited each season's finds at the Musée Guimet and in 1901, after his sixth season, the textiles began to be parcelled out to several French museums. A public auction was held comprising forty-one lots, with some lots containing over 500 pieces. This sale started the circulation of these textiles in private and public collections around the world. It became *de rigueur* for the status of a museum to acquire examples (Gayet 1902; Calament and Durand 2013).

Gayat arranged three tableaux of this material in the Palais du Costume during the 1900 Exposition Universelle de Paris where it caused a sensation and would have been seen by the Duncan family when they visited the exhibition (I. Duncan 1927: 68–9). The catalogue of the finds was illustrated with images of the tunics, and details of woven and embroidered decorations (*Palais du costume* 1900). Gayat (1902, 1904) also published the finds along with colour plates of fanciful renderings of the costumes on the mummies, and in 1903 gave a public lecture with replicas of the Coptic robes, mantles, shawls and tunics modelled in tableaux that was lavishly illustrated and discussed in *Femina* (Ravidat 1903: 621–2).

Gayat's exciting finds and his promotions created a popular interest in Late Antique and early Christian culture that influenced the arts. It was first seen in the novel *Thaïs* (1890), by Anatole France, and became the basis for Jules Massenet's opera of the same name, first performed in 1894 at the Opera Garnier. In 1902, actress Sarah Bernhardt appeared in *Théodora* by Victorien Sardou dressed in a Coptic tunic and shawl that was directly inspired by Gayat's finds and the Byzantine mosaics in Ravenna (Rutschowscaya 2013: 97–8). Modern designers and artists, including Henri Matisse, Raoul Dufy, Georges Rouault and Auguste Rodin were inspired by these finds (Hoskins 2004: 9; Spurling and Dumas 2004: 52; Curtis 2003) as was Raymond Duncan. The Antique was a key element in fashion seen in Mariano Fortuny's Coptic tunic printed with clavi and decorative bands, and Margaine Lacroix's robe Tanagréenne that created a furore in 1908 (Ralph 2012). That same year the *New York Times* reported that:

> All of the great couturiers of Paris are buried up to their eyes now, studying the tales of mythology and fables of ancient lore. They are scanning the history of Byzantine architecture, and burning the midnight oil . . . sketch artists are working night and day copying and adapting designs from the friezes of the Parthenon, from the Roman Forum and from wherever they find them. ('Paris Planning a Radical Change' 1908: 65)

Clearly Raymond Duncan's designs were in tune with the leading artistic interests of the day and not an eccentric anomaly.

Unravelling the designs

The ROM's collection of Raymond Duncan dress and textiles comprises one tunic, which he called '*la robe sans couture*' (L. Duncan 2014), one long shawl and three smaller squares that could also be used for small headcoverings or pillows, and recall Late Antique shawls in the configuration of the borders. All are printed and painted to shape as complete designs.

FIGURE 8.3 A Raymond Duncan *robe sans couture*, an unsewn tunic. Block printed and dry brush cotton tabby called *crêpon de coton*, c. 1920s, Paris, France (ROM 2010.102.1). Courtesy of the Royal Ontario Museum, ©ROM. This acquisition was made possible with the generous support of the Louise Hawley Stone Charitable Trust.

The tunic is a complete selvedge-to-selvedge length with unhemmed ends, and could be worn with a belt and seamed at the sides (Figure 8.3). It is a simpler version of the one worn by Aia Bertrand in Duncan's performance of *Oidipous* at Kolonos (Figure 8.1). The block-printed decorations are configured like early Byzantine tunics with decorative bands at the neck, arms, hem and roundels at shoulders. The pattern is a simple and effective repeat employing only three blocks for the deep hem, neck opening and shoulder decorations. The colouration of this tunic is also similar to Antique models with a white ground dominated by purple and gold colours painted in by hand. The geometric and curvilinear animal and abstract designs, rondels and rectangles are all motifs found in the early Egyptian wool tapestry woven borders (ROM 910.1.11). A Late Antique fourth- or fifth-century wool and linen tunic fragment (ROM L982.7.52) with Dionysiac and

Nilotic figures, animals, and stylized wave scroll border is the type of design Duncan assimilated. The other Duncan textiles in the ROM also have influences of Late Antique designs in the borders such as interlacing meandering forms and can be compared to those in an early Egyptian *tiraz* textile dated 718–750 that is woven with a band of tangent pearl-rings that runs above a simple Kufic inscription (ROM 976.298.1).

Initially I tried to analyse all the designs in terms of ancient mythology because some of the motifs are easily identifiable. For instance one repeat pattern shows Narcissus and his reflection, alternating with a nymph or dryad metamorphosing from a tree (ROM 2010.102.4) (Plate 16). The textile with a repeated arched design with a male figure (ROM 2010.102.5) (Plate 17) recalls the Dionysiac figures in arcades seen in a typical Egyptian, Byzantine sixth-century linen tunic (ROM 910.1.1). I first thought this might be an interpretation of the Prometheus myth depicting the making of man from clay and making of fire, however the figures bear no relation to the illustrations in Duncan's book *Prometeus* (1919) so this did not seem likely. When I showed the design to Ligoa Duncan she immediately identified it as 'le moissonneur', a harvester, depicting sowing and reaping wheat, actions that she said are emulated in Duncan's gymnastic movements (L. Duncan 2014).

The large printed shawl with a repeat pattern of a runner holding a ball with two leaping dogs was immediately identified by Ligoa as Diana the Huntress (ROM 2010.102.2) (Plate 18). This design is framed with a border pattern of apples, that she said were fun to paint, and the head of an ibis, a common motif also found in Egyptian fragments and depicted in a rare printed textile in the ROM (978.76. 549). The final Duncan textile in the ROM collection is a repeat pattern of a seated figure with one arm up and one down. In each hand he holds a round blue orb or ball, framed on either side of a central dark brown-purple I-shaped geometric frame (ROM 2010.102.3). I could not make out the meaning of this design and Ligoa suggested that the blue balls represent the earth and that the action is that of a potter (L. Duncan 2014). A ball is part of the design of Diana the Huntress and, as in the ancient gymnasium, the ball is also used in Duncan's gymnastics. Thus each of the textile designs is a unique fusion that unite Raymond Duncan's philosophy of Actionalism, work and movement, with a modern twentieth-century rendering of Greek Revival art and design.

Meanings and metaphors 'at once classical and modern'

The Raymond Duncan textiles in the collection of the Royal Ontario Museum first piqued my interest because the artefacts are beautiful and they would build the collection of twentieth-century printed textiles. But this alone was not enough to answer the question of 'who cares?' Only by conducting lengthy, diverse and circuitous research could I begin to answer the question. Duncan's textiles initially offered a visual link to the past and specifically to Late Roman – Early Byzantine textiles, but research has shown how they are linked specifically to the turn of the century excavations at Antinoe in Egypt and to the popular Greek Revival culture of the day. This is important for the Royal Ontario Museum as it holds the largest collection of this material outside of Egypt (ROM 2014). However, this research has shown that archaeological textile sources are only one influence, and that the textiles represent more complex contemporary ideas of art, design, archaeology, architecture, dance, drama and music. By understanding Raymond Duncan's textiles in a much broader and more complex way, links can now be forged with more diverse objects in the museum's collections from the ancient world to the twentieth century.

Taken together, these directions and associations suggest that what initially seemed to be a small collection of dress and textiles by an obscure, and even dismissed designer about whom few people currently care, is in fact something that is of wider interest to a range of scholars within and beyond dress history, and inside and outside the museum. Lou Taylor concludes her book, *The Study of Dress History*, by noting that things acquire meaning only once they are woven into complex cultural conversations (2002: 273); this case study has aimed to do just that. It demonstrates that through open-minded, multidisciplinary enquiry, artefacts can offer complex trajectories suggesting new research directions. By researching the man beyond the textiles to include his entire oeuvre – his books, printing, art, music and gymnastics – the complexity and significance of his work has radically changed. Oral history with the family has afforded the invaluable opportunity to discuss Duncan, his work and philosophies with those who were witnesses at the time. These discussions have extended this project far beyond my initial interpretation of the designs and freed it from erroneous interpretation and conjecture. The Duncan family input confirmed my thoughts about his modernity that was based on his prodigious scholarship on the ancient world in order to create an alternative lifestyle that was, as shown, *au courant* with his time.

Raymond Duncan's inspiration was the Antique, but his work needs to be set alongside the other stylistic influences of the era including Japonisme, Chinoiserie, primitivism, folk art, Orientalism, African, Egyptian, Indian and Persian art. His life and work should also be related to other contemporary international art movements operating throughout Europe: the Weiner Werkstätte, the Ecole Martine, Charles Rennie Mackintosh and the Glasgow School, and Bloomsbury and the Omega workshops. His dress and textiles are part of an important group of hand-crafted objects created by artist-designers that include Maria Gallenga, Madame Pangone and Paul Poiret, who was patronized by Isadora, and is said to have copied designs from Raymond (L. Duncan 2014). Duncan's designs were not slavish copies of the Antique. They are clearly his own modern interpretation, and need to be understood wholistically within the world that he created as an alternative *modern* life centred at the Akademia in Paris.

The reason Duncan's dress and textiles and output of art, print, theatre, music and movement have never been evaluated academically or included in publications on the arts and crafts is simply because they have not been researched. This chapter begins to correct this omission by establishing his work within the canon of dress and design history. It is the first step in a larger project that will further explore the many facets of Raymond Duncan and situate the significance and resonance of his life and work in the first half of the twentieth century.

References

Bonney, T. and Bonney, L. (1929), *A Shopping Guide to Paris*, New York: Robert M. McBride.

Bowman, S. and Molinare, M. (1985), *A Fashion for Extravagance: Art Deco Fabrics and Fashion*, New York: E.P. Dutton.

Boyle, K. ([1934] 1986), *My Next Bride*, London: Virago Press.

Boyle, K. and McAlmon, R. (1984), *Being Geniuses Together, 1920–1930*, San Francisco: Northpoint Press.

Calament, F. and Durand, M. (2013), *Antinoé, à la vie, à la mode: visions d'élégance dans les solitudes*, Lyon: Fage.

Curtis, P. (2003), 'Deco Sculpture and Archaism', in C. Benton, T. Benton and G. Wood (eds), *Art Deco 1910–39*, London: V&A Publications.

Daly, A. (1995), *Done into Dance: Isadora Duncan in America*, Bloomington and Indianapolis: Indiana University Press.

Duncan, D., Pratl, C. and Splatt, C. (1993), *Life into Art: Isadora Duncan and Her World*, New York and London: W.W. Norton.

Duncan, I. (1927), *My Life*, New York: Boni and Liveright.

Duncan, L. (2014), interview by author, 3 July.

Duncan, R. (1908), *Hellenic Vase Painting*, Athens: Fodotera.

Duncan, R. (1912), *Le Vrai But du Travail*, Paris: Akademia Raymond Duncan.

Duncan, R. (1914), *La Danse et la Gymnastique*, Paris: Akademia Raymond Duncan.

Duncan, R. (1919), *Prometeus: (les grands crucifiés)*, Paris: Raymond Duncan.

Duncan, R. (1929), *Winter Exhibition of Parisian Art, Raymond Duncan*, Norfolk, VA: Norfolk Society of Arts; Paris: Raymond Duncan.

'Duncan's Clothes Catch Eye: He Regrets Philosophies Don't' (1947), *Reading Eagle*, 9 February: 16.

'Duncan Amazed at Interest People Show in His Robes and Sandals' (1946), *Milwaukee Journal*, 31 December: 1.

'Exhibit Lacks Americans: Decorative Art Show at Paris May Have Only One "Representative"' (1925), *New York Times*, 6 March: 23.

Fensham, R. (2011), 'Nature, Force and Variation', in A. Carter and R. Fensham (eds), *Dancing Naturally: Nature, Neo-classicism and Modernity in Early Twentieth-century Dance*, Houndmills, Basingstoke, Hampshire and New York: Palgrave Macmillan.

Field, J. (2001), 'Dyes, Chemistry and Clothing: The Influence of World War I on Fabrics, Fashions and Silk', *Dress*, 28 (1): 77–91.

Fiorentini, A. (2007), 'Vionnet Is the Best Known and the "Chicest" Couturiere of the World, no dico altro!"', in D. Degl'Innocenti et al., *Thayaht, Un artista alle origini del Made in Italy*, Prato: Museo del Tessuto Edizioni.

Gayet, A. (1902), *Antinoë et les sépultures de Thaïs et Sérapion*, Paris: Society française d'éditions d'art.

Gayet, A. (1904), *Fantômes d'Antinoë: les sépultures de Leukyoné et Myrithis*, Paris: Société française d'éditions d'art.

'Gazette des tribunaux' (1912), *Le Figaro*, 14 January: 4.

'Greek Ideals: Mr. R. Duncan's Aims' (1912), *Times of India*, 12 November: 9.

Gulliver, L. (1952) 'An Easy Swing', *Lilliput*, 30, no. 3 (178): 39–45, 128.

Hambidge, J. (1920), *Dynamic Symmetry: The Greek Vase*, New Haven: Yale University Press.

Hambridge, J. ([1926] 1967), *The Elements of Dynamic Symmetry*, New York: Dover Publications.

Hawhee, D. (2004), *Bodily Arts: Rhetoric and Athletics in Ancient Greece*, Austin: University of Texas Press.

Hoskins, N. A. (2004), *The Coptic Tapestry Albums and the Archaeologist of Antinoé, Albert Gayet*, Seattle: University of Washington Press.

'The I.C. M'Keevers Give Unique Reception' (1929), *New York Times*, 23 November: 16.

'Isadora Duncan Girls Assailed by Raymond' (1922), *New York Times*, 4 March: 15.

Kennedy, R. G. (2010), *Greek Revival America*, New York: Rizzoli.

Kirke, B. (1998), *Madeleine Vionnet*, San Francisco: Chronicle Books.

Lambourne, L. (1980), *Utopian Craftsmen: The Arts and Crafts Movement from the Cotswolds to Chicago*, Salt Lake City, UT: Peregrine Smith.

'Lost Beat Generation Helps Duncan Celebrate' (1962), *Evening Independent*, 2 November: 2A.

'New Styles Costly Despite Hard Times' (1931), *New York Times*, 25 February: 22.

'Painting Slashed in Salon' (1924), *New York Times*, 16 March: 6.

Palais du costume, le costume en Egypte du IIIe au XIIIe siècle d' après les fouilles de Al. Gayet (1900), Paris: Ernest Leroux.

Palmer, A. (2013), 'Looking at Fashion: The Material Object as Subject', in S. Black, A. de la Haye, J. Entwistle, A. Rocamora, R. A. Root and H. Thomas (eds), *The Handbook of Fashion Studies*, London, New Delhi, New York, and Sydney: Bloomsbury.

'Paris Planning a Radical Change in Winter Fashions' (1908), *New York Times*, 27 September: 65.

Ralph, S. (2012), 'Inspired by the Antique: Margaine Lacroix and the Robe Tanagréene', paper presented at Costume Colloquium III: Past Dress – Future Fashion, Florence, Italy, 8 November.

Ravidat, M. (1903), 'La toilette d'une élegante d'Antinöé' *Femina*, 1 August: 611, 622.

'Raymond Duncan' (1925), *L' Officiel de la couture*, 45: 53.

'Raymond Duncan Evicted in Paris' (1924), *New York Times*, 8 June: 13.

'Raymond Duncan, son portrait par Emile-Antoine Bourdelle' (1921), *Exangelos*, 5 December: n.p.

'Raymond Duncan, Symbol of La Vie Boheme Dies' (1966), *New York Times*, 17 August: 31.

Roatcap, A. S. (1991), *Raymond Duncan: Printer, Expatriate, Artist*, San Francisco: The Book Club of California.

Royal Ontario Museum, Toronto (ROM) (2014), 'Cairo Under Wraps', https://www.rom. on.ca/en/exhibitions-galleries/exhibitions/cairo-under-wraps-early-islamic-textiles, accessed 3 July 2014.

Rutschowscaya, M.-H. (2013), *Le châle de Sabine*, Soleb: Paris.

Silver, Kenneth E. (2010), *Chaos and Classicism: Art in France, Italy, and Germany 1918–1936*, New York: Guggenheim Museum.

Spurling, H. and Dumas, A. (2004), *Matisse, His Art and His Textiles*, London: Royal Academy of Arts.

Stein, G. ([1933] 1961), *The Autobiography of Alice B. Toklas*, New York: Random House, New York.

Taylor, L. (1996), 'Men in Black', *Journal of Design History*, 9 (4): 301–3.

Taylor, L. (2002), *The Study of Dress History*, Manchester: Manchester University Press.

'Toga-togged Exponent of "Actionalism" has a New Phrase for US Ambition' (1948), *Globe and Mail*, 26 January: 12.

9 AN 'UNEXPECTED PEARL': GENDER AND PERFORMATIVITY IN THE PUBLIC AND PRIVATE LIVES OF LONDON COUTURIER NORMAN HARTNELL

Jane Hattrick

The London couturier Norman Hartnell (1901–79) is best remembered for dressing British royalty, particularly the current British monarch Elizabeth II for her coronation in 1953. Hartnell was far more than a royal dressmaker, however, he was the first of a new generation of young couture designers who replaced London's West End court dressmakers in the early twentieth century. Also, as this chapter argues, existing research has overlooked core aspects of Hartnell's identity. With access to previously unseen private archival papers and artefacts, this chapter offers a new view on a well-known couturier.

Lou Taylor argues that dress history now exists within an 'open-minded, multi-disciplinary atmosphere' (2004: 279). It is within the context of this atmosphere that this chapter examines one particularly pertinent, yet hitherto sidestepped, aspect of the life and work of Hartnell, that of his sexual identity. How this identity manifested itself through Hartnell's cross-dressing, and how this act impacted his signature couture designs is of particular interest. This chapter adopts a multidisciplinary approach, one that combines queer theory with methodologies from dress, design and life histories and social science in its analysis of the couturier. Specific critical issues including taste, self-presentation and performance of sexual, gender, personal and public identities have emerged from a close reading of the material culture in the Hartnell archive. Sociologist Steph Lawler argues, in relation to the study of identity, that individual actions and responses can be understood as 'part of a wider social order that permits some actions and disallows others' (2008: 104). Thus identity is not really about who we really are, but who it is possible for us to be in the context in which we construct our identities, for example the period in time in which we live out our lives, and the constraints this puts upon us. As this chapter will explore, Hartnell lived out his life as an effeminate, cross-dressing gay man within the constraints of pre-liberation, as homosexuality was illegal in Britain until 1967.

The House of Hartnell and the Hartnell-Mitchison Archive

Using legacies left to them by their mother Emma, and with financial help from their father, Norman Hartnell and his sister Phyllis opened a couture house on a small scale at 10 Bruton Street, Mayfair in 1923. By 1934 Hartnell had become a very successful and wealthy couture fashion designer, and the firm moved to much larger premises at 26 Bruton Street, employing up to 500 staff and producing thousands of couture garments a year by 1939. A close study of reviews of his fashion collections in the British and international press reveals that he was considered cutting-edge during the interwar period. By the early 1930s he was perceived as a quintessentially English, leading figure in the London couture industry, providing work-a-day wardrobes for women in the upper echelons of British society. He expanded the House of Hartnell into an international fashion brand in the immediate post-war period, branching out into franchised and licensed products lending his name to perfume, stockings and costume jewellery. Hartnell had international business interests in the Commonwealth countries of South Africa, Canada and Australia, and also in Argentina, Japan, Germany and Switzerland. In 1973 there were at least sixty-six known trademarks in the name of Norman Hartnell in fifteen countries worldwide. Throughout his career he designed two seasonal fashion collections a year until his death in 1979. The House of Hartnell remained open until 1992, with his house style kept alive by a series of later designers.

What remains of Hartnell's business archive, generated over a fifty-year period, is kept in the house once lived in by Hartnell's business manager, friend and heir George Mitchison and his wife, which is now the home of their daughter Claire Williams. This material was largely unexamined and unanalysed until research by this author, begun in 2005 (Hattrick 2011, 2012, 2014). Archival material was stored in wardrobes, suitcases and bags, combined with a wide range of personal material associated with Hartnell's life from his baby photographs to his hair brushes. This eclectic collection has been identified and catalogued by the author and together the objects and paperwork form the newly constituted Hartnell-Mitchison archive. Along with business paperwork, correspondence between the couturier and his British royal clients, personal snapshots, fashion photographs, studio portraits of the designer, press-books and hundreds of sketched designs, the archive includes over 200 Hartnell-designed garments including a collection of model gowns taken from fashion collections that were used in charity shows and for publicity events. It is these evening gowns in colours and fabrics favoured by Hartnell, such as pink and turquoise silks and velvets, decorated in his signature beaded embroidery, that I argue represent examples of Hartnell's personal taste in colour, fabric and embellishment. These are the garments he selected to keep as representative of his house style. In addition, the archive contains clothing and accessories owned and worn by the designer. Selected examples from these collections are drawn on here.

A close examination of this collection of photographs has unlocked many of the stories behind the mute objects found in the archive and the house in which it is kept, revealing their biographies and the contexts in which they were originally made, displayed and used. Studio and personal portraits taken of Hartnell between 1921 and 1979 provide evidence of Hartnell's own style in dress and accessories, and have enabled identification of surviving clothing and personal effects as once worn and used by the designer. In order to gain a closer understanding of Hartnell's personal identity and self-fashioning, draft versions of his memoir *Silver and Gold*, heavily edited throughout 1954 and published in 1955 by Evans Brothers, along with unpublished writing by Hartnell, have also been studied.

Using selected samples of Hartnell-Mitchison archive material, this chapter investigates how Hartnell's consumption of fashionable clothes in both men's and women's styles both reflected his personal taste and contributed to the construction of his private and public identities. I argue that his personal taste in normative feminine styles translated into the garments he designed, resulting in his signature looks and house style. Aside from curator Edwina Ehrman's brief examination of his career in the interwar years (2006: 80–5) and Amy de la Haye's analysis of his post-war work (2007: 102–6), most recent publications, and exhibitions examining his work (including annual Buckingham Palace summer exhibitions since 2005 and the V&A's 2007 *The Golden Age of Couture*) have done so largely with reference to royal dressing. Any critical writing about Hartnell's life and work can no longer sidestep the fact and significance of his homosexuality as a core aspect of his identity and therefore his creative practice. In Wendy Moffat's 2010 biography, *A New Life of E.M. Forster*, which she subtitles *A Great Unrecorded Story*, she begins by recounting a conversation between Christopher Isherwood and John Lehmann as they discuss how to go about publishing Forster's novel *Maurice,* hidden from view for decades until Forster's death in 1970. Considering all the books already published about E. M. Forster, Isherwood turns to Lehmann and exclaims: 'Of course all those books have got to be re-written . . . Unless you start with the fact that he was homosexual, nothing's any good at all' (Moffat 2010: 20). I apply the same principle to my reappraisal of Hartnell's life and work.

A personal identity in context

Hartnell was often described in the press as a lifelong bachelor. He lived alone except for a brief period of time during which Mitchison lived with him at Tower House in Regent's Park just before the Second World War. Hartnell's 1924 article 'Why I am a Dressmaker', published in *Woman*, demonstrates his burgeoning sense of self and his understanding of how shared 'worldly, manly' tastes might 'put me on a footing with other men'. Hartnell described his realization that he 'was different from everybody else' (1924: 499). A particular version of his life was constructed for the purposes of his autobiography, published in 1955, aided by two ghost writers and heavily edited by Stanley Jackson at Evans Brothers. Preliminary drafts of Hartnell's memoir and personal letters in the archive evidence how, as an effeminate gay man, Hartnell continually wrestled with his sexuality. He worried how others might judge him, especially as he lived his life as a well-known fashion designer from his mid-twenties and a celebrated royal couturier from the mid-1930s to the peak of his career in the mid-1950s. This was the time when, as statistics published in *The Wolfenden Report* underline, the largest numbers of gay men were arrested in Britain (1963: 5). In a draft chapter, left out of his published memoir, Hartnell reflected on the potential effects of the success of his first fashion collection the day after it was launched to critical acclaim by the fashion press on 16 March 1924. He wrote:

> I was convinced my sister would be proud of me when she knew. But my father – what would he say? He had warned me that in return for the work I had chosen to do I would be called effete, to put it politely, by the rest of the world. I was doing an unusual thing and as most people are usually unused to the unusual I was baring my bosom . . . as a target to the acid darts of criticism and calumny . . . was this sudden success, I wondered, fame to be enjoyed henceforth without falter, or was it merely a transient and unwelcome notoriety. (c. 1954a: 6)

In a subsequent, undated draft of the complete autobiography, called at this stage *Living for Design* or *Living by Design*, Hartnell begins his first chapter with a description of a conversation between his father and his headmaster, John McClure at Mill Hill School's Foundation Day. He was fourteen years old. The two men were discussing a future career for the young Hartnell. Hartnell remembered:

> It was a ticklish question and after a time I heard my father say:

> 'You know, Sir John, I feel sometimes that I am like a hen that has laid a duck's egg.'

> Sir John McClure seemed momentarily taken aback. He paused for a minute, adjusted his large spectacles and gazing straight at my father, said:

'May I suggest, Mr. Hartnell, that you might feel rather more like an ordinary oyster that has produced an unexpected pearl!' (c. 1954b: 1–2)

These examples of Hartnell's autobiographical writing between 1924 and 1955, albeit with input by ghost writers and editors, indicate that anxiety about his perceived effeminacy and sexuality continued to be problematic for a life lived under the spotlight. While Hartnell tried to acknowledge these tensions, the excisions made by the editor make it clear that they were considered unpublishable in this period.

Garments in the archive, together with studio portraits, and snapshot photographs of the designer, provide evidence that Hartnell bought and wore fashionable clothes in both men's and women's styles. Photographs of Hartnell in fancy dress and school magazine cuttings demonstrate that Hartnell enjoyed dressing in this way from an early age, and had played the female lead in several school productions. When Hartnell was at school between 1914 and 1919, it was still common practice for boys and young men in all-male environments such as schools and all-male colleges at universities to take on female roles in theatrical productions. Photographs of Hartnell dressed in women's clothing for these productions demonstrate his ability to pose and style himself as feminine. Hartnell's expression of his sexual subjectivity involved the performance of an internalized femininity through gesture and the adoption of women's clothes made up in ultra-feminine textiles, colours and embellishments. Hartnell saw his inner self as feminine and one can read what he considered his internal gendered self through his external fashioning through clothing and accessories associated with normative femininity. Hartnell did not see himself as a 'macho man', but performed what he understood as his gendered identity through his dressing up.

Hartnell lived out the majority of his queer life within the decades before homosexuality was legalized in 1967, as he died only a decade after the law changed. Avoiding detection was essential. As a gay man he walked what Richard Dyer has described as 'the thin line between passing and flaunting' (2002: 64), either passing as heterosexual or visibly flaunting his queer sexuality according to the context in which he found himself. In public, after 1923, Hartnell largely dressed in a three-piece suit of either dark wool suiting fabric or tweed. Within the constraints of pre-liberation British society, Hartnell's performance as feminine, in clothing styles designed and made up at the House of Hartnell, took place in the privacy of his own home, behind closed doors.

Hartnell as actress

Hartnell studied for two years at Cambridge University between 1920 and 1922, a factor that was important in his introduction to a British elite clientele. His first clients were the fiancées, sisters and mothers of his fellow students. Wedding invitations in Hartnell's archive dating from the 1920s include two inviting Hartnell and his sister to the marriages of Thelma Schofield in 1927 and Joy Schofield in 1929. A. H. B. Schofield was at Cambridge with Hartnell, and played the female character Marcelle in *Folly*, the Footlights production of 1923, in which Hartnell played Gwen. Both men designed their own dresses for this production. Hartnell's career at university was more celebrated for his contribution to the Footlights theatricals than his achievements as a student of modern languages, and he left without completing his degree to pursue a career in fashion design in the summer of 1922. Hartnell played the female lead in three Footlights productions between 1921 and 1923, designing all of his own costumes. In the early days of his career in dress design, this acceptable side of female impersonation was seen as a positive aspect of his life to be applauded, and which impacted on his career in a favourable way. A picture article from 1922 cited Hartnell as 'one of London's newest and cleverest dress designers', and included a picture of him as Kitty Fenton in the Footlights 1921 show, *What a Picnic!* stating that 'amongst other accomplishments Mr. Hartnell is a very clever female-impersonator' ('University Man Takes Up Dress Designing' 1922: n.p.).

Five studio portraits, stored among damp sketches and documents of the Hartnell archive in the cellar of the Mitchisons' house, appear to show, at first glance, a young actress dressed according to fashionable styles worn by the ingénue of the early 1920s. On closer study, however, the young actress is revealed as Norman Hartnell, cross-dressed. Viewed alongside portraits of Hartnell dressed in lounge suit and tie, photographed at roughly the same age, Hartnell seems more at ease in a silk dress and picture hat than he does in his masculine guise. Initially these photographs appeared to have been taken solely to promote the Footlights production of 1921, *What a Picnic!* However, on closer investigation, and by comparing these images with those on the pages of the French fashion magazine of the period, *Les Modes* from the same year, it became clear that Hartnell had an alternative agenda. The ensembles designed by Hartnell bear a very close resemblance to several contemporary couture models with almost the exact same fabrics, silhouettes and accessories. In the studio photographs therefore, Hartnell is not presenting himself as a male actor, dressed in glamour-drag for the sake of a theatrical performance and parody, but as a model or fashion mannequin, wearing the fashionable styles of 1921.

According to Shaun Cole's research, effeminate gay men identified with the feminine, and up until the 1960s, 'the effeminate queen was the dominant public image of male homosexuals' (2000: 159). Queer theorist Judith Butler has argued, more broadly, that 'gender . . . operates as an interior essence that might be disclosed, an expectation that ends up producing the very phenomenon that it anticipates'. This internalized gender, she writes, is constructed through 'a sustained set of acts, posited through the gendered stylization of the body . . . what we take to be an "internal" feature of ourselves is one that we anticipate through certain bodily acts, at an extreme, an hallucinatory effect of naturalized gestures' (1990: xv–xvi). Gender is therefore performed according to a set of sociocultural norms including dress, gestures and postures. To become a girl, one must act like a girl. Butler uses the example of male to female drag to expose the constructed nature of gender and '(hetero)sexuality' and enable an exploration of the ways in which Hartnell performed his inner gender.

The photographs of Hartnell dressed in feminine styles and adopting feminine gestures reveal Hartnell's aptitude for acting 'like a girl'. As Butler has explained, 'there is no necessary relation between drag and subversion' (1993: 125). Hartnell's performance is not, to apply the words of Butler, 'an imitation based in ridicule and degradation' (1993: 126), but an example of what she describes as 'realness'. As she puts it: 'the artifice works, the approximation of realness appears to be achieved, the body performing and the ideal performed appear indistinguishable' (1993: 129). In these portraits, Hartnell strives to deceive, but not to parody. He performs his internalized, feminine ideal through dress and gesture and strives to pass as a woman.

The ensembles that Hartnell wears in these photographs reveal his use of fabric in different weights, textures and finishes. In wearing these soft silk gowns, Hartnell was exposed to the feel of luxury dress fabrics, defining his taste in both the types of fabrics with which he preferred to work, and those he chose for his personal use. He often wrote that he loathed working with 'manure coloured' tweed (1971: 26). An understanding of these preferences is central to an analysis of his work as a fashion designer. These photographs also display the origins of his signature house styles designed for clients (including himself) throughout his career, as will be discussed.

In a photograph dating from 1921, Hartnell poses in a dress of shimmering silk tissue and tulle decorated with small flowers at the waist. The short sleeves are also trimmed with flowers. The silk tissue forms a front panel through the bodice to the hem, seen in more detail in a head-and-shoulder shot of Hartnell in which he also wears a headdress of silver or gold leaves with a spray of lilac over his right ear. His wig is carefully coiffed in the fashionable styles of the day, and his make-up is applied with expertise. In another photograph from this series (Figure 9.1), Hartnell wears a stiff, silk taffeta dress with side frills and a blown rose at the waist along with a picture hat decorated with egret feathers. He is photographed wearing a different pair of high-heeled shoes in fashionable styles with each of the three 1921 ensembles, which must have been made to measure, as his feet were a British size 9.

The programme from this production shows that these garments were made up at the court dressmaker Myra Salter, in Hanover Square, London. Hartnell must therefore have experienced being a couture client first hand, having fittings and possibly making alterations during the making-up. This would also have

FIGURE 9.1 Norman Hartnell as Kitty Fenton in the Cambridge Footlights production, *What a Picnic!*, 1921. Courtesy of the Hartnell-Mitchison Archive.

contributed towards his understanding of the creative process of *haute couture*. Hartnell continued to have such personal fittings throughout his life, undertaken by workroom staff in his private apartment at 26 Bruton Street who made women's couture garments for him (Wright 2010).

Hartnell as dandy

Hartnell could not be seen in public wearing his own designs after 1923 when his performances in the Footlights theatrical productions ceased. Instead he had to dissimulate his feminine persona, and adopt the sartorial codes appropriate to gender norms of the day, albeit with the touch of glamour associated with the dandy. Cultural theorist and dress historian Elizabeth Wilson defines the dandy as a performer and as the epitome of glamour. As a combination of person and dress, the dandy 'created glamour by means of daring departures from the conventionally well dressed, combined with an aura of defiance' (2007: 98). She explains that the dandy aesthetic was an attitude that exemplified 'exquisite restraint', and continues:

> it creates a seamless perfection, as impenetrable as the carapace of a beetle. It is not surprising that this mode of being led to the idea that dandies were androgynous, asexual, and even if deviant, deviant in an opaque and hidden way. (2007: 97–8)

She explains, 'dandyism came to be associated with eroticism outside the conventions of marriage, even homosexuality' (2007: 97). Hartnell's homosexuality was reflected in this dandy aesthetic, which is represented in the many studio portraits in his archive.

Hartnell was identified as a 'Regency buck' in an article for *Woman's Illustrated* in 1949 by Godfrey Winn, who stated:

> Hartnell's office, like his country home near Windsor, where he does most of his actual designing, is full of delightful Regency furniture. And now that I come to think of it, there is quite something of the Regency buck about this most famous of British couturiers, in his high colouring and his sporting air – he rides every week-end without fail, whatever the weather – his Georgian figure, and instinctive good manners. (1949: n.p.)

At the root of Hartnell's sartorial presentation sits a performative function that can best be summarized through a description of the evolving image of the dandy, originating with the socialite George Bryan 'Beau' Brummell (1778–1840). Brummell patronized Savile Row tailors who, as dress historian Christopher Breward has noted, offered:

> a sartorial signature style suited to the demands of English aristocrats who required practical items for the equestrian pursuits of the rural landowner alongside a form of dress appropriate for the rounds of court, ceremonial, commercial transactions, and leisured display expected of the gentleman in town. (2003: 161–4)

Although Breward refers to a historical figure, fashion theorists Adam Geczy and Vicki Karaminas equate dandyism with 'a state of mind'. They write that after the First World War and the collapse of the 'old feudal world order', sartorial elegance and luxury could be bought by any man with the necessary financial capital. To distinguish oneself as a dandy within the simplified styles of dress for men at this time meant: 'a return to the refinements of detail: cufflinks, the cut of a jacket, hand sewing and the like. As always, these were by far the provinces of gay men, but gay men were apt to cherish these signs as worthy of the upper-class sensibility of queer taste' (Geczy and Karaminas 2013: 73). The portraits of Hartnell display these distinctions clearly.

Hartnell adopted a particular look appropriate to his country house lifestyle lived at Lovel Dene, his house in Windsor Forest, and his town life lived at The Tower House in Regent's Park and in the flat above the workrooms at 26 Bruton Street. He assembled a particular set of accessories with which to complement his dark three-piece double-breasted lounge suit, which he wore in town with a navy and white spotted tie, cufflinks and signet ring. He wore a red carnation in his buttonhole, and his wavy hair parted on the left (Figure 9.2). Examples of Hartnell's shoes, ties, jewellery and cufflinks, including the cufflinks monogrammed with 'ER' that Queen Elizabeth the Queen Mother gave him in 1938 after his White Wardrobe designs for the State visit to Paris, correspond exactly with items that he wore to be photographed in over time. His collection of diamond, pearl and sapphire tie-pins were designed in floral

FIGURE 9.2 Photograph of Norman Hartnell, De Groot (Amsterdam), c. 1943. Courtesy of the Hartnell-Mitchison Archive.

shapes to mirror his signature, beaded embroideries. It would seem that once Hartnell was content with this look he never wavered from it. A collection of his shoes in the archive reveal his longstanding taste for black patent Gucci loafers, and show that he wore navy suede loafers from Crocket & Jones of Harrow into the 1970s.

The other aspect of the dandy look adopted by Hartnell was that of a rural landowner and country gentleman. Hartnell was often photographed at his country home in Windsor, with his horses and dogs, usually wearing a tweed jacket and tie, or jodhpurs and a white shirt with tightly rolled-up sleeves. Photographs of him at work also show him wearing this look on occasions, again accompanied by a carnation worn in his buttonhole. Hartnell adopted the carnation as his favoured buttonhole from the mid-1930s. The fashion journalist Anne Scott-James, who had worked for both *Vogue* from 1934 and was Editor at *Harper's Bazaar* after the war, wrote a comic account of life at a fictitious fashion magazine, first published in 1952, which she named *Venus*. Although she stated in the Foreword that she had 'taken the greatest care not to "put in" anyone I really knew', she described the various characters who worked at the magazine, and was particularly disparaging of the queer men:

Apart from Directors . . . the men on *Venus* were nearly all effeminate . . . They copied each other's clothes, voices, houses, mannerisms, photographs, coiffeurs, slavishly picking up any new fashions set by one more adventurous than the rest . . . At that time their clothes were already markedly Edwardian, and tight trousers, waisted, skirted jackets, velvet collars and carnations were universal for the fraternity. Their hair was wavy, and perfumed with tonic or Cologne; their nails were manicured; but only the most advanced cases wore make-up. Their voices were usually high and drawly and their conversation was marked with many stresses. (Scott-James 1952: 60–1)

All of the studio portraits where Hartnell's hands are visible show that his fingernails were long and manicured. There is a collection of pale blue silk ties in the archive made by Harvie & Hudson, Jermyn Street, SW1, and New & Lingwood. These are similar to the tie worn in Madame Yevonde's portrait of Hartnell taken in the mid-1930s. These suppliers were also the makers of several navy and white spotted ties in the collection. Shaun Cole cites the findings of a 1949 Mass Observation survey on sexual attitudes, that found that 'amongst its study group "pale blue was a queer's 'trade colour'"; the group studied favoured pale blue for short socks, ties and pullovers' (Cole 2000: 63). Hartnell also wears a pale blue pullover in the portrait by Madame Yevonde.

In a collection of copies of letters from Hartnell to various makers and suppliers of men's clothing, written in 1945 and typed up on the back of blank workroom order forms, Hartnell placed orders for suits from Messrs.

Lesley & Roberts, Hanover Square, and shirts from Messrs. Coles Limited, Knightsbridge. He enquired about having a coat and suits made at Messrs. Benson & Clegg, and wrote to J.A. Murdoch at Messrs. Kilgour, French & Stanbury, Dover Street to the same end. To G.F. Curtis Esq., of Messrs. Hawes & Curtis Ltd., Piccadilly, in a letter dated 23 May 1945, he wrote:

> I daren't accept smart week-end parties, because I have no shirts to wear. My London and country suits are frayed and faded, and when I visit Buckingham Palace once or twice a week, my neck is so raw after having worn your splendid collars which are now torn and frayed, that discomfort is added to my embarrassment.

> I have had three cream taffeta shirts on order for some time. Is there any chance of having them within the next month or two? Mr. Sandford also has some materials for pyjamas, but they don't matter. But I would like some cream shirts and a few stiff collars. (Hartnell 1945)

These letters reveal the tailors and gentlemen's clothing suppliers Hartnell frequented for his London and country suits, taffeta shirts and men's pyjamas. In her 1934 guide to London shopping, Thelma Benjamin wrote that 'Kilgour & French in Dover Street made "Ultra-modern clothes for the most dashing type of young man". Lesley & Roberts in George Street catered for the "man-about-town" and film stars Clark Gable and Gary Cooper' and Hawes & Curtis in Jermyn Street were patronised by the Prince of Wales (Benjamin 1934 in Ehrman 2004: 99). Hartnell closely associated his public self-fashioning with the Savile Row suppliers of clothing to these celebrity dandy figures.

Biography in an embroidered pyjama suit

From actress to dandy, Hartnell performed a series of identities through photographs and clothing. Above all, his particular signature style of beaded evening wear, executed in Hartnell's favourite pastel shades of chiffon, holds the key to one important aspect of his private life in terms of his identity as it is present in his design work. Of all the Hartnell garments in the archive, a two-piece pastel blue lace pyjama suit embroidered with pink sequins and featuring a pink rose corsage and matching beaded sandals with ankle straps, found in the attic of the Mitchison house separate from the rest of the dress collections, seemed incongruous (Plate 19). The ensemble is very well worn and not very clean. The fastenings at the trouser waist have been mended repeatedly, cobbled together with a large tacking stitch, and the measurements of the jacket and trousers are larger and of a different shape to those of the model gowns in the collection. The aqua satin sandals with beaded embroidery were also rather wider and larger than the women's shoes in the collection.

Following an interview with former Hartnell employee Maureen Markham, who embroidered this ensemble, this pyjama suit was identified as having been owned and worn by Hartnell himself. Further garments in the collection include a well-worn, turquoise embroidered chiffon evening dress made to the same measurements, which may well have also belonged to the designer. As Markham divulged, Hartnell had garments, including crinoline gowns, made up and embroidered in his own couture workrooms, going by the name of 'Mrs Freeman' in the order books (2010). This pseudonym, chosen by Hartnell for purposes of discretion, may well have had a double function as a pun, playfully representing how wearing couture garments in feminine styles offered a sense of freedom. Hartnell's personal struggle with his 'effete' persona, as has been noted, was referred to in several early drafts of his memoir yet was never included as part of his published narrative. No reference to his female impersonation, celebrated in early articles about him in 1922, was included in his autobiography. This aspect of his private world is only present within the few, well-worn women's garments that were made for him by discreet members of his loyal staff in his workrooms at Bruton Street. This element of his private life has remained locked away, embedded in these silent clothes and in Hartnell's personal photograph collection.

On a summer's day in 1953, possibly June, the month of Elizabeth II's coronation, Hartnell was photographed dressed as the country gentleman in the drawing room of his country house, Lovel Dene, by the photographers De Groot of Amsterdam. That same day, a friend took two snapshot photographs of Hartnell upstairs in his bedroom. In one, Hartnell poses at the door to the balcony, wearing the exact same clothes and accessories as he wore for the De Groot photograph. In the other, Hartnell lies on his four-poster bed decorated with cherubs and floral chintz curtains (Figure 9.3). Here he wears a pale-coloured silk polka dot pyjama suit with rose corsage identical to the one pinned to the pale blue lace pyjama suit already discussed. Hartnell – the confirmed bachelor, the country gentleman, the dandy, the 'Regency buck' – is replaced by Hartnell the gay, effeminate, cross-dresser, performing his queer, internalized feminine identity in the private interior world of his bedroom. These two small snapshots reveal a private moment between himself and the photographer in the secret world of the Queen's couturier. These small faded snapshot photographs are so private that they are not reproduced here; I show the pyjama suit and the bed, but leave private depictions to the private world from which they came.

FIGURE 9.3 Photograph of Norman Hartnell's bed at Lovel Dene, Windsor, Marian Stephenson, c.1953. Courtesy of the Hartnell-Mitchison Archive.

Conclusion

Hartnell had written in 1924 that he was not like other men. An analysis of the samples of autobiographical writing, photographic portraits, garments and accessories discussed here, offers up some interpretation of what, perhaps, he felt made him different. What has become clear is that the impact of his lifelong gender play on his house style cannot be underestimated. It has been possible, by using a broad range of hitherto unstudied sources, to understand how within British society, pre-liberation, Hartnell was only able to act like a woman in private. Material including snapshot photography, personal interviews with staff and the silent garments once worn by Hartnell offer a glimpse of how he navigated between his public identity as an aspirational middle-class man and his private identity as a cross-dressing homosexual who displayed feminine traits performing what Butler has called his 'interior essence' (1990: 9) behind closed doors. His identity was forged in the liminal spaces between the upper echelons of society and his middle-class origins, and between his public, dandy masculinity and private gender performance as feminine. In both senses he was outside of the boundaries of convention.

The rose corsage attached to the white satin collar of Hartnell's beaded pyjama suit and his blue and white spotted tie, both established accessories worn by Hartnell in the early 1920s, represent Hartnell's life lived between genders. Hartnell thought that he was different from everybody else, but he was in fact like other gay men of his period. As he stated, 'for a long time I was uncertain. But gradually I came to realize that it meant merely that I was *myself* and *not* everybody else' (1924: 499), indicating that perhaps, over time, he became more comfortable with his sexuality. In more open-minded times, by reading archival garments against the grain, unexpected pearls may be revealed.

References

Benjamin, T. (1934), *London Shops and Shopping*, London: Herbert Joseph, in E. Ehrman (2004), 'Broken Traditions; 1930–55', in C. Breward, E Ehrman and C. Evans (eds), *The London Look: Fashion from Street to Catwalk*, London: Museum of London.

Breward, C. (2003), *Fashion*, Oxford: Oxford University Press.

Butler, J. (1990), *Gender Trouble: Feminism and the Subversion of Identity*, London and New York: Routledge.

Butler, J. (1993), *Bodies That Matter: On the Discursive Limits of 'Sex'*, London and New York: Routledge.

Cole, S. (2000), *Don We Now Our Gay Apparel: Gay Men's Dress in the Twentieth Century*, Oxford and New York: Berg.

de la Haye, A. (2007), 'Material Evidence: London Couture 1947–57', in C. Wilcox (ed.), *The Golden Age of Couture: Paris and London, 1947–57*, London: V&A Publications.

Dyer, R. (2002), *The Culture of Queers*, London and New York: Routledge.

Ehrman, E. (2004), 'Broken Traditions; 1930–55', in C. Breward, E. Ehrman and C. Evans (eds), *The London Look: Fashion from Street to Catwalk*, London: Museum of London.

Geczy, A. and Karaminas, V. (2013), *Queer Style*, London, New Delhi, New York and Sydney: Bloomsbury.

Hartnell, N. (1924), 'Why I am a Dressmaker', *Woman*, 1 (6): 499.

Hartnell, N. (1945), letter from Norman Hartnell to J. A. Murdoch, Kilgour, French and Stanbury, 23 May, Hartnell-Mitchison Archive, Box 2/1945, File 19.

Hartnell, N. (c. 1954a), 'The Following Day' (draft chapter of autobiography, *Silver and Gold*), Hartnell-Mitchison Archive, Box 3, File 1, 2–5.

Hartnell, N. (c. 1954b), 'Possible Alternative Titles: *Living by Design* or *Living for Design*' (draft of autobiography), Hartnell-Mitchison Archive, Box 3, File 12.

Hartnell, N. (c. 1971), untitled memoir, Hartnell-Mitchison Archive, Box. 3.

Hattrick, J. (2011), *A Life in the Archive: The Dress, Design and Identity of the London Couturier Norman Hartnell, 1921–1979*, PhD thesis, University of Brighton.

Hattrick, J. (2012), 'Collecting and Displaying Identity, Intimacy and Memory in the Staged Interiors of the Royal Couturier Norman Hartnell', in S. Dudley et al. (eds), *Narrating Objects, Collecting Stories: Essays in Honour of Professor Susan M. Pearce*, London and New York: Routledge.

Hattrick, J. (2014), 'Seduced by the Archive: A Personal Relationship with the Archive and Collection of Objects Pertaining to the London Couturier, Norman Hartnell', in A. Moran and S. O'Brien (eds), *Love Objects: Emotion, Design and Material Culture*, London, New Delhi, New York and Sydney: Bloomsbury Academic.

Lawler, S. (2008), *Identity: Sociological Perspectives*, Cambridge and Malden, MA: Polity Press.

Markham, M. (2010), interview by author, 30 April.

Moffat, W. (2010), *A Great Unrecorded History: A New Life of E.M. Forster*, New York: Farrar, Straus and Giroux.

Scott-James, A. (1952), *In The Mink*, London: Mermaid Books.

Taylor, L. (2004), *Establishing Dress History*, Manchester: Manchester University Press.

'University Man Takes Up Dress Designing' (1922), *Sunday Illustrated*, 31 December: n.p.

Wilson, E. (2007), 'A Note on Glamour', *Fashion Theory*, 11 (1): 95–107.

Winn, G. (1949), 'Norman Hartnell: A Profile', *Woman's Illustrated*, 26 (638), 22 January: n.p.

The Wolfenden Report: Report of the Committee on Homosexual Offences and Prostitution (1963), New York: Stein and Day.

Wright, A. (2010), interview by author, 5 July.

10 FROM KAYS OF WORCESTER TO *VOGUE*, PARIS: THE WOMEN'S INSTITUTE MAGAZINE, RURAL LIFE AND FASHIONABLE DRESS IN POST-WAR BRITAIN

Rachel Ritchie

'Our inspiration is totally with rural life as it can be lived', wrote Laura Ashley in the late 1970s in a statement that underlines the centrality of the countryside in the British designer's vision for her successful chain of high street stores (Sebba 1990: 106). Comments made by Ashley's husband in 1990 reinforce this importance; the couple walked and talked, 'endlessly rambling in fields, lanes and in the hills. Most of our ideas, plans and design philosophies were formed on these walks' (Sebba 1990: xv–xvi). The example of Laura Ashley and her evocations of rural romanticism may be one of the most well known in recent fashion, but this is only one instance of rural life and the countryside influencing trends in dress. From Marie Antoinette's eighteenth-century pastoral idyll to Cath Kidston's twenty-first-century 'shabby chic' look, visions of the countryside have proved alluring despite (or perhaps even because of) fashion's status as an inherently modern concept, inextricably linked to key features of modernity such as urbanization, industrialization and commercialization. As Mary Lynne Stewart notes in her study of haute couture in interwar France,

> It is widely acknowledged that fashion is modern. If one adopts David Frisby's
> definition of *modernité* as 'the more general experience of the aestheticization

of everyday life, as exemplified in the transitory qualities of an urban culture shaped by the imperatives of fashion, consumerism, and constant innovation,' fashion is proto-typically modern. (Stewart 2008: xii)

The countryside is rarely included within these definitions of modernity. Rural areas are associated with the past, a time before modernity. Such cultural constructions render country-dwellers as pre-modern, un-modern or anti-modern, hence also either anti-fashion, un-fashionable or somehow outside of fashion. These images are deeply entrenched within the collective imagination. As Raymond Williams observed in *The Country and the City*, 'Powerful feelings have gathered and have been generalised. On the country has gathered the idea of a natural way of life: of peace, innocence, and simple virtue . . . a place of backwardness, ignorance, limitation. A contrast between country and city, as fundamental ways of life, reaches back into classical time' (Williams 1973: 1). Such visions of the countryside obscure and deny both the historically varied lived experiences of rural-dwellers and the connections between rural and urban areas: 'The country and the city are changing historical realities, both in themselves and in their interrelations' (Williams 1973: 288).

Williams was writing in 1973, following two decades of enormous change in the British countryside. In his wide-ranging study of post-war Britain, Brian Harrison goes as far as to state 'The face of the country was changing at least as fast between 1951 and 1970 as at any other time' (2009: 123). Technological developments had an enormous impact, revolutionizing various aspects of country life from agriculture and transport to living conditions. Electricity, for example, became almost universal in rural homes for the first time (Harrison 2009: 123–75; Howkins 2003: 142–206). While dramatically altering the lives of those who lived in rural areas, such changes also signal the extent to which the British countryside was being modernized on different fronts in these decades. Despite the continued prevalence of ahistoricized and romantic visions of a timeless countryside, key features of modernity increasingly shaped rural life too.

These experiences of modernity away from large urban centres remain marginalized within accounts of post-war British modernity even though rural-dwellers accounted for a sizeable minority of the population, around 20 per cent throughout the 1950s and 1960s (Harrison 2009: 146). Likewise, scholars of dress have paid little attention to the relationship between those who live in the countryside and fashion, an oversight noted by those involved in the Fields of Fashion Research Centre at Nottingham Trent University: '[f]ashion consumption, retailing and production in rural areas has been neglected in academic studies. A rash of work exists on fashion in so-called "world cities" but the richly textured, vibrant landscapes of fashion away from the metropolis have yet to be considered through any sustained academic research' (Fields of Fashion 2011).

This chapter not only addresses this neglect but also demonstrates the insights that can be gained from exploring notions of fashion within rural contexts. It does so via a case study of the British magazine *Home and Country* during the late 1950s and 1960s, the time of huge changes in the countryside. *Home and Country* was the official publication of the National Federation of Women's Institutes (NFWI), a non-sectarian, non-party political organization for rural women in England and Wales. Institute branches held monthly meetings with a visiting speaker, often about an educational topic or handicrafts, alongside classes, outings and other social events. In the first academic study of the organization, Maggie Andrews highlights the significance of such gatherings: 'the very existence . . . of a women's group within a village in the 1920s, or even now precipitates a change in rural life . . . Within the village a local WI provided for the development of hitherto unknown female networks' (Andrew 1997: xi). Networks were created nationally too, with the NFWI campaigning on a variety of issues. In 1964, for example, the AGM passed a resolution calling for regular cervical cancer screening (Beaumont 2009: 71). By this time, the movement was the largest women's organization in Britain with over 500,000 members from working-, middle- and upper-class backgrounds and from all age groups, although attracting younger members was becoming increasingly difficult (Beaumont 2001: 274; Andrews 1997: xiii–xiv).

The chapter begins by exploring how *Home and Country* writers and advertisers presented fashion as modern before moving on to discuss the roles played by mail order, home-dressmaking and knitting in providing access to fashionable dress. It then considers how the magazine's producers tried to use links to brands with high levels of symbolic capital in an attempt to validate its rural interpretation of fashion. Such efforts reveal the extent to which fashion was an integral part of the rural modernity found within *Home and Country*'s pages. In her exploration of domestic identities, femininity and modernity, Judy Giles asserts that the city and the suburb 'express two different ways of responding to modernisation' (Giles 2004: 35); likewise, the countryside provided another way of responding. In certain settings, in this instance a publication catering for a readership composed of countrywomen, rural experiences shaped constructions of the modern; country life supplied the conceptual framework for understandings of modernity in the magazine.

This perspective challenges scholars interested in dress as well as modern historians in general. As literary scholar Janet Galligani Casey notes in one of the few investigations of rural modernity, '[a]n underexamined and perpetually flat backdrop . . . Twentieth-century rural culture has remained in the shadows of a modern urbanity'. Yet women's 'lived and represented rural experiences' can contribute to 'a remapping of modernity itself' (Casey 2009: 20). This chapter adds to such remapping by exploring the particularities of how contributors to *Home and Country* understood, experienced and depicted rural modernity through dress. This also provides a new perspective on dress history by moving away from the current focus upon fashion in metropolitan settings. The use of women's magazines as a source in dress history is well-established: Stewart (2008), for example, used periodicals when exploring the relationship between interwar female fashion and modernity. As Lou Taylor notes, however, dress historians have tended to rely on elite magazines that focus on urban dwellers, such as *Vogue* and *Harper's Bazaar*, ignoring other periodicals and mail-order catalogues (Taylor 2002: 140). By drawing upon a complete cover-to-cover analysis of a sample of *Home and Country* issues selected at six monthly intervals across the years in question, this study highlights valuable material for the investigation of dress history in rural areas. I also consulted the Kay and Co. archive, comparing their catalogue's cover imagery with the company's magazine advertising, and examined the minutes of the NFWI sub-committee who were responsible for producing *Home and Country*. This material, part of the Women's Institute collection at The Women's Library in London, provides invaluable background information about the publication, as will be discussed below.

Fashion and the modern

Each cover of *Home and Country* in this period reminded readers that it was 'The WI Magazine'. As such, its perspective echoed that of the movement, with its focus on the lives of countrywomen. This particular geographic outlook was distinctive, with most women's magazines at this time containing a tacit assumption that readers lived in urban, or at least suburban, locations. Offering a gendered perspective, however, was typical (Winship 1987: 67). Women's magazines have long had an important role as sites for the formation and dissemination of feminine identities. Ellen McCracken explores this process in *Decoding Women's Magazines*, arguing that their pages provided 'a pleasurable, appealing consensus . . . [an] ostensibly common agreement about what constitutes the feminine' (McCracken 1993: 3).

In the mid-1960s, audited sales figures for *Home and Country* stood at around 148,000 copies per month, with readers paying 6d for thirty-seven pages (*Home and Country* Minutes 5 January 1966). Every issue contained articles and regular features about the WI alongside the kinds of items found in mainstream women's periodicals, including content about personal appearance. There were, for instance, articles about beauty. Due to scholars largely focusing on NFWI campaigning activities and incorporating discussions of *Home and Country* within this, these elements of the magazine have only recently begun to receive academic attention (Ritchie 2014a).

While such issues are important, other aspects of the organization and its publication warrant consideration too. Advice and instruction on personal appearance formed part of the NFWI's remit and evidence suggests that Institute members, who also comprised *Home and Country*'s readership, enjoyed participating in fashion and beauty culture. The movement's college, for example, regularly ran short courses such as 'Looking Your Best' (Ritchie 2014a: 15). Furthermore, the publication's sub-committee regarded this as an integral component of the magazine, recurrently commissioning one of the regular freelancers to write fashion and beauty content (*Home and Country* Minutes 5 January 1966, 4 April 1967).

Unfortunately little is known about these writers as they often used pseudonyms and are thus difficult to trace. Their work relied heavily on text, with a few illustrations and only occasionally photographs (e.g. see *Home and Country* October 1968: 390). This reflects the magazine's limited production values. Most of the fashion imagery appeared in the designer reports, discussed in the final section, or as largely black-and-white photographs in some clothing advertisements. In October 1965, for instance, an Antartex advertisement showed one of their sheepskin coats being modelled (October 1965: 395). Sheepskin, along with tweed and wool, is typical of the country wear advertised in *Home and Country*. Manufacturers often used the moniker of 'country' for items made of traditional materials or alongside adjectives such as practical, sensible and classic to describe the aesthetic style. Skerry, for instance, presented a pair of low heeled brogue court shoes as a country style but also claimed they were fashionable enough for the transition to town wear: 'Town elegance with a gentle country smile' (October 1966: 385). Country was also used interchangeably with county, as in 'For quality with the county touch look for Skerry Shoes', from another Skerry advertisement showing two pairs of small square heel shoes (October 1964: 345).

In Britain, 'county' refers to an administrative and geographical area, but has longstanding symbolic associations linked to the countryside and the rural elite. Likewise, country dress carried connotations of an upper- or upper-middle-class lifestyle. The WI, however, was composed of members from across the social class spectrum. The tone of *Home and Country* echoed this diversity, even in its advice on personal appearance (Ritchie 2014: 12). Some advertising aside, contributors to *Home and Country* did not heavily promote country wear. On the contrary, descriptions and depictions of clothing often highlighted fashion rather than a distinctly country style. This emphasis reflects the symbolic relationship between fashion and the modern, as the earlier quotation from Stewart highlights. If fashion symbolized modernity, then being 'fashionable' or 'in fashion' equated to being modern and thus dressing in fashionable clothes functioned as a sign of one's own modernity.

Even reading about fashion, regardless of whether one then acted upon the information given, provided a means to claim the same status. Not all contributors shared this standpoint, with many advertisements selling garments in styles out of sync with contemporary trends, but the language found in the magazine's fashion features reinforced and encouraged these positive associations between fashion and the modern. Writers often used temporal phrases that presented fashion trends as modern by virtue of being the newest innovation. Within such a schema, being 'up-to-date' was a virtue and 'the latest' was the style to which to aspire to, as in the 1969 title 'Creating the "Now" Look in Fashion' (Figure 10.1). This headline was also a pun on Christian Dior's hugely influential 1947 New Look. Twenty plus years later, this double reference no longer signalled fashionability per se but operated as a knowing joke that positioned the writer and those readers who understood it as members of the fashion cognoscenti.

The 'Creating the "Now" Look in Fashion' feature included a discussion of fur coats, with fashion writer Julia Kent observing that 'It's the ambition of many a woman to own a fur coat – seen as a sign of her husband's success, of acquired position, as a reward, perhaps, for years of going without'. However, Kent then shifts the emphasis away from prestige, wealth and status: 'Look at the exciting way modern furriers design coats' (*Home and Country* October 1969: 394–5). This encouragement to view fur coats as fashionable (and modern) items as well as a status symbol mirrors changes in popular taste from the mid- to late-1950s, when the material's cachet began to decline (Dyhouse 2012: 147–8). The

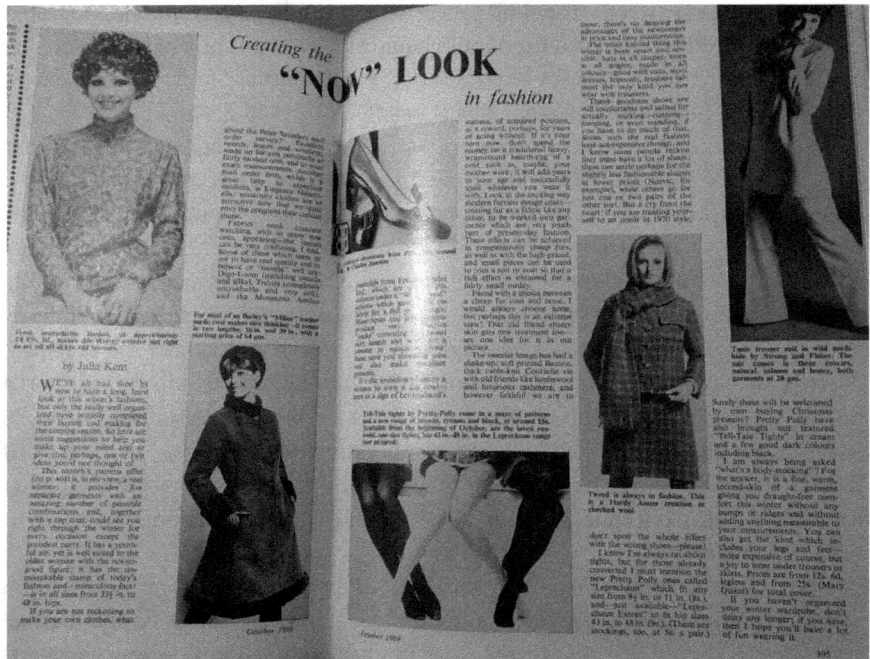

FIGURE 10.1 'Creating the Now Look in Fashion', *Home and Country*, October 1969: 394–5. Courtesy of National Federation of Women's Institutes.

negative impact of this on the fur industry, and their attempts to respond, are discernible in *Home and Country*. Two furriers that advertised in the magazine, L and D Goodkind and Derella Fur Models, amalgamated in 1957, suggesting financial difficulties in one or both companies. Their advertisements appeared regularly and Kent's 1969 endorsement of fur coats may have been a reward for loyalty to the publication. Her language certainly echoes their publicity. These firms similarly attempted to update the image of fur, moving away from its old-fashioned and traditional associations by emphasizing the new, up-to-date styles available. As well as 'cash for that fur coat', underlining the literal value such items had for women, the advertisements offered part exchange 'for one of our modern styled furs' or restyling, 'This beautiful jacket made from your outmoded Fur Coat' (May 1954: inside cover). Such offers continued throughout the 1960s, with advertisements promoting a remodelling service or a (that phrase again) 'new look' for ten guineas (April 1963: 145).

Contributors such as Julia Kent and the furrier advertisers were trying to convey a sense of connection between the magazine, its readers and the world of fashion. In doing so, they positioned the countryside and rural-dwellers as part of fashionable modernity, not removed from it. Still despite such imaginings, *Home and Country* writers and advertisers could not ignore the practical difficulties that many countrywomen faced in trying to access fashionable clothing, or indeed any clothing. As a result, the magazine offered readers a number of solutions to help overcome such problems and assist them in creating a fashionable and modern appearance. The following section explores how.

Buying fashion

In the post-war decades, clothing stores were common in the provincial towns that served Britain's countryside. In the early 1950s, menswear tailor Burtons, for instance, opened a store in the small market town of Devizes in the rural county of Wiltshire, reflecting their commitment to nationwide coverage (Mort and Thompson 1994: 110, 112). Fashion coverage in *Home and Country* acknowledged this availability. In October 1965, an article informed readers that square hats were the latest trend emanating from Paris and '[t]he pleasing results can be seen in any hat shop in the country'; the same piece also promoted some shoes from the multiple retailer Clarks (October 1965: 389). Women living outside urban centres, however, continued to lack easy, straightforward, reasonably priced access to shops, especially those in larger towns and cities that sold the most up-to-date goods. Even in the late twentieth century, rural consumers faced certain distinctive problems, with women being particularly disadvantaged because of their low mobility (Westlake 1993: 177). Although the number of cars in Britain rose fivefold between 1950 and 1970, only 13 per cent of women held driving licences in the mid-1960s compared to 56 per cent of men (O'Connell 2007: 117). At the same time, public transport provision in rural areas was in decline, with decreases in bus services and massive closures across the rail network (Gant and Smith 1991: 109; Bell and Cloke 1991: 128). Potential access to shops is thus not necessarily an indicator of actual ability to frequent them (Westlake 1993: 174).

Those who dismiss geography and accessibility as factors influencing consumer choice ignore these very real difficulties (Coopey et al. 2005: 2). The NFWI, however, was well aware of these issues. While the organization campaigned vigorously for improvements to rural public transport (Ritchie 2011: 78–9), contributors to *Home and Country* offered other solutions. One aspect of this was alternative forms of retailing. This included direct sales. Thanks to the post-war consumer boom, ready-to-wear clothing was a growth area by the 1960s, a trend reflected in the increasing number of advertisements placed by garment manufacturers peddling their wares directly to the public rather than (or as well as) in shops. By utilizing the nationwide postal service, firms such as Watkins and Cole, who promised 'Immediate Delivery' of their dresses and suits (October 1968: 407), allowed consumers to purchase goods from their own homes, meaning distance from retailers was not an issue.

During this decade there was also an increase in the number of advertisements for mail-order catalogues selling clothes and other goods. This reflects the huge growth of mail-order sales in the post-war period, with their proportion of the UK retail market increasing from 0.9 per cent in 1950 to 2.5 per cent and 4 per cent in 1961 and 1969 respectively (Coopey et al. 2005: 53). There were several factors behind this rise. Easy access to credit was one of them, but convenience was hugely important too (Coopey et al. 2005: 56–9). This was especially the case for countrywomen due to their particular problems with transport and mobility. Home-shopping catalogue companies, like firms involved in direct sales, could reach rural consumers far more easily than standard retailers were able to.

With one or more mail-order catalogue advertisement appearing in most issues of *Home and Country* during the 1960s, it appears that these companies regarded the publication as a vital channel through which to appeal to rural consumers. Kay and Co. advertised most regularly, a commitment rewarded with additional publicity in the magazine's 'Advertising Extra' feature in October 1968. This promotional page informed readers that the Kays catalogue contained 'a range of "in" gear – including Mary Quant's – to suit any teenager, and delightful classic styles in clothes for the whole family' (October 1968: 403).

While the presence of licensed clothing by on-trend designer Mary Quant points to efforts by Kay and Co. to present themselves as a purveyor of fashionable wares, the juxtaposition of 'in gear' with 'delightful classic styles' highlights a broader friction in the company's identity. Kay and Co. was based in Worcester, a small historic city in the English Midlands. Although not the countryside per se, the surrounding county of Worcestershire was a traditional farming area and this shaped the town's identity. Kay and Co. incorporated this sense of being located in the rural provinces into their corporate imagery. Catalogue covers drew heavily on idealized notions of a bucolic past, regularly showing the town's riverside vista and its ancient cathedral, thus evoking a bygone era that reinforced the already strong association of the country with times long ago. Such depictions of an historic idyll were at odds with the fashionable modern world within the catalogue's pages or on other covers (Ritchie 2014b). These tensions are apparent on the front of the autumn/winter 1963 Kays catalogue (Plate 20), a reproduction of which appeared in that season's Kay and Co. advertising (October 1963: 335). The picture positions the modern and the traditional in the same frame, with a contemporary apartment and equally up-to-date occupant in the foreground and the centuries old cathedral and riverbanks in the background. It is, however, an imaginary scene; no building faced the cathedral from that angle.

This rural provincial identity belied the modern-day communications infrastructure that was essential to the successful expansion of mail-order retailing in this period (Coopey et al. 2005: 54). Kay and Co. were able to cater to rural consumers by providing quick and easy access to goods when visiting clothing stores was difficult, costly and time-consuming. As their advertisement stated, 'Fast 48 hour dispatch' was available. Kay and Co., along with other mail-order and direct sales retailers, were therefore vital to efforts within *Home and Country* to offer opportunities to readers to surmount the practical difficulties that they faced when trying to access fashion. They were not, however, the only solution that the magazine presented.

Making fashion

The other solution presented by *Home and Country* was to make one's own clothes. Home-dressmaking and knitting were significant elements within post-war women's magazines, although the presence of dressmaking and knitting on the pages of a magazine does not of course necessarily reveal how widespread either activity actually was; nor, in the case of dressmaking, does it reveal whether readers made their own garments or commissioned a dressmaker to create items on their behalf. Even though home-dressmaking was common in the early decades of the twentieth century, there is some evidence to suggest that it was in decline after the Second World War (Hackney 1999: 88–9). Yet as Barbara Burman observes in her introduction to *The Culture of Sewing*, the 1999 edited collection which significantly advanced research in this area, 'the work and habits of home dressmakers is multifaceted and susceptible to so many variables that they remain outside precise measurement and are best understood in richer terms than mere numbers' (1999: 5–7).

Despite such reservations, the high level of home dressmaking and knitting coverage in *Home and Country* indicates that both activities remained popular with its readers. For example, when *Home and Country* carried advertisements for other publications, these often emphasized either or both home-dressmaking and knitting as means of attracting its audience to read that magazine too. A 1957 advertisement for *Woman* used the headline '16-page pull-out knitting booklet' (October 1957: 316); similarly, three years later, an advertisement for a craft magazine declared 'Knit Alma Cogan's Sweater – Make Brigitte Bardot's dress! – Two of the 50 exciting patterns in the grand new April number of *Pins and Needles*' (April 1960: 142).

Furthermore, when discussing comparative circulation figures in 1958, *Home and Country*'s editorial committee noted that one of the reasons given by Institute members for declining readership was the desire for more knitting patterns (*Home and Country* Minutes 2 April 1958). The publishers responded to this desire by greatly increasing the number of patterns included; compared to the sample for the four years prior to that meeting, the four years that followed saw a rise of 200 per cent. Around the same time, the wool brand Emu became an important advertiser in *Home and Country*, which may also help to explain the increase; these patterns, which appeared in full, came 'courtesy of' various major yarn manufacturers. They provided an important supplement to direct advertising, offering firms an opportunity to promote their goods with an implicit endorsement from the magazine's producers.

Whereas entire knitting patterns could be provided cheaply and easily, sewing patterns were more expensive and difficult to reproduce within the pages of a magazine. Like other publications, *Home and Country* thus promoted home-dressmaking by postal service. In April 1956, for example, readers wanting the 'All-Season Pinafore Dress' pattern had to write to Department P and enclose a postal order for 2s 9d (April 1956: 149). Such provision played a crucial role in the democratization of home-dressmaking during the twentieth century (Walsh 1979; Moseley 2001: 477). Moreover, both this form of pattern service and the reproduction of manufacturers' knitting patterns were integral to the commercial culture of home-dressmaking evident across women's magazines since 1900 (Hackney 1999: 76–7, 83; Maynard 1995: 50).

Advertising was another crucial element within this commercial culture. Advertisements for items such as wool and dressmaking fabric averaged over ten per issue in the 1960s, suggesting that companies selling these kinds of products regarded the magazine as a lucrative forum for advertising. This was because handicrafts were a significant part of the NFWI's collective organizational culture. This is apparent in the level of coverage that they received in *Home and Country*, with articles by the Institute's Handicrafts Sub-Committee and reviews of craft-related events and publications, as well as regular listings for courses at such as 'Staging and Displaying of Handicrafts' and 'Methods of Teaching (Handicrafts)' at the WI college (e.g. see April 1956: 133). This not only made the magazine popular among vendors of handicraft goods; it also attracted home-dressmaking marketers, particularly as the two areas could converge: a 1969 advertisement promoting a crochet book emphasized that its patterns were 'for wardrobe and home', while an article on leather-craft in the same issue encouraged readers to make leather garments too (October 1969: 389, 403).

There has been relatively little attention paid to this complex arena in which commercial goods were produced and sold to facilitate the domestic creation of garments. The terminology used, notably the phrase 'home-made clothes', denies the involvement of industry and manufacturing in the process, creating the misleading assumption that home-dressmaking and knitting are outside of commercial and consumer circuits. This is clearly not the case. By highlighting the commercial aspects of home-dressmaking and knitting, the patterns, pattern services and related advertising on the pages of *Home and Country* expose the highly ambiguous nature of such endeavours. Its contents demonstrate that making one's own clothing was part of consumer culture, not divorced from it, supporting the argument that such activities resist and challenge standard divisions between production and consumption (Burman 1999: 3).

The home-dressmaking and knitting content within *Home and Country* also disputes the derisory and elitist assumption that the items created through such activities were outside the canon of fashion (Buckley 1998: 165–6; Burman 1999: 12). On the contrary, the magazine's writers actively utilized the concept of fashion in discussions of home-dressmaking and knitting. For example, the captions that accompanied patterns contained the same discourses found in descriptions of fashionable manufactured garments, such as references to the current season or year. A pattern service offer for a dress thus stated that it had 'at least two 1963 features – elbow-length, slightly full sleeves, and a skirt with a panel front flare, nipped at the waist with a (bought) patent belt' (April 1963: 137). Advertisers likewise used the concept of fashion when promoting items for use in home-dressmaking, professing that 'Fashion runs smoothly with NyZip . . . It's fashion's smoothest zip!' and promising that their products would 'accentuate fashion features' (October 1961: 326; April 1961: 118).

This kind of language was not unique to *Home and Country*. Nor was it entirely a hollow marketing ploy. Scholars such as Rachel Moseley have recognized the critical role of home-dressmaking in providing women with an economical way of keeping up with fashion (2001: 477; see also Burman 1999: 3; Hackney 1999: 80). Saving on cost was not the only benefit to making one's own clothing. Home-dressmaking and knitting also made fashion accessible for rural women who were geographically isolated. As a substitute for or even simply a supplement to shopping (whether in person or by using postal services), these creative pursuits gave countrywomen another opportunity to create fashionable and modern appearances for themselves.

The perception of geography as a hindrance to shopping for the latest trends, and the importance of *Home and Country*'s pattern provision in providing an alternative solution, is clearly articulated in a 1968 'Dear Nancy Fielding' column. Responding to a reader's query about why the magazine's patterns were 'so expensive', the publication's agony aunt for all WI-related issues evoked the difficulties encountered by country-dwelling NFWI members. At the same time, she positioned the pattern service as resolving this difficulty, stating 'Since readers demand smart and up-to-date patterns, only the best makes are used, and it seems that the service is particularly appreciated by members in rural areas who would have bus or rail fares to pay if they went to choose from pattern books in town shops' (April 1968: 139).

Fielding's comment that 'only the best makes are used' referred to the inclusion of *Vogue Paris Original* patterns. During the 1960s, these became an important component within *Home and Country*'s presentation of rural fashion. While the pattern manufacturers were seeking to widen their market (Emery 1999: 250), this brand appealed to the magazine's editorial committee and readers for several reasons. Part of the attraction was economics. Moseley found such paper patterns made couture styles 'available to women whose finances would not have stretched to Dior and Givenchy' (2002: 57). Furthermore these licensed designs allowed wearers to perceive themselves as being dressed in couture, even though garments made from a designer pattern would differ from those created in a couture workroom. This even extended to knitting; one spring the magazine featured a blouse pattern that was 'One of the many attractive designs in the latest Vogue Knitting Book' (April 1964: 143).

A second crucial factor in explaining why *Vogue*-branded patterns were important was geography. While *Home and Country* readers may or may not have been able to afford the originals, their provincial and often isolated rural location certainly meant they lacked convenient access to purveyors of designer clothing whereas the patterns could be made up in their own homes or by a local dressmaker. At the same time, their allure went beyond the practicalities of money and geography. As the final section demonstrates, the presence of *Vogue Paris Original* patterns in *Home and Country* was an attempt to legitimate the vision of rural fashion that the magazine presented.

Legitimating rural fashion

Among all of the home-dressmaking content in *Home and Country*, *Vogue Paris Original* patterns were significant because of the high status accorded to the *Vogue* brand. Due to its reputation as 'the twentieth century's most influential fashion magazine', the very name *Vogue* is synonymous with fashion (O'Hara Callan 1998: 253). The dressmaking division grew out of pattern provision in the magazine (Emery 1999: 245). The inclusion of Paris, the home of haute couture, within the trademark name further enhanced the aura of connection to the heart of the fashion industry. The statement that accompanied the first *Vogue Paris Original* pattern to appear in *Home and Country* (Figure 10.2) clearly articulated this sense of prestige:

> As we visit Counties from time to time and note your requests, one above all has been voiced. 'Please', we have been asked, 'may we have a really special pattern, a Paris pattern, so that some of us may have a chance to make something really exclusive for our wardrobes'. So here for your delight is a *Vogue Paris Original* pattern of a Jacques Heim model. (October 1961: 351)

Even if individual readers did not send off for a 'special pattern' to make up themselves or pay a seamstress to create it for them, the inclusion of this Jacques Heim model and the other *Vogue Paris Original* patterns in *Home and Country* during the 1960s assisted the magazine's producers in their attempt to construct

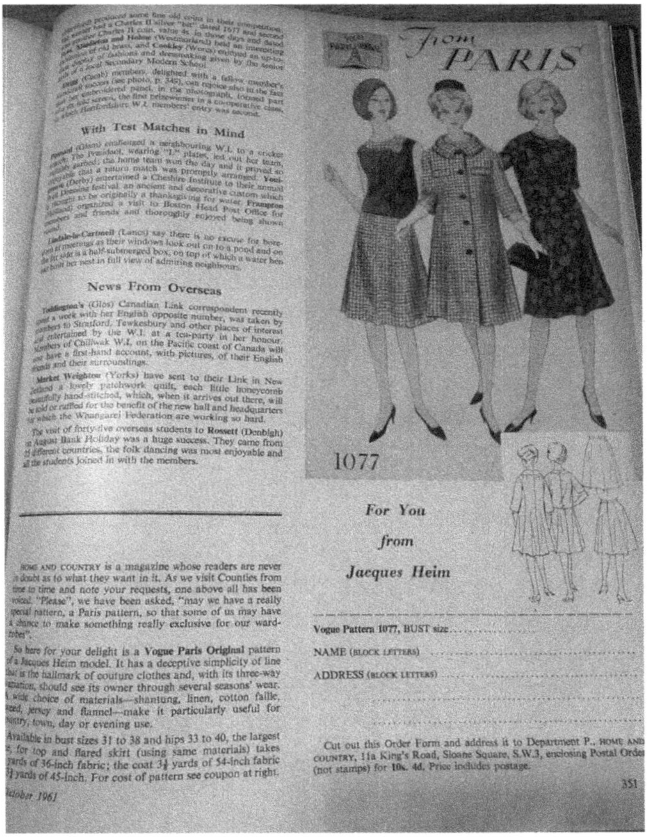

FIGURE 10.2 'From Paris', *Home and Country*, October 1961: 351.
Courtesy of National Federation of Women's Institutes.

a rural vision of fashion in two ways. First, these patterns created a sense of fashionable glamour within the magazine's pages, an atmosphere that the NFWI themselves could not evoke given their rather sensible reputation and practical focus on issues and campaigns that would benefit members' lives. The *Vogue* brand, with which the pattern company was indelibly linked, was sufficiently strong that even the name conjured up an array of cultural connotations that allowed the country housewife readers a brief moment of escapism. That the world of *Vogue* was so far removed from their daily lives was part of the appeal, allowing them (even if momentarily) to dream of transformation (McCracken 1993: 168).

Second, since neither the NFWI nor its publication had a reputation for being interested in personal appearance (Ritchie 2014a: 15–17), *Home and Country*'s editors needed assistance if they wanted to claim justifiably that the home-dressmaking patterns offered were fashionable. The reputation of *Vogue* bestowed such legitimacy. The concept of symbolic capital, 'typified as "prestige" or "honour" . . . largely unconscious in all but effect' (Keeble 2007: 99), helps to explain this attempt to secure validation via association with a prestigious brand. The producers of *Home and Country* tried to counter their lack of cultural authority in this sphere by aligning, however tenuously, their fashion content with those aspects of the fashion industry that did have symbolic capital, specifically *Vogue*.

This link had particular importance because the vision of rural fashion presented on the magazine's pages had little symbolic capital on its own merits. As seen throughout the chapter, it relied heavily on postal services (mail order and direct sales), home-dressmaking and knitting, all of which had low levels of status and value. The Kays catalogue, for instance, may have been a useful resource for readers, but in terms of perceived symbolic capital Kay and Co. was somewhat down-market. The firm definitely did not possess fashion prestige and legitimacy, partly because of continued negative attitudes towards credit, but also because of the popularity of home-shopping catalogues among working-class consumers (Coopey et al. 2005: 5–6, 65).

Another attempt by the magazine's producers to validate their vision of rural modernity by allying with a prestigious element of the fashion industry is evident in the 1960s as well. Alongside articles about fashion, discussed earlier, the publication contained reports from recent fashion shows (Figure 10.3). The source of these is unknown, but they focused on couture and high-end fashion brands; 'Paris in Spring', for instance, mentions Pierre Cardin, Nina Ricci and Jacques Griffe (April 1961: 142). The producers of *Home and Country* perhaps hoped that the aura of symbolic capital conveyed by such references to famous designers would permeate other aspects of its sartorial coverage as well.

Nevertheless success in accruing symbolic capital was not assured; as Bev Skeggs notes in her research on working-class women and respectability,

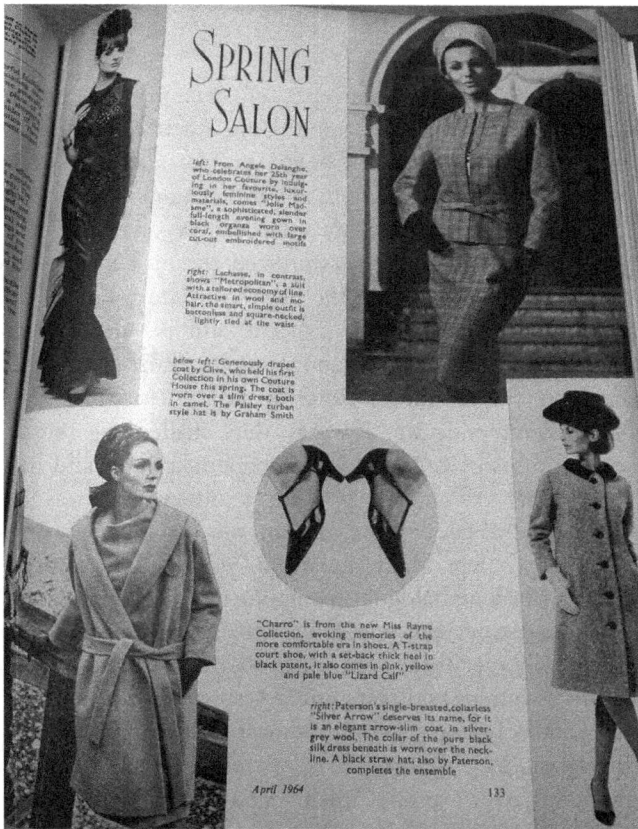

FIGURE 10.3 'Spring Salon', *Home and Country*, April 1964: 133.
Courtesy of National Federation of Women's Institutes.

'proximity to the "right" knowledge and standards does not guarantee acceptance' (1997: 11). Indeed, such acceptance was not forthcoming and the rural vision of fashion seen in *Home and Country* received little or no recognition, let alone elevation of status, in other fashionable arenas. It remained isolated and accorded little value because its focus on home-shopping catalogues and home-dressmaking, the very elements that catered to rural consumers, were so far removed from metropolitan visions of fashion in which aesthetic styles were more important than logistical solutions. In particular, the image of Swinging London, with its mini-skirts and little boutiques, came to exert an enormous influence over understandings of late 1950s and 1960s fashion both at the time and in subsequent scholarship. Casey commented that 'Twentieth-century rural culture has remained in the shadows of a modern urbanity' (2009: 20); in the realm of fashion, the capital overshadows the countryside.

Conclusion

Throughout this chapter, the concepts of fashion and modernity have intertwined. Scholars have long recognized the inextricable links between the two and evidence from *Home and Country* supports this connection. At the same time, this case study has demonstrated that understandings of who and what is fashionable and/or modern are subject to negotiation and redefinition. The magazine's writers and advertisers utilized certain common and accepted discourses, such as an emphasis on the newest or latest, but they also shaped both notions according to their own needs and perspectives, for example describing fur coats as fashionable and modern. Most notably, contributors to *Home and Country* presented a vision of fashion in which the experience of living in the countryside was integral, thus challenging the very basis of mainstream definitions of and assumptions about fashion and modernity. As one of the biggest sartorial challenges facing countrywomen was limited access to clothing retailers, this rural vision of fashion focused heavily on solutions to help overcome this problem. Many *Home and Country* advertisers offered postal services, with mail-order catalogues being particularly prominent. Advertisers along with the magazine's producers also portrayed home-dressmaking and knitting as alternative means through which to dress fashionably.

Both mail-order clothing and home-made garments again contravene standard definitions of what is fashionable and modern, as the tensions and refutations discussed throughout have shown. The editors of *Home and Country* were aware of this; hence they tried to legitimate their vision of rural fashion by forging links with brands that had high levels of symbolic capital, namely *Vogue Paris Original* patterns and the high-end designers named in the Paris fashion show reports. Such connections remained rather tenuous and confined to within the publication. Despite this, contributors to *Home and Country* presented solutions that, on a representational level at least, allowed readers access to fashionable clothing and therefore a modern appearance. Outside of the magazine, the symbolic capital of such representations may have been limited, but inside its pages, such depictions created an inclusive vision of fashion and the modern that incorporated rural areas and the countrywomen who lived in them. In doing so, this vision disputed widely held views about both conceptualizations of fashion and the modern. As a result, it provides an alternative perspective on dress history during this period while also contributing to a remapping of post-war British modernity.

References

Andrews, M. (1997), *The Acceptable Face of Feminism: The Women's Institute as a Social Movement*, London: Lawrence and Wishart.

Beaumont, C. (2001), 'The Women's Movement, Politics and Citizenship, 1918–1950s', in I. Zweiniger-Bargielowska (ed.), *Women in Twentieth-Century Britain*, Harlow: Pearson Education.

Beaumont, C. (2009), 'Housewives, Workers and Citizens: Voluntary Women's Organisations and the Campaign for Women's Rights in England and Wales in the Post-war Period', in M. Hilton, N. Crowson and J. McKay (eds), *NGOs in Contemporary Britain: Non-state Actors in Society and Politics Since 1945*, Basingstoke: Palgrave Macmillan.

Bell, P. and Cloke, P. (1991), 'Public Transport in the Countryside: The Effects of Bus Deregulation in Rural Wales', in T. Champion and C. Watkins (eds), *People in the Countryside: Studies of Social Change in Rural Britain*, London: Paul Chapman Publishing.

Buckley, C. (1998), 'On the Margins: Theorizing the History and Significance of Making and Designing Clothes at Home', *Journal of Design History*, 11 (2): 157–71.

Burman, B. (1999), 'Introduction', in B. Burman (ed.), *The Culture of Sewing: Gender, Consumption and Home Dressmaking*, Oxford: Berg.

Casey, J. G. (2009), *A New Heartland: Women, Modernity, and the Agrarian Ideal in America*, Oxford: Oxford University Press.

Coopey, R., O'Connell, S. and Porter, D. (2005), *Mail Order Retailing in Britain: A Business and Social History*, Oxford: Oxford University Press.

Dyhouse, C. (2010), *Glamour: Women, History, Feminism*, London: Zed Books.

Emery, J. S. (1999), 'Dreams on Paper: A Story of the Commercial Pattern Industry', in B. Burman (ed.), *The Culture of Sewing: Gender, Consumption and Home Dressmaking*, Oxford: Berg.

Fields of Fashion Research Centre, Nottingham Trent University, https://ntu.ac.uk/research/groups_centres/art/81396.html, accessed 14 November 2011.

Gant, R. and Smith, J. (1991), 'The Elderly and Disabled in Rural Areas: Travel Patterns in the North Cotswolds', in T. Champion and C. Watkins (eds), *People in the Countryside: Studies of Social Change in Rural Britain*, London: Paul Chapman Publishing.

Giles, J. (2004), *The Parlour and the Suburb: Domestic Identities, Femininity and Modernity*, Oxford: Berg.

Hackney, F. (1999), 'Making Modern Woman, Stitch by Stitch: Dressmaking in Women's Magazines in Britain, 1919–1939', in B. Burman (ed.), *The Culture of Sewing: Gender, Consumption and Home Dressmaking*, Oxford: Berg.

Harrison, B. (2009), *Seeking a Role – The United Kingdom 1951–1970*, Oxford: Oxford University Press.

Home and Country, 1954–1956, National Federation of Women's Institute Collection, The Women's Library, London School of Economics, 5/FWI/G/2/3/49, box 262.

Home and Country, 1957–1961, National Federation of Women's Institute Collection, The Women's Library, London School of Economics, 5/FWI/G/2/3/51, box 263.

Home and Country, 1962–1964, National Federation of Women's Institute Collection, The Women's Library, London School of Economics, 5/FWI/G/2/3/55–58, box 264.

Home and Country, 1965–1969, National Federation of Women's Institute Collection, The Women's Library, London School of Economics, 5/FWI/G/2/3/59–62, box 265.

Home and Country Sub-committee Meeting Minutes (*Home and Country* Minutes), 1954–1958, National Federation of Women's Institute Collection, The Women's Library, London School of Economics, 5FWI/G/2/1/2, box 250.

Home and Country Sub-committee Meeting Minutes (*Home and Country* Minutes), 1958–1966, National Federation of Women's Institute Collection, The Women's Library, London School of Economics, 5FWI/G/2/1/2, box 251.

Howkins, A. (2003), *The Death of Rural England: A Social History of the Countryside Since 1900*, London: Routledge.

Kay and Co. catalogue, 1960–1969, University of Worcester Research Collections.

Keeble, T. (2007), 'Domesticating Modernity: *Woman* Magazine and the Modern Home', in J. Aynsley and K. Forde (eds), *Design and the Modern Magazine*, Manchester: Manchester University Press.

Maynard, M. (1995), '"The Wishful Feeling about Curves": Fashion, Femininity and the "New Look" in Australia', *Journal of Design History*, 8 (1): 43–59.

McCracken, E. (1993), *Decoding Women's Magazines: From* Mademoiselle *to* Ms., Basingstoke: Macmillan Press.

Mort, F. and Thomspon, P. (1994), 'Retailing, Commercial Culture and Masculinity in 1950s Britain: The Case of Montague Burton, the "Tailor of Taste"', *History Workshop Journal*, 38 (1): 106–27.

Moseley, R. (2001), 'Respectability Sewn Up: Dressmaking and Film Star Style in the Fifties and Sixties', *European Journal of Cultural Studies*, 4 (4): 473–90.

Moseley, R. (2002), *Growing Up With Audrey Hepburn*, Manchester: Manchester University Press.

O'Connell, S. (2007), 'Motoring and Modernity', in F. Carnevali and J. Strange (eds), *Twentieth-Century Britain,* 2nd edition, Harlow: Pearson Longman.

O'Hara Callan, G. (1998), *The Thames and Hudson Dictionary of Fashion and Fashion Designers*, 2nd edition, London: Thames and Hudson.

Ritchie, R. (2011), 'The Housewife and the Modern: The Home and Appearance in Women's Magazines, 1954–1969', PhD diss., University of Manchester.

Ritchie, R. (2014a), '"Beauty Isn't All a Matter of Looking Glamorous": Attitudes to Glamour and Beauty in 1950s Women's Magazines', *Women's History Review* 23 (5): 723–43.

Ritchie, R. (2014b), 'Worlds within Kays: British Modernity and Representations of Place in the 1960s', in B. Mitra and R. Johnson (eds), *Constructions of Gender and Identity through Kays Catalogue (1920–2000)*, Cambridge: Cambridge Academic.

Sebba, A. (1990), *Laura Ashley: A Life by Design*, London: Weidenfeld and Nicolson.

Skeggs, B. (1997), *Formations of Class and Gender: Becoming Respectable*, London: Sage.

Stewart, M. L. (2008), *Dressing Modern Frenchwomen: Marketing Haute Couture, 1919–1939*, Baltimore: Johns Hopkins University Press.

Taylor, L. (2002), *The Study of Dress History*, Manchester: Manchester University Press.

Walsh, M. (1979), 'The Democratization of Fashion: The Emergence of the Women's Dress Pattern Industry', *Journal of American History*, 66 (2): 299–313.

Westlake, T. (1993), 'The Disadvantaged Consumer: Problems and Policies', in R. D. F. Bromley and C. J. Thomas. (eds), *Retail Change: Contemporary Issues*, London: UCL Press.

Winship, J. (1987), *Inside Women's Magazines*, London: Pandora.

11 RADICAL SHOEMAKING AND DRESS REFORM FROM FABIANS TO FEMINISTS

Annebella Pollen

In a famous polemic from 1937, George Orwell denounced the 'cranks' that he considered were giving left-wing politics a bad name. As he put it, 'One sometimes gets the impression that the mere words "Socialism" and "Communism" draw towards them with magnetic force every fruit-juice drinker, nudist, sandal-wearer, sex-maniac, Quaker, "Nature Cure" quack, pacifist and feminist in England' (2001: 161). Following Orwell's claims, in this chapter I examine the distinct political associations that have become attached to certain types of footwear – such as sandals – and to hand-made footwear in particular. To do this, this chapter traces a historical story of reform practices and political ideals in relation to shoes and their making since the nineteenth century, whether as concerns for health, as anti-industrial alternatives or as anti-fashion statements.

The principal focus for these debates in the present day is the British company Green Shoes. Founded in 1981, the South Devon all-women shoemaking collective has long promoted footwear with a social conscience. From early advertisements in the back pages of women's liberation magazine *Spare Rib* to a close engagement with the current ethical fashion movement, the company combines a practical politics with the design, production, promotion and sale of comfortable and stylish footwear. As a small-scale business, maintaining traditional hand-making techniques and underpinned by a variety of ethical principles, and as a part of the longstanding alternative economy of Totnes and Dartington and its environs, the company holds a distinct position at the nexus of a number of intersecting social and political, historical and geographical concerns. As such, Green Shoes offers a pertinent case study for reviewing the changing fortunes and meanings of the twenty-first-century craft economy, for assessing the legacy of dress reform principles in the present day, and an alternative vantage point from which to examine the enduring, if complex, relationship between women and shoes. Contrasting documents and garments from nineteenth-century dress reformers with texts and images from the Green Shoes company archive, and drawing on my own experience as a former shoemaker, alongside interviews with the directors and feminist dress history and theory, this chapter puts radical handmade footwear in historical, social and cultural context, as objects of refusal as well as objects of desire.

Reform practices hold a particular place in the historiography of dress studies. The pioneering work of Stella Mary Newton's *Health, Art and Reason* (1974) remains a standard point of reference; this has been followed by a second generation of studies including important work by Crane (2000), Cunningham (2003), Stern (2004) and Wahl (2013) who variously examine aesthetic, rational and futurist campaigns to overthrow conventional clothing. Publishing on shoes, while rarely interconnected with histories of dress reform, is extensive if not always scholarly; notable exceptions of collections that cross cultural studies and dress history include Benstock and Ferris (2001) and Riello and McNeil (2006). Most recently the work of sociologists Hockey, Dilley, Robinson and Sherlock (2013) emerging from the University of Sheffield project 'If the Shoe Fits', while sidestepping any explicit discussion of shoes and politics, has explored the rich connections between shoes and personal identity evident in the present day. This chapter builds on these studies to position the humble, practical handmade shoe as a means by which complex cultural and historical stories can be told.

Edward Carpenter's socialist sandals

The sandal-wearing, vegetarian 'crank' that Orwell referred to so disparagingly in the 1930s remains a stock figure of ridicule in the present; 'sandal-wearing' along with 'muesli-eating' and '*Guardian* newspaper-reading' have become standard accusatory descriptors in British conservative journalism for those perceived to be of a certain liberal disposition. In the interwar period, Orwell's invective was specifically prompted by a trip to Letchworth Garden City; the 'simple-lifers' that he encountered there, however, were bearers of a longer tradition. Although a number of early reformers could stand in the firing line of Orwell's accusation, Edward Carpenter (1844–1929), in particular, is the person most associated with socialism in sandals. As an openly gay, libertarian poet, philosopher, mystic and nudist at the centre of a bohemian, literary circle, his pioneering ideas about the simplification of life, from the pursuit of a fruitarian diet to the promotion of market gardening and outdoor living, prefigure many of the core aspects of alternative lifestyles in the present day with their environmental and humanitarian ideals.

In particular, Carpenter's beliefs about clothing, especially in relation to footwear, are revealing. No doubt influenced by the dress reformers of his social circle, and by the associated exhibitions of rational and hygienic dress popular during the 1880s (Cunningham 2003), Carpenter dismissed the conventional fashions of his day on a number of aesthetic and political grounds. He considered, for example, the clothes of the wealthy man to be restrictions, 'in which', he argued, 'it is impossible for him to do any work of ordinary usefulness'. A gentleman's prevailing anxieties about soiling his garments, he complained, meant that 'his dress is a barrier to all human relation with simple people' (Tsuzuki 1980: 55). Carpenter burned his own conventional formal clothing as symbols of class privilege. He dressed instead in an artistic style comprised of a broad brimmed hat, silk cummerbund and knee breeches, when he was clothed at all, for he combined his dress reform with a love of 'sunbaths', in pursuit of what he called 'the sturdy Simplification and debarrassment of daily life by the removal of those things which stand between us and Nature, between ourselves and our fellows' (Carpenter 1916).

As a part of this, Carpenter believed the liberation of the feet to be of principal importance, arguing that only the bare foot could experience 'the pleasure of grasping the ground – the bare earth' (Rowbotham 2009: 95). However, it was Carpenter's discovery of sandals that was to prove revelatory. After requesting examples in the mid-1880s from his friend Harold Cox who was living in India and, being 'anxious to try some' (Carpenter 1916), Carpenter not only adopted sandals as a core part of his moral dress code, but also began to make his own. Believing shoes to be 'leather coffins' for the feet (Tsuzuki 1980: 64), Carpenter's enthusiasm for the sandal was evangelical and connected to his mystical Eastern spirituality as well as to more earthly concerns. Of his own made-to-order designs (Figure 11.1), available either in a 'most elegant' Cashmere style or in his own favourite, the Millthorpe – named after his rural smallholding in Derbyshire – Carpenter claimed: 'By freeing the foot from the confinement of the closed shoe or boot they render it in a short time as healthy and vital as the hand' (Carpenter/MSS/408). Carpenter practiced what he preached and wore his sandals proudly. Several photographs show him wearing reform dress and his own sandal designs over knee-length stockings, in an early illustration of the sock-and-sandal combination so often derided in the present day as a fashion faux pas (Figure 11.2). Although some have claimed that the socks under Carpenter's sandals demonstrate his residual adherence to convention and reveal a partial commitment to liberation in dress (de Abaitua 2012), in fact the wearing of layer of pure woollens over the whole body, as promoted by the German physiologist Dr Gustav Jaeger for 'sanitary' purposes, was a core principle of dress reform for health in the 1880s (Cunningham 2003). Newton (1974) even suggests that Jaeger's striking 'digital' socks – with divided toes – were particularly suitable for thonged sandals. Carpenter's sock and sandal arrangement was thus a moral as well as a practical choice.

While much attention has been paid to debates about specific controversial objects of dress such as corsets and bifurcated clothing in nineteenth-century women's reformist ideals, the sandal was also central to endeavours to liberate

SANDALS

MADE TO ORDER.

Millthorpe.

These sandals, which are made of the best leather, and are very durable, can be worn either with or without stockings, and are suitable for indoor use at all times and for out doors in dry weather. By freeing the foot from the confinement of the closed shoe or boot they render it in a short time as healthy and vital as the hand; its comfort is greatly increased; the circulation is improved, and the feet become much warmer and less liable to chill than before.

For children the "Millthorpe" pattern is specially recommended.

Cashmere.

Prices of	Infant's	— Sizes	1	to	3	...	4/9
Sandals:	Children's	— ,,	4	,,	6	...	5/–
"Millthorpe"		— ,,	7	,,	9	...	5/6
"Cashmere"	Women's	... ...	...	...	...	...	10/6

Millthorpe Heel Caps, 1/– extra for children; 1/6 extra for adults.

Postage: Children's 3d. Adults 4d. extra.

Measurements: give careful outline of foot on paper, and length from instep round extreme point of heel to instep again.

Cash to be sent with order.

Millthorpe, with Heel Cap.

George E. Adams, Holmesfield, near Sheffield.

N.B.,—Owing to the great demand for the sandals in the summer, orders should be sent early in the year if possible.

FIGURE 11.1 Advertisement for handmade sandals by Edward Carpenter and George Adams, c. 1900. Courtesy of Sheffield Libraries and Archives.

the body from its clothed restrictions. Men, women and children were all to be included. As part of a move away from high heels and narrow toes, Carpenter's footwear was proposed as a healthy and liberating alternative to conventional boots and shoes in a campaigning letter to *The Chronicle* newspaper in 1894 by dress reformer and illustrator Mabel Dearmer. She writes:

> if we must reform, why start half-way? Why not begin humbly and practically with our feet, and see that they are clean, healthy and beautiful? For centuries we have tortured our feet into uncouth and horrible shapes, and we have so distorted our eye that we actually admire pointed, shiny patent-leather boots.

Dearmer then notes that the footwear designs by Carpenter 'are most lovely and graceful in their delicate arrangement of straps, and are a comfort and a joy to the wearer'. She states that the sandals, 'although not "new", constitute a most important point of dress reform' (Sheffield Archives/Carpenter/MN/4/111/a).

Inspired in part by Grecian ideals – whose classical drapery in dress was such a central motif in health reform practices (Challis 2012) – sandals were ancient in form. Wearing them in public in the late nineteenth century, however, was highly novel. Carpenter (1913) notes that his rural Derbyshire neighbours were puzzled by his choices, having 'never seen such things anywhere except in illustrated Bibles' (Sheffield Archives/Carpenter/363/17); they were also radical enough to

FIGURE 11.2 Edward Carpenter, c. 1895. Courtesy of Sheffield Libraries and Archives.

cause offence. An amusing letter by Carpenter to the *Westminster Gazette* serves as a telling illustration of their public effect. Under the title 'The British Museum and Sandals', Carpenter writes:

> Some of your readers may like to know that the British Museum authorities, who give us so many and such valuable opportunities of studying ancient, and, as some of us think, very sensible opinions about foot-gear, are decidedly averse to seeing such opinions put into practice. It appears that Mr. W. A. Macdonald, who is in some degree known as a reformer in the very important matter of dress, and whose sincere personality is respected by everyone who knows him, has committed the enormity of coming to the Museum Reading-room in sandals. For this he has been excluded the use of the room till such time as he returns to the common commercial boot!

Carpenter complains that it is hard to understand how 'educated persons' evidently do not understand that 'the sandal is obviously in every way a much more clearly and hygienic thing than the more modern covering', and he suggests that 'the authorities should put themselves on the side of that larger culture and broadmindedness which they are supposed to represent'. Carpenter, characteristically, as a person who lived his politics, lets his feet do the talking. He ends the letter with the promise: 'I shall certainly take an early opportunity of visiting the Reading-room in my largest and most conspicuous sandals, and hope other friends will do likewise' (Sheffield Archives/Carpenter/NC/1/73).

Radical shoemaking in historical context

It is significant, amidst this humorous complaint, that 'the common commercial boot' should come in for criticism, for Carpenter not only wore sandals but also made his own. Although this could be seen, in part, as a pragmatic decision based upon the limited opportunities to purchase such items and their evident popularity among his bohemian social circle (as archival orders and correspondence during the 1890s attest), hand-making also accords with a number of Carpenter's other personal and socialist principles of hands-on local solutions to larger political and economic problems, such as growing his own food. Carpenter was, it must be remembered, firmly rooted in Arts and Crafts socialist ideals about the nobility of labour; as a socialist he campaigned against sweated industry. He drew inspiration from John Ruskin, had a close political affiliation with William Morris, and his close friendship with artist C. R. Ashbee would surely have influenced him in the social and aesthetic value of handcraft. Carpenter stated that he 'got two or three lessons from W. Lill, a bootmaker friend in Sheffield, and soon succeeded in making a good many pairs for myself and various friends'. From 1889, with trade growing, Carpenter made his shoes alongside George Adams, a working-class man from Sheffield who became a close friend and resident at Millthorpe. During the 1890s, Adams was making 'a hundred or more pairs a year' (Carpenter 1916). Adams was, significantly, himself the son of a cobbler, and a gifted artist in his own right; after later falling out with Carpenter, he set himself up as an independent sandal maker among the radical community at the newly established Letchworth Garden City at the turn of the twentieth century (Plate 21) (Marsh 1982; Hardisty 1997).

Contemporaneous shifts in the shoe and boot industry more broadly in the last years of the nineteenth century make the establishment of a small-scale, hand-making enterprise at this time all the more striking. Elizabeth Brunner has provided a detailed account of the major unrest in the British shoemaking industry in the 1890s, which contemporary writers go so far as describing as less of a strike and more of an 'industrial war' (in Brunner 1949: 251). Brunner points out that while other industries had had significant struggles over industrialization, 'the boot and shoe industry was later than most in changing over from the old handcraft to the modern machine trade, which perhaps made the struggle all the more bitter' (1949: 251). In the case of the shoemaking industry, a number of changes in the late nineteenth century had been significant in the reorganization of labour, from the shift from bespoke to sale production, the scaling up of individual makers' workshops to centrally controlled factories, the increasing subdivision of operations, the progressive introduction of machinery and, in particular, the changes to the conditions under which the machinery was to be operated. All of these accumulating factors culminated in acrimonious disputes and industrial action in the 1890s at the time when Carpenter and Adams were drawing around the feet of their bohemian friends and simplifying the shoemaking process back to the basics of an artisanal cottage industry.

Before the specific industrial unrest of the 1890s, however, shoemaking had long held radical political associations. Social historians Eric Hobsbawm and Joan Wallach Scott (1980) begin their fascinating article on the topic with a revealing quotation:

> the makers of new and old shoes are always distinguished by a restless, sometimes aggressive spirit and by an enormous tendency to loquacity. Is there a riot? Does an orator emerge from the crowd? It is without doubt a cobbler who had come to make a speech to the people. (Sensfelder 1865 in Hobsbawm and Scott 1980)

What they describe as a reputation for radicalism can mean one or more of three things: 'a reputation for militant action in movements of social protest, whether confined to the trade in question or not; a reputation for sympathy or association with, or activity in, movements of the political left; and a reputation as what might be called ideologists of the common people' (1980: 86). They continue, 'Shoemakers as a trade had, in the nineteenth century, a reputation for radicalism in all three senses' (1980: 87). These associations with activism, the authors point out, mark shoemakers out as politically distinctive, as does their tendency, as a trade, to produce an impressive number of artisan-intellectuals during, and long before, the time of industrial capitalism. Hobsbawm and Scott put it, 'Who says cobbler surprisingly often says journalist and versifier, preacher and lecturer, writer and editor' (1980: 89). After an impressive account of the range and reach of radical shoemakers, historically and geographically, the authors finally ask, 'What eventually happened to the radicalism of the gentle craft?' Their answer is inevitable and rueful. They conclude:

> there seems little doubt that, on the whole, the role of the radical shoemaker was no longer as prominent in the era of the socialist mass labour movements as it was before them. No doubt this is partly due to the transformation of shoemaking from a numerically large artisan or semi-artisan craft into a numerically much smaller industry distributing its products through shops. [. . .] Most men and women manufacturing shoes increasingly became a subspecies of the factory operative or outworker of developed industrialism; most who sold shoes had

no connection with their making. The radical shoemaker as a type belongs to an earlier era. (1980: 112–13)

Radical shoemaking in revival: the case of Green Shoes' feminist footwear

Yet, at the point at which Hobsbawm and Scott were writing, seemingly unbeknownst to them, the craft of handmade shoemaking, based on radical principles, was enjoying a renaissance. Clare Rendell (1987) positions this revival in the 1970s. She credits British shoemaker Rachel Floater and her partner Robert Lusk as early agents of change. Floater made ethnic sandals at a time 'when demand was high and British suppliers were rare', selling firstly in Portobello Road market and later expanding into a chain of London shops, including the enduring Natural Shoe Store in Covent Garden in 1977 (1987: 110). In America, at the same time, informed by similar hippy concerns for natural health and tastes for handcraft, publications such as David and Inger Runk's *Shoes for Free People* (1976) suggested a do-it-yourself method and aesthetic for making simple, handmade shoes.

In South Devon in the late 1970s, among the rolling hills of Totnes, following decades of radical and bohemian influx into the area begun by the establishment of the progressive Dartington Hall school by Dorothy and Leonard Elmhirst (Bonham-Carter 1958), a clustering of new enterprises based around vegetarian food, alternative education, holistic health, organic agriculture and mystic spirituality began to flourish. As a part of this, inspired by E. F. Schumacher's 1973 text, *Small Is Beautiful: Economics as if People Mattered*, Andy Langford, a former time and motion manager from Clarks Shoes in Somerset and Graham Kitchener, a leatherworker, came together to found Conkers, a small-scale shoemaking workshop and outlet in the town, selling simple handmade designs. They were joined a year after their founding by Alison Hastie, fresh from an English Literature degree at Exeter University at twenty-one years old, disillusioned with academia and idealistic about making a living with her hands. A year later, frustrated by the mechanizing ambitions of Langford and by his primary interest in manufacturing at the expense of design, Hastie picked up her tools and walked out, along with her fellow shoemaker and former student colleague Sarah Almy. They rented a workshop space in the Totnes Women's Centre and in 1981, Green Shoes, the women's shoemaking collective, was born.

Named jointly after the verdant countryside of Devon as well as the emerging ecological political movement, Green Shoes was founded on a number of core principles: that the company should be run on an egalitarian basis, that the shoes should be handmade as far as possible, that the makers should be involved in every part of the shoemaking process and that there should be a direct relationship between making and selling. Additionally, the company was set up on distinctive feminist foundations. Early on the partners stated that they intended to break the mould of traditional work patterns, 'particularly those of a male-dominated society' (Almy in Oates 1984). The company has only ever employed women, in order to foster skills and confidence in an environment where women can work at their own pace. No-one works more than four days a week to fit with family life; offspring in prams are a regular feature in the workshop.

Echoing the dress reformers' complaints of a century before, the company argued: 'For decades now most footwear has been anything but foot-shaped, ostensibly in the name of elegance. But a foot shaped shoe which is healthier for the foot can be elegant too, as our original last shape and many designs show' (Green Shoes promotional brochure, c. 1987). Green Shoes's ambitions, particularly in the very early days, were to prioritize foot-health, comfort and durability above and beyond what they called 'transient fashion' (in Oates 1984). As such, their ambitions were political as well as aesthetic. Hastie put it, in a 1984 interview in *The Guardian* newspaper:

There's a wonderful woman who runs a shoe museum in Northampton. She believes that shoes are very much a political statement. The platform shoes of the 1960s, for example, represented men and women getting on to their political platform. I see a lot of fashion today as a Right-Wing back-lash. It's all high heels and pointed toes. (Oates 1984)

Green Shoes' political motivations are seen most clearly in their advertisements in the back pages of feminist magazine *Spare Rib* during the 1980s, where they coexist with a striking number of other handmade footwear makers. Despite the fact that there was only a page or so of classified ads in the magazine each month, an assessment of the full print run during the decade shows that handmade shoemakers feature in almost every issue. This is testament, in part, to the contemporaneous rise of feminist-run handmade shoemakers: there are advertisements from Nell Crispen, with her rainbow-painted boots, and from a range of all-women cooperatives: Orchid Shoes and Marged Shoes in Wales, On the Peg and Made to Last in Yorkshire. Notably, there are also advertisements by Adams and Jones of Somerset, who were not all-women; these simple, colourful, hand-stitched boots were not only footwear made by feminists, but also feminist footwear; they are Fuck You rather than Fuck Me shoes. The footwear is advertised alongside rape alarms and abortion advice, appeals for charitable and political campaigns and a small but regular selection of other dress items: dungarees from Ragged Robin's women's clothing co-op, hand-knitted rainbow striped or mohair jumpers and a range of jewellery featuring political symbols. Together, these items could constitute a feminist wardrobe; certainly it is hard to argue that they would have been bought for reasons of style rather than statement when the sketchy line-drawn illustrations that describe each of them are, in many cases, so poorly executed. Green Shoes' products are notably sold using adjectives such as 'tough' and 'comfortable' rather than, say, 'pretty' or 'trendy'.

All this may seem a very long way from Edward Carpenter, precisely a hundred years before, but there are a number of correspondences, from the line-drawn advertisements, the simple shoe designs and the priority towards natural comfort to the practical method of drawing around the customer's feet. Although Green Shoes were not aware of Carpenter's existence, many of their principles and practices of shoemaking and wearing are shared. Additionally, as dress historian Elizabeth Wilson pointed out in 1985, 'Since contemporary feminism, in Britain at least, has been greatly influenced by the socialist tradition, it is hardly surprising that the feminist debate about dress has been [. . .] simply a re-run in very different circumstances of the whole nineteenth-century dress reform project' (1985: 235). She saw feminist clothing in the 1970s and 1980s as 'a latter-day version of the Fabian style' (1985: 243).

Wilson has highlighted the contradictions in feminist debates about fashion, between the irreconcilable desires for utilitarian renunciation on the one hand and creative self-expression on the other, and has argued that this is a false dichotomy. Feminism may have set itself up to be anti-fashion (Davis 1992) but in practice this was not borne out, as Clare Rose (2009) has also shown. As Wilson argues, in an observation that is very relevant to the *Spare Rib* shoemakers, 'Even feminists who never wore a skirt or make-up went crazy about Kickers, or wore beautifully hand-painted boots in rainbow colours [. . .]. Fashion, banished from clothing, reappeared more surreptitiously in forms of adornment that were less obviously feminine or sexualised' (1985: 241). Arguments found in Green Shoes' promotional literature fit with this approach. As they put it, 'Our design criteria are dictated by our "foot shaped" nature-form last and our desire to make comfortable shoes that we would all want to wear' (Green Shoes promotional brochure 1990s). Elsewhere, they state: 'We have no interest in making shoes that are 95% fashion and restrict the wearer, but we do make innovative and challenging shoes that mean our customers can be brave and make a more individual statement' (Green Shoes promotional brochure 2000s). Making a statement, in this context, can be aesthetic as well as political; as dress historian Lou Taylor has argued, '[t]he pleasure in constructing shifting patterns of personal appearance is one of the significant features of subcultural style' (2002: 81).

Additionally, as Wilson sees it, 'in so far as feminists have dressed differently from other women (and most have not) their style of dress has still borne a close relationship to currently circulating styles' (1985: 240). Fashions of the 1970s and 1980s for casual clothing and thrift-shop chic corresponded with contemporaneous feminist dressing. Hastie observes that the mixture of vintage dresses, second-hand tweed and hand-knitted jumpers worn by Green Shoes staff in the early days were very much part of the look of the period, but also points out that much of the stylistic impetus for the company was that the shoes that they wanted to wear were not widely available to buy (Hastie 2013). Simple, colourful – not least multi-coloured – comfortable flat footwear was not commonly on sale in the shops; companies such as the Natural Shoe Store were set up precisely to fill this gap. Hastie noted that early Green Shoes designs (Figure 11.3) were modelled on Clarks patterns from the 1940s and 1950s. Styles were necessarily limited by making skills; these were shoes, particularly in the early days, with a very basic

FIGURE 11.3 Green Shoes, mail order brochure, late 1980s.

construction, but that too was part of the aesthetic of simplification. To be able to look at an artefact and see how it was made was part of the same desire to have the workshop and the shop combined. It demystified production at a time of highly technologized and increasingly globally outsourced industry.

Crafting solutions to contemporary problems: radical shoemaking today

Taking a longer historical view, it is perhaps this craft aspect of Green Shoes that has proved most revolutionary. Of all of the companies listed in the back of *Spare Rib* throughout the 1980s, in 2013 only one remains in business. Although Hastie states that she is proud to call herself a feminist and says that the company would not have happened if it was not for feminism, Green Shoes' own promotional material has not included reference to the company being women-only since the late 1990s (Plate 22). When I worked for the company as a shoemaker during those years, feminism was very much part of the everyday conversation; we took our morning coffee break to coincide with BBC Radio Four's *Woman's Hour*. This aspect remains present, but is now rarely discussed. Hastie says that she cannot think of a single other women-only shoemaking business in Britain. As she notes, of the changes to the industry more generally, 'There are only around a dozen small businesses like us now that are still going.' She observes, 'nowadays the radical element seems to come from having the sheer audacity to run a small workshop and to still be producing handmade shoes' (Hastie 2013).

In 1999, before their demise, all-women shoemaking cooperative Made to Last set up the annual Independent Shoemaker's Conferences. As Hastie's business partner since 1991, Steph Crutchley, described it:

> They rang round all these old guys in sheds doing it completely in the old-fashioned way with twenty stitches to the inch – or even more than that – making one pair of shoes a fortnight at the bottom of the garden. They got everyone together to share experiences and suppliers. Everyone feels so threatened by the shrinking of the industry and you can't get any components these days – nothing's made in this country and you simply can't get rivets, buckles, threads. (Crutchley 2013)

Despite craft's twenty-first-century fashionability – where knitting has become sexy, and so-called craft beers are all the rage – handmade shoemakers find it ever harder to survive, and the handmade shoe industry, even in the model of its 1970s renaissance, is in decline. Crutchley feels that new shoemakers starting up now, where they exist, tend to be 'high fashion and high heels', and British shoemaking courses, such as those in Northampton, Leicester and at London College of Fashion, 'emphasize design rather than manufacture'. Core principles of Green Shoes and their 1970s and 1980s counterparts were simplicity and an ethos of do-it-yourself. As Crutchley put it, in a striking parallel with the famous 1970s punk dictum, 'Here's three chords; now form a band': 'all you needed was a last, some leather and some thread – and just go for it!'

So why does Green Shoes survive where others fail? In part, Hastie insists, it is 'a practical thing. It's harder to weave and make a living. And people pot and can make a living – just. But shoes are an enduring commodity. If you can get it right for people and they like it, then they will come back'. Getting it right for people means, in part, making a desirable product that moves with the times. Hastie says:

I am by no means a slave to fashion but I quite like to be aware of things that are going on. I find it intellectually stimulating. And I like that young people are now liking our vintage styles. I like that, with a little bit of a tweak, some of our styles can be a bit steampunky. I'm interested in all those kinds of trends. I'm massively sad that we don't do enough design work. We do *just* enough. I'd love to do more, but it's difficult to do research and development when you need to earn your bread and butter. (Hastie 2013)

In part, Green Shoes' survival owes much to its location. After a regional clustering of all things alternative in the late 1970s, by 1986, Martin Stott, in his satirical book *Spilling the Beans: A Style Guide to the New Age* could state:

The area of Britain to live in is Devon. There are more natural healers, holistic health practitioners, alternative therapists and other inner-directed souls than any other part of the country. [. . .] The Totnes-Ashburton area is the veritable Californian Marin County of Britain. Living there is what all ATs [Alternative Types] ultimately aspire to. (1986: 10)

These utopian associations continue in the present day. The municipal sign that welcomes drivers on the main approach road was vandalized in 2010 to read, 'Totnes: Twinned with Narnia'. Certainly, the town has long been a centre for handmade shoemaking, hosting two companies since 1981 despite a population of only 5,000. As such, Green Shoes can be defined as a kind of local dress (Hastie in Longhurst 2010). After more than thirty years of production, they may even be local heritage. Yet, after many years of dismissal as goods that might only appeal to feminists and hippies, since the 1990s, Green Shoes' consumer base has broadened, perhaps influenced by the way that very many seemingly radical ideas of so-called alternative and counter-cultures have become absorbed into the mainstream, from the personal politics of gay liberation and the women's movement to the shifting reappraisal of arts centres as 'cultural industries' and a widespread shared concern for the environment (Green 1998). Hastie has noticed this shift, saying, 'Well, I do think that many things – from organic vegetables to brown rice – are consumed by more people now. And I think in a way we are part of that.'

As well as the designs shifting, then, culture too has changed. As part of the renaissance of interest in ethical fashion – albeit under a newer nomenclature of sustainability – and as part of the contemporaneous renaissance of interest in craft, Green Shoes have been overwhelmed by the popularity of their recently introduced shoemaking classes. Here, sometimes with and sometimes without machinery, participants can make a pair of sandals, shoes or boots from start to finish in under two days. Being able to construct yourself something wearable and durable in an age where traditional skills are almost lost and manufacturing, even on its largest scale, is almost invisible, is clearly more appealing than ever. In the twenty-first century, the need for radical approaches to production and consumption is arguably more pressing than ever; Green Shoes' present-day promotional literature remains politically uncompromising (Plate 23).

Conclusion

A wealth of analysis has been undertaken on the stiletto heel (see, for example, Wright 1995; Semmelhack 2008; Steele and Hill 2013), perhaps because it remains so baffling and ultimately irrational. Much less has been written about flat shoes. Despite the fact, as Steph Crutchley from Green Shoes puts it, 'most humans have been wearing sensible shoes for thousands of years', scholars can equate them with being badly dressed (Steele 1991), although their status as a means of communicating resistance has also been acknowledged (Brydon 1998; Lyon 2001; Lomas, McNeil and Gray 2006). This chapter argues that the comfortable shoe is unjustly overlooked, given its dominance historically and in everyday wear, and offers a defence of the artefact as much more interesting than has previously been thought. In its handmade manifestation, in particular, the comfortable shoe can be seen as both sensible and radical, as fashion and anti-fashion, as alternative and mainstream, as historically enduring and as a last stand for craft. This chapter has also sought to offer some context for contemporary interest in ethical clothing production and consumption; it has a much longer history than is usually discussed. These political ideas, in their own ways, are patently fashions that go in and out of style. Ideals about the simple life and dress reform have been periodically held up to ridicule as much as they have been embraced; feminism has been variously celebrated and overlooked in different periods; both appear to be currently having their methods reappraised for a new generation. Perhaps, in the twenty-first century, as journalist Paul Laity (2005/6) has put it, in his consideration of 'cranks' in the present day, 'we are all sandal wearers now'.

Finally, this chapter is based on the understanding that clothing is not trivial. In the case of each of the examples featured, there is a sense of radicalism, whether it is in the early days of shoemakers as political organizers, in Edward Carpenter's building of a utopian lifestyle, or in Green Shoes, who hold on to creative artisanship and small-is-beautiful economics within a globalized capitalist system. As Hastie argued in 1984, shoes are very much a political statement. Although they may be what Crane (2000) describes as non-verbal resistance, with them, you walk your talk.

References

Benstock, S. and Ferriss, S. (1994), *Footnotes: On Shoes*, New Brunswick: Rutgers University Press.

Bonham-Carter, V. (1958), *Dartington Hall: The History of an Experiment*, London: Phoenix House.

Brunner, E. (1949), 'The Origins of Industrial Peace: The Case of the British Boot and Shoe Industry', *Oxford Economic Papers*, 1: 247–59.

Brydon, A. (1998), 'Sensible Shoes', in A. Brydon and S. Niessen (eds), *Consuming Fashion: Adorning the Transnational Body*, Oxford: Berg.

Carpenter, E. (1916), *My Days and Dreams*, London: George Allen and Unwin.

Carpenter, E. Papers. Sheffield Archives. Carpenter/MSS/408.

Carpenter, E. Papers. Sheffield Archives. Carpenter/MN/4/111/a.

Carpenter, E. Papers. Sheffield Archives. Carpenter/Carpenter/363/17.

Carpenter, E. Papers. Sheffield Archives. Carpenter/Carpenter/NC/1/73.

Challis, D. (2012), 'Fashioning Archaeology into Art: Greek Sculpture, Dress Reform and Health in the 1880s', *Journal of Literature and Science*, 5 (1): 53–69.

Crane, D. (2000), *Fashion and Its Social Agendas: Class, Gender and Identity in Clothing*, Chicago: University of Chicago Press.

Crutchley, S. (2013), interview by author, 2 February.

Cunningham, P. A. (2003), *Reforming Women's Fashion, 1850–1920: Politics, Health and Art*, Kent, OH and London: Kent State University Press.

Davis, F. (1992), *Fashion, Culture, and Identity*, Chicago: University of Chicago Press.

de Abaitua, M. (2012), 'On Sandals and Socks', *The Art of Camping*, http://www.cathandmathcamping.com/on-sandals-and-socks/, accessed 18 September 2014.

Green, J. (1998), *All Dressed Up: The Sixties and the Counterculture*, London: Jonathan Cape.

Green Shoes, company archives, 1981–2014.

Hardisty, O. (1997), 'George Adams: Socialist Sandal Maker and Letchworth Pioneer', *The Letchworth Garden City Society Journal*, 68 (March), www.lgcs.org/georgeadams.htm, accessed: 18 September 2014.

Hastie, A. (2013), interview by author, 22 February.

Hobsbawm, E. and Scott, J. W. (1980), 'Political Shoemakers', *Past and Present*, 89 (1): 86–114.

Hockey, J. et al. (2013), 'Worn Shoes: Identity, Memory and Footwear', *Sociological Research Online*, 18 (1): 20, www.socresonline.org.uk/18/1/20.html, accessed 18 September 2014.

Laity, P. (2005/6), 'A Brief History of Cranks', *Cabinet*, 20 (winter), http://cabinetmagazine.
org/issues/20/laity.php, accessed 18 September 2014.

Lomas, C., McNeil, P. and Gray, S. (2006), 'Beyond the Rainbow: Queer Shoes', in G. Riello
and P. McNeil (eds), *Shoes: A History from Sandals to Sneakers*, Oxford: Berg.

Longhurst, N. (2010), *Twinned with Narnia? The Postcapitalist Possibilities of a
Countercultural Place*, PhD thesis, University of Liverpool.

Lyon, T. (1994), 'Big Feets; or, How Cinderella's Glass Slippers Got Smashed under the
Heel of a Size Ten Doc Marten', in S. Benstock and S. Ferriss (eds), *Footnotes: On Shoes*,
New Brunswick, NJ: Rutgers University Press.

Marsh, J. (1982), *Back to the Land*, London: Faber and Faber.

Newton, S. M. (1974), *Health, Art and Reason: Dress Reformers of the 19th Century*,
London: John Murray.

Orwell, G. ([1937] 2001), *The Road to Wigan Pier*, London: Penguin.

Rendell, C. (1987), 'The Wider Last of Shoemaking', in G. Elinor et al. (eds), *Women and
Craft*, London: Virago.

Riello, G. and McNeil, P. (eds) (2006), *Shoes: A History from Sandals to Sneakers*, Oxford:
Berg.

Rose, C. (2009), 'Opinion: The Liberation Look', *Times Higher Education*, http://www.
timeshighereducation.co.uk/story.asp?storycode=409273, accessed 18 September 2014.

Rowbotham, S. (2009), *Edward Carpenter: A Life of Liberty and Love*, London: Verso.

Runk, D. and I. (1976), *Shoes for Free People*, California: Unity Press.

Schumacher, E. F. (1973), *Small Is Beautiful: Economics as if People Mattered*, London:
Blond and Briggs.

Semmelhack, E. (2008), *Heights of Fashion: A History of the Elevated Shoe*, Pittsburgh, PA:
Periscope.

Steele, V. (1991), 'The F Word', *Lingua Franca*, April: 17–20.

Steele, V. and Hill, C. (2013), *Shoe Obsession,* New Haven and London: Yale University
Press.

Stern, R. (2004), *Against Fashion: Clothing as Art 1850–1930*, Cambridge, MA: MIT Press.

Stott, M. (1986), *Spilling the Beans: A Style Guide to the New Age*, London: Fontana.

Taylor, L. (2002), *The Study of Dress History*, Manchester: Manchester University Press.

Tsuzuki, C. (1980), *Edward Carpenter 1844–1929: Prophet of Human Fellowship*,
Cambridge: Cambridge University Press.

Wahl, K. (2013), *Dressed as in a Painting: Women and British Aestheticism in an Age of
Reform*, Durham: University of New Hampshire Press.

Wilson, E. (2003), *Adorned in Dreams: Fashion and Modernity*, London: I.B. Tauris.

Wright, L. (1995), 'Objectifying Gender: The Stiletto Heel', in J. Attfield and P. Kirkham
(eds), *A View from the Interior: Women and Design*, London: Women's Press.

12 DRESS AND TEXTILES IN TRANSITION: THE *SUNGUDI* SARI REVIVAL OF TAMILNADU, INDIA

Kala Shreen

Among contemporary consumers in India, traditional techniques of textile production can contribute to creating desirable, fashionable clothing. In the south-eastern state of Tamilnadu, one such technique, *sungudi*, has enjoyed a recent renaissance. This chapter will explore the production and consumption of this sari textile with specific reference to the World Crafts Council (WCC) project, titled 'Reviving *Sungudi*'. An international non-profit, non-governmental organization, the WCC works to strengthen the status of crafts in regions of Africa, Pacific Asia, Europe, Latin America and North America. This chapter is the outcome of my work as an Associate Researcher in the Humanities in the European Research Area (HERA)-funded project 'Creativity and Innovation in a World of Movement' (CIM) between 2010 and 2013. While the other researchers in the CIM project study objects and images in areas such as the Caribbean, Africa and Europe, my research focuses primarily on the material religion, visual arts, textiles and crafts among the Tamils in Tamilnadu and the Tamil diaspora in North America.

'Tying and dyeing, knotting and dotting': *sungudi* and its revival

What is *sungudi*? A craftsperson ties a thread around a tiny portion of fabric, knots it tightly and repeats. Once the fabric is dyed and the knots untied, the previously knotted areas will transform into tiny dots (Plate 24). Traditionally *sungudi* was used for cotton saris. Thousands of such dots decorate a *sungudi* sari; it contains

20,000 knots on average. Depending on the number of knots tied, a *sungudi* sari may take seven to fifteen days to make. According to the documents produced by the Government of Tamilnadu, the *sungudi* craft is believed to have to come into the town of Madurai during the Nayak dynasty that ruled Madurai from the sixteenth century. These government records state that the craft was brought by weavers of the Saurastran community, who migrated to southern India from their native region in western India, and who continued to pursue their craft in their new place of settlement (Department of Handlooms and Textiles 2005). Madurai remains closely associated with *sungudi*, having received Geographical Indication status for this craft in 2006.

In November 2009, two Tamil women, one of whom was Usha Krishna, the then President of the WCC, went to a leading store in Madurai that sells traditional textiles, hoping to buy examples of the *sungudi* saris which are synonymous with the town. They were shocked to discover that saris with machine-printed *sungudi* designs were being sold as authentic *sungudi*. To their dismay they learned from the retailer that traditional handmade *sungudi* saris were not easily available and were therefore not part of his stock. The two women also received similar responses to their requests in other shops. As these women were active members of local organizations in Tamilnadu, they decided to research the state of *sungudi* production in Tamilnadu. The investigation showed them that there were only four *sungudi* craftspersons remaining, of whom one was in her late sixties and one had failing eyesight. This discovery led to Krishna's launch of the project 'Reviving *Sungudi*' in 2011, which received funding from the Ministry of Textiles, Government of India.

With the help of a Madurai-based heritage activist, Uma Kannan, 'Reviving *Sungudi*' organized a ten-day workshop and training programme in *sungudi* tying, and recruited thirty-nine women (with little or no previous craft experience) to take part. The training programme was delivered by two of the artisans identified during the initial study. The textiles generated by this workshop resulted in an exhibition and sale at the Apparao Art Gallery in Chennai, the capital city of Tamilnadu, in October 2011; this forms the central focus of this chapter.

The research for this project has included interviews with those who make, promote and purchase *sungudi* saris in Madurai and Chennai in Tamilnadu. In this chapter, I draw on my fieldwork in Chennai during the exhibition and sale of these textiles. As one of the primary aims of the research was to understand how a disappearing craft might be revived, I conducted individual interviews with the project organizers and also observed and participated in several craft-related group discussions to understand their pivotal role in reframing this traditional craft in contemporary Tamilnadu. The chapter also draws on the publicity materials generated by the organization, to understand their advertising strategy and to provide a perspective on how this particular initiative was constructed in public media. During the exhibition and sale at Chennai, I was also able to observe and record the opinions of several customers. My interviewees also included the two craftswomen who attended the event and provided craft demonstrations. This chapter, however, concentrates on *sungudi* from the point of view of craft organizations, retailers and consumers, rather than that of the craftspeople, which will be explored in future papers.

Several anthropological studies dealing with material culture, commodities and things have placed great importance at comprehending them through their movement. Values and meanings continuously change as people and things travel through their lives, constantly bumping into each other (Boradkar 2010). To study the dynamics of objects in a moving world, different concepts have been used, from social life (Appadurai 1986) to cultural biography (Kopytoff 1986; Hoskins 1998). In this study, I employ Maruška Svašek's terms of 'transit', 'transition' and 'transformation' (2007, 2012). These terms help to understand the movement of the *sungudi* sari across geographical boundaries and sociocultural contexts, as well as its changing values and the correlated production of different subjectivities. Svašek, the CIM project leader, is an anthropologist whose research has concentrated on the dynamics of objects and images in the various geographical regions including Africa, Europe and India. Svašek defines 'transit' as the movement of the things and people across time and space, and 'transition' as transit-related changes in terms of artefacts' meanings, value and agency. The concept of 'transformation' refers to the dynamic ways in which people in transit relate to changing social and material environments and any corresponding changes in human subjects in terms of their social status, identity formation and emotional subjectivity. This provides a perspective on the ways in which the producers and patrons of the *sungudi* sari have situated themselves in specific social and political settings, particularly with respect to perceptions of heritage in contemporary India.

Authentic *sungudi*, artistic *sungudi*

The term 'authentic' has a range of meanings specific to different cultural milieu. Drawing on definitions utilised by Gloria Hickey (1997) and Henrietta Lidchi (2012), I have identified the ways in which the concept is understood in the *sungudi* project. Authenticity, in this context, attributes paramount importance to the provenance of the *sungudi* and the process of *sungudi* making, with specific reference to the traditional handmade technique. The important association between *sungudi* and its geographical origins was incorporated in the project by using craftspeople from Madurai, by having the same artisans train other Madurai-based women and by bringing Madurai artisans to the Chennai exhibition for a demonstration. As Hickey has argued, 'The craftsperson, the materials, the activity of making and consequently the object are regarded as characteristic of a place'

(1997: 91); location was thus an essential aspect in establishing the authenticity of the craft. The crucial defining aspect of authenticity in the *sungudi* textiles is the handmade technique. The hand-tied status of the knots was a key element that was constantly reiterated during the sale and also in the publicity materials. According to Hickey (1997), the fact that something is handmade makes it more authentic for the buyer. Lidchi also argues that 'it is the manual working of these materials that has been at the core of definitions of authenticity and value' (2012: 71); the fact that the *sungudi* saris were handmade set apart these garments from other similar-looking machine-printed saris in mainstream retail outlets.

Hickey (1997) equates tradition with value in craft, particularly when it is executed using a 'centuries-old' technique. Similarly, Lidchi (2012) observes that the value and popularity of an object depends 'on the aura of primitiveness' that surrounds it. In the case of the *sungudi* project this 'age' quotient was implemented by using the same handmade skill that had been used in ancient times, and by employing artisans with longstanding experience. Commenting on producers of the saris, Usha Krishna said:

> These saris were produced by craftswomen who received training from senior, experienced artisans hailing from Madurai. In fact one of our trainers Saroja is about seventy years old and whose grandmother had been practising this craft. Therefore her knowledge of the craft has been passed down to her through generations. This ensured that she in turn would be able to train more women in the authentic craft. (2011a)

Thus, as well as being handmade, the production of the saris by senior craftspeople from Madurai (the original site of *sungudi* production) using a traditional skill was an important selling point for the promoters of the saris.

While the organizers were keenly focused on maintaining this craft tradition, they willingly innovated with fabric and design. In addition to using traditional weight cotton fabric, they experimented with other types of lighter weight cottons such as *kotta* and *venkatagiri*. Likewise they produced newer designs in an effort to appeal to modern urban customers and the younger generation. As well as producing the traditional sari, they also exhibited and sold new *sungudi* products such as *dupattas* (similar to stoles) and blouse materials (which would be tailored to be worn with a sari). Thus, the WCC members felt that the authenticity of the textiles was determined by its handmade traditional technique, yet the production of the *sungudi* in new fabrics, new designs and new products did not undermine the authenticity of the craft.

To draw further attention to the authenticity of the craft, two *sungudi* craftswomen were stationed at the retailing venue to provide live demonstrations of the technique to visitors and buyers. The staging of craft demonstrations, apart from visually authenticating the products, also emphasized the uniqueness and individuality of the work on display and sale. As Irene Stengs has explained, 'crafting-in-the-open is a ritualized practice that singularizes the end product through the added value of craftsmanship' (2012: 60). Individualization or singularization (Kopytoff 1986) of goods can be achieved by rendering them unique through the addition of particular values. The added value of beauty through design, apart from singularizing the *sungudi* products, clearly inflated the price of the hand-tied works. Customers paid a premium for the manual labour and increased status of revival *sungudi* textiles. While a machine-made *sungudi* sari costs approximately 400 Indian Rupees, the hand-tied *sungudi* sari sold at the exhibition was priced at Rs.4,000.

Another facet of the *sungudi* initiative which added singularity was that every sari bore the name of the individual craftswoman who made it. These name tags presented *sungudi* saris as unique, individually made works of art. They produced a new image of the craftswoman; that of the individual artist. This individualization of labour shown by the name tags also individualized the *sungudi* saris for customers, one of whom commented:

> First of all, to me when I see the name of a person on an object, I know immediately that it is handmade and not machine-made. I instantly relate to the human element behind the craft. It is therefore not a run-of-the-mill product but to some extent renders a personal touch. Because it is handmade I know that no two saris will look identical. Therefore the sari in my possession will look different and there won't be some ten other women having the exact same sari that I have. The handmade attribute to me feels like a customized sari even though I did not order one to be done specially for me. (Varadaraja 2011)

While for this customer, the name of the maker added uniqueness to the garment she purchased, for the project coordinators it served a different agenda. Design historian Judy Attfield has argued that non-government organizations and craft organizations that work with governmental ministries 'preserve ancient craft techniques while at the same time develop a contemporary aesthetic with which to evaluate it on equal terms with fine art' (2000: 66). While the challenges in raising the status of craftwork and craftspeople has been discussed by several scholars, notably in the innovative boundary-challenging work of Glenn Adamson (2007), Attfield's work on the organized voice of the crafts councils and their attempt to elevate the position of the crafts is of particular relevance to the *sungudi* revival. Attfield notes that the fight for a higher status for crafts has led to the redefinition of 'craftwork as a creative art and craftsmen as designer-makers with a right of entry into the circle of respectability enjoyed by fine artists' (2000: 67). She contends that the integration of design into craft is a means by which craft promoters have tried to draw a relationship between craft and fine art; certainly this can be observed among the *sungudi* organizers. The project coordinators of the WCC played an important role in mediating and attempting to transform the status of craft. By displaying the saris artistically between paintings and individually crediting every *sungudi* product to an artisan, they attempted to attribute an elevated art-like status to the craft.

In response to my question as to why these saris had the names of the individual *sungudi* craftswoman on the textile, Sudha Ravi, one of the project coordinators, said, 'Why not? Among fine artists, it has always been the practice to put his or her name on their individual works. So, why shouldn't the craftspeople put their names on their works? After all, every single piece that is exhibited is handmade; something that the individual artisan has painstakingly worked on for days' (2011). Adding to these words of her team member, Krishna said:

> During my forty years of service in craft organizations, one of my personal aims has always been to reinforce the importance of crafts in our society and culture . . . Why should crafts take a back seat to other forms of art such as paintings, sculptures, music, dance and films? Crafts are also works of art in their own way . . . Therefore, I also feel that craftspeople should be given the same kind of respect and social status that fine artists are given. I try to achieve this goal in one way or another in all the events organized by me. (2011b)

Dress historian Lou Taylor (2002: 232–3) has surveyed the ways in which dress and textiles have been variously classified as craft and art since the nineteenth century. In the present day, she notes that dress and textiles may be framed as art as a form of upward commodification in the marketplace and as a means by which makers can be valued – and even romanticized. Krishna's comments illustrate the efforts of the WCC project coordinators to showcase reputed makers who produce objects worthy of respect. Following Svašek (2012), this illustrates the transformation of the *sungudi* maker from an unknown craftswoman to an individualized artist.

This presentation of *sungudi* craftspeople as artists exists in stark contrast to their role in the production of the textiles on sale, which was limited only to the manual tying of *sungudi* knots. While describing the materials on display, the project coordinators explained to me that they had provided the designs and supervised the choice of colours for the saris and the uniformity of colour dyeing. They observed that the 'aesthetic sense' of the *sungudi* craftspeople did not align with that of the coordinators, who considered themselves better informed about the tastes of potential consumers. When the *sungudi* makers produced a few saris on their own, the project coordinators considered the colours that they chose too traditional or gaudy, the dyeing inconsistent and the designs not very appealing. In their opinion, the *sungudi* makers did not possess the skills to produce aesthetically superior textiles. The coordinators therefore allocated the manual labour of knot-tying to the *sungudi* craftspeople and took responsibility for the design of the saris themselves.

This segregation of tasks brought to light the underlying hierarchy of knowledge systems and the place of the makers and project coordinators in a stratified society based on hereditary class structure. The coordinators perceived the craftspeople to be only capable of manual, technical execution and lacking the creative ingenuity and imagination to produce visually appealing designs and colour schemes. This contrasts with their public representations of craftspeople as fine artists and with the practice of crediting each *sungudi* maker for her individual pieces. On the one hand, the artisans are celebrated and cherished, as they are portrayed holding the cultural heritage of a region in their hands. At the same time they are seen to be struggling, unable to survive without the intervention and support of the rich and the powerful. In this duality, the *sungudi* producers and promoters exist in tension. According to David Whisnant, cultural institutions shape the image of the folklore of indigenous people. The office bearers of these institutions, 'by virtue of [their] status, power and established credibility, [are] frequently able to define what the culture is, to normalize and legitimize that definition in the larger society, and even to feed it back into the culture itself' (1983: 260). Marleen De Witte and Birgit Meyer (2012) have also argued that heritage is formed by state officials, chiefs, ethnic activists and cultural entrepreneurs who seek to convince the public of its appeal.

Sungudi as heritage

In this revival project, ancient craft has been given a privileged position in contemporary practices of heritage consumption. The heritage industry in contemporary India thrives by amalgamating the past and the present, tradition and modernity, the historic and the contemporary. Modernity in India is experienced through the relationship between the present and its past (Das 2000). Today's interest in the past and its traditions should not be interpreted as out of sync with modernity, but rather as an aspect of modernity. In relation to dress and its temporalities, Christopher Breward and Caroline Evans have argued, 'The unstoppable trajectory forwards results in nostalgia . . . and modernity repeatedly clothes itself in reconstructions of the past' (2005: 10). Modernity allows traditions to be disembedded from the constraints of situated and localized interaction, and to be redefined in new and diverse contexts within the multiple forms of mediated spectacle (Thompson 1995). Bella Dicks has argued that 'heritage is not a retreat from the present but is stimulated by the present. It is late modernity itself which allows the past to be represented in forms which seem so real particularly in wrap-around, interactive living history simulations. The desire to access the past can be seen as a manifestation of contemporary modes of representation' (2003: 131–2); thus the revival of the ancient craft of *sungudi* is enthused by a modern Tamil ethos.

During the exhibition and retailing of *sungudi* in Chennai, the project coordinators created promotional materials and advertisements that drew on this understanding of heritage. In their efforts to market and sell the saris, they highlighted history, tradition and difference and thereby exoticized and romanticized these objects. In the promotional and publicity materials, the craftswomen were depicted as 'clothiers of the royalty' and an 'ancient community of textile making'. As 'regal *Sungudi*', the craft was 'given the pride of place by King Thirumalai Nayak', which 'began on the banks of the famous Vaigai river', and hailed 'from the temple town of Madurai'. As such, they constructed a romantic view of the region's past through images of an idyllic rural setting and sacred landscapes (WCC 2011).

The *sungudi* advertising served as an example of some of the key characteristics of the process of exoticization, such as a curiosity or a fascination with something strange and different, an indigenous, remote place or a distant era (Santaolalla 2000). The advertising also alludes to the 'indigenous' attribute of the craft by incorporating the word *pattunoolkarars*, which is the transliteration of the Tamil word used by the natives of the region to refer to artisans working with silk threads. *Sungudi* was therefore promoted as a craft that dates back to the seventeenth century and received royal patronage under the Nayak Dynasty in Madurai. Arjun Appadurai contends that imagination is central in the social practices of the modernizing world and is 'the key component of the new global order' (1994: 327). The promotional materials thus establish a relationship between *sungudi* and the imagined past of Madurai. Despite its recent fast-paced development, improved infrastructural facilities and rising technological profile, Madurai has been frozen in the romanticized royal period. *Sungudi* has become the material evidence of this imagined presence of the past and a materialization of the discursive representation of the state. Thus, *sungudi* is an example of how the past can be reconstructed in the present and how, in its transit through time, it acquires new values. By recreating its glorious life from a distant past in an effort to make it more appealing to the elite urban retail market, *sungudi* saris are imbued with additional value and can be perceived as exotic objects. Thus the transition of the *sungudi* into an exotic textile is evident in its movement into the urban retail market.

Sungudi as responsible fashion and status object

In their mission statement, the WCC refers to crafts as 'the living treasures of our cultural heritage' (WCC 2013). *Sungudi* was thus reframed as something historic and precious, as a dying craft which needed to be protected and perpetuated.

Promotional and publicity materials depicted the craftswomen as 'Saroja and Mahalakshmi, last surviving craftspeople' of an 'ancient community of textile making', exploited due to 'meagre wages'. Publicity blamed modern industry for its demise – the 'influx of mill-made cheaper cottons . . . drove out the *sungudi*' – and carried an accompanying plea to 'keep *sungudi* alive' (WCC 2011). These phrases position *sungudi* as disappearing and its practitioners as victims of industrialization and economic exploitation. *Sungudi* saris were represented as cultural products on the brink of extinction. Organizers sought the support and patronage of the consumers by emotively appealing to their moral and social consciences.

This perception of heritage can be understood in the context of the contemporary proliferation of discourses of social responsibility in India. These elements of morality and responsibility are common in many craft initiatives today. In fact, most projects run by craft organizations and non-governmental organizations in Tamilnadu have a strong aspect of social responsibility. For example, crafts are often produced using eco-friendly materials, traditional handcrafting skills or by indigenous artisans. To increase this activity, in 2014, the Government of India passed a Constitutional Act requiring all corporate organizations with a certain minimum turnover or profits to donate to charitable causes. This is expected to lead to an exponential increase in contribution to heritage-related initiatives, as heritage is one of the government-approved sectors for these corporate social responsibility projects.

Alongside the exhibition and sale organized in Chennai, the team members also sent some of the textiles produced to other retail outlets, which in turn had a great impact on the visibility of *sungudi*. The saris were well received by various Chennai-based shops, including Shilpi, a leading boutique. Its owner told me with enthusiasm, 'Of course, I was thrilled to have these saris in my shop. They are an essential part of our cultural heritage. As retailers we must do our bit in promoting such traditional authentic garments by giving them shelf space' (Narayan 2012). Another sari retailer, Sundari Silks, which caters to an elite consumer base and has a record of supporting regional cultural heritage events, also acquired *sungudi* saris from the project coordinators to sell in their showroom. Krishna also collaborated with Sabyasachi Mukherjee, an esteemed Indian fashion designer, because she felt that the usage of *sungudi* textiles in his fashion line would draw attention to *sungudi*. Subsequently this designer utilized *sungudi* textiles in a range of *salwar kameez* (traditional attire of North Indian origin) produced by his brand. Since Bollywood actresses and fashion models wear clothes designed by Sabyasachi Mukerjee, *sungudi* has acquired a new glamorous image.

Sungudi revival saris were also sold in the Indian capital of New Delhi at the Kamala store in the Rajiv Gandhi Handicrafts Bhawan (named after the former Prime Minister of India and late husband of Sonia Gandhi, the leader of the Indian National Congress Party). Sonia Gandhi purchased a light blue *sungudi* sari from this shop, so *sungudi* now has a home in her wardrobe. Krishna recounts with enthusiasm that this was a significant moment for the project; this single buy enormously augmented the spirit of all the coordinators as well as boosting the status of the craft at a national level. Gandhi's purchase of the *sungudi* sari also stimulated discussions among the coordinators of the *sungudi* project. One expressed immense satisfaction, happiness and pride that a sari that she helped design and produce would be worn by a national leader. It was also felt that this could be used as an effective marketing strategy, using phrases such as '*Sungudi* goes to Parliament', '*Sungudi*: The Chosen One of Sonia Gandhi' or 'Sonia's *Sungudi*'. Gandhi is noted for always being clad in authentic Indian handloom saris, so her choice of a *sungudi* sari also emphasizes the socially responsible fashion of these objects. Indira Gandhi, former Prime Minister of India and mother-in-law of Sonia, owned a legendary sari collection and was, according to Mukilika Banerjee and Daniel Miller, 'the epitome of the carefully casual, power-dressing sari wearer' (2003: 220); Sonia thus continues her mother-in-law's practice.

Describing the influence of celebrities on consumer choices, Banerjee and Miller note:

> For many middle-class women Indira Gandhi was thus a trend-setter, a modern professional woman who wore traditional saris. She also contributed to the growing taste for the ethnic style, which she promoted through her patronage . . . Even today, Mrs Gandhi's is by far the most commonly cited sari wardrobe . . . Following her example, other women too aspired to collect saris from all over India . . . Mrs Gandhi set the trend for their enthusiastic acquisition. (2003: 221)

A coordinator of the project said that it was important to incorporate the names of these notable wearers and users in *sungudi* advertisements. Krishna agreed, 'This could be a good idea . . . just like how the Naga bead necklace has received greater visibility and sales because it was purchased by Michelle Obama during her visit to Delhi' (2012). As celebrity emulation in fashion is a common behaviour among many Indian consumers (Banerjee and Miller 2003; Nayar 2009), the project coordinators believed this advertising strategy would increase awareness about and sales of *sungudi* saris. Thus the value of craft is accentuated by patronage from celebrities and the social elite and is consequently perceived as fashionable, glamorous and a responsible consumer choice. Anthropologist Emma Tarlo (1996) observed an 'ethnic chic' trend in India in the 1990s, where women's fashions were guided by rural motifs and ethnic Indianness. From subsequent visits in the 2000s, she observed that this was followed by a trend of 'luxury chic'; here, women's clothes imitated the lifestyles of India's past royalty and aristocracy. In the contemporary fashion scenario in India, as shown in the examples above, it may be profitable to add a further trend to Tarlo's structure: that of 'responsible chic'.

Conclusion: dualities and dynamics

The value of the *sungudi* craft has been portrayed via a dual vision of past opulence and present obsolescence, past magnificence and present moribundity, past exquisiteness and present-day extinction. On the one hand *sungudi* can be perceived as a visual reminder of its past glory, vibrancy and celebrated status. The visual construction of past luxury is achieved through the re-invoked imagery of precolonial material aesthetics of kings and queens. Heritage value is assigned to *sungudi* by citing its ancient provenance and its patronage among the precolonial Tamil royalty. This constructed image of *sungudi* in the craft discourses of the organization draws heavily on its nostalgic image. On the other hand, *sungudi* is perceived as a handmade craft that has been superseded by machine-made goods in this age of fast-paced industrialization. It is projected as a dying craft that is not capable of self-sustenance but in need of resuscitation in order to survive. It is portrayed as a craft that is subject to poverty, inequity and exploitation. While the former vision substantiates the projected exoticism of the craft, the latter vision connects the *sungudi* craft with social responsibility. Just as 'one could justify buying exquisite saris by reminding oneself that one was supporting the handloom weavers who would otherwise become extinct' (Banerjee and Miller 2003: 221), the framing of *sungudi* as an ancient, once thriving and currently languishing craft has turned the textiles into ideal commodities for responsible patronage.

Throughout this chapter I have delineated the reframing and revaluation of *sungudi*. As introduced at the beginning of this chapter, while studying the life of the *sungudi* sari with reference to their exhibition and sale, the concepts of 'transit', 'transition' and 'transformation' (Svašek 2012) prove particularly useful. *Sungudi* as a craft does not have a fixed status or value in its movement across various geographical and sociocultural contexts. When the *sungudi* sari of Tamilnadu was taken up as a revival project by the international craft organization it took part in a transition, becoming a signifier of Tamil and Indian heritage. The depictions of the *sungudi* during its transit from the erstwhile precolonial era of Tamil royalty to the postcolonial contemporary Tamilnadu have enabled a further transition, whereby the *sungudi* sari becomes an exotic object. The indigenous craft was brought from its production site in the town of Madurai to the capital city of Tamilnadu in order to be made into an economically viable commodity. In its transit to the art gallery during the exhibition in the metropolitan city of Chennai the *sungudi* textile was perceived as a worthy craft with an elevated artistic status. In its transit to the wardrobes of celebrities and the social elite, the *sungudi* saris were also made glamorous and part of socially responsible fashion. Thereby, one can observe the shifting boundaries between various categories such as everyday textile, craft, heritage, art, exotic commodity and responsibly fashionable apparel.

These dynamic values of *sungudi* in various contexts did not exist readily. They had to be made, constructed and framed. The project coordinators, who belong to large industrial families, have an impact on what should be perceived as crafts and heritage, what is valuable and worth preserving and what the crafts should mean to their makers, retailers and consumers. Thus they play an active role in shaping the course of Tamilnadu's crafts. The new values of the *sungudi* saris had to be engineered by the coordinators of the revival project. For example, they had to dig out records pertaining to the history of the craft to assign it an exotic value. Likewise, they made conscious efforts to collaborate with an eminent national designer and large retailers and consequently, the *sungudi* was revalued as glamorous and fashionable in ways that could be used as marketing strategies.

Another process connected to the transition of the *sungudi* is the notion of transformation which captures the corresponding change in human subjects and the production of renewed social status and subjectivities. I have expanded this concept to include not only the actual transformational effects experienced by individuals, but also the projected transformation in the social status and social image as imagined by themselves, attributed by others or as perceived in public. During the *sungudi* exhibition and craft demonstrations, the craftswoman was presented as an individual artist as opposed to an unknown labourer by the project co-ordinators. The patrons of the *sungudi* textiles produced by the struggling craftswomen are also perceived as socially responsible citizens and conscious consumers. The transformation most evident in this chapter is that of the members of the crafts council who coordinated the *sungudi* project. The intermingling of the local craftswomen and people working for this transnational organization has impacted the reconstruction and revaluation of the *sungudi* as cultural heritage and artistic and therefore rendered it worthy of preservation and perpetuation. The support of disappearing crafts by craft organizations enhances the social image of the working members of these organizations who are produced as protectors of craft. The craft coordinators are now imagined as the torch bearers of a nation's cultural heritage. It is apparently due to the intervention, influential networks and benevolent patronage of the social elite that the destiny of *sungudi* is being rewritten.

The manufactured values of *sungudi* textiles and the projected transformations of individuals, however, also present a state of paradox while comprehending the practices and perceptions amidst the *sungudi* products, producers and protectors, wherein the *sungudi* makers are provided an artistic status, but are deputed only with the task of manual labour in the production of *sungudi* textiles. Similarly, the *sungudi* is portrayed as the treasure of India's cultural heritage and at the same time penurious in patronage. This chapter has analysed how the *sungudi* craft mediates the creation of new values for its textiles and the production of renewed social status and social image for the associated individuals. Thus, the trajectory of *sungudi* sari reflects the dynamics of cultural production and consumption in contemporary Tamilnadu which is an essential part of the modern Indian ethos.

References

Adamson, G. (2007), *Thinking Through Craft*, Oxford: Berg.

Appadurai, A. (1986), 'Introduction: Commodities and the Politics of Value' in A. Appadurai (ed.), *The Social Life of Things: Commodities in Cultural Perspective*, Cambridge: Cambridge University Press.

Appadurai, A. (1994), 'Disjuncture and Difference in the Global Cultural Economy', in P. Williams and L. Chrisman (eds), *Colonial Discourse and Post-Colonial Theory: A Reader*, New York: Columbia University Press.

Attfield, J. (2000), *Wild Things: The Material Cultures of Everyday Life*, Oxford: Berg.

Banerjee, M. and Miller, D. (2003), *The Sari*, Oxford: Berg.

Boradkar, P. (2010), *Designing Things: A Critical Introduction to the Culture of Objects*, Oxford: Berg.

Breward, C. and Evans, C. (2005), 'Introduction', in C. Breward and C. Evans (eds), *Fashion and Modernity*, Oxford: Berg.

Das, V. (2000), 'The Making of Modernity: Gender and Time in Indian Cinema', in T. Mitchell (ed.), *Questions of Modernity*, Minneapolis: University of Minnesota Press.

De Witte, M. and Meyer, B. (2012), 'African Heritage Design: Entertainment Media and Visual Aesthetics in Ghana', *Civilisations*, 61 (1): 43–64.

Department of Handlooms and Textiles (2005), Application for the Registration of Geographical Indication, Government of Tamilnadu, www.ipindiaservices.gov.in/GI_DOC/21/, accessed 13 September 2014.

Dicks, B. (2003), *Culture on Display: The Production of Contemporary Visitability*, Maidenhead: Open University Press.

Hickey, G. (1997), 'Craft Within a Consuming Society', in P. Dormer (ed.), *The Culture of Craft*, Manchester: Manchester University Press.

Hoskins, J. (1998), *Biographical Objects: How Things Tell the Stories of People's Lives*, New York and London: Routledge.

Kopytoff, I. (1986), 'The Cultural Biography of Things: Commoditization as Process', in A. Appadurai (ed.), *The Social Life of Things: Commodities in Cultural Perspective*, Cambridge: Cambridge University Press.

Krishna, U. (2011a), interview by author, 2 December.

Krishna, U. (2011b), interview by author, 5 December.

Krishna, U. (2012), interview by author, 3 June.

Lidchi, H. (2012), 'Material Destinies: Jewelry, Authenticity and Craft in the American Southwest', *The Journal of Modern Craft*, 5 (1): 69–92.

Narayan, B. (2012), interview by author, 12 June.

Nayar, P. (2009), *Seeing Stars: Spectacle, Society and Celebrity Culture*, New Delhi: Sage.

Ravi, S. (2011), interview by author, 5 December.

Santaolalla, I. (ed.) (2000), *'New' Exoticisms: Changing Patterns in the Construction of Otherness*, Amsterdam: Rodopi B.V.

Stengs, I. (2012), 'Sacred Singularities: Crafting Royal Images in Present-day Thailand', *The Journal of Modern Craft*, 5 (1): 51–68.

Svašek, M. (2007), *Anthropology, Art and Cultural Production*, London: Pluto Press.

Svašek, M. (2012), 'Affective Moves: Transit, Transition and Transformation', in M. Svašek (ed.), *Moving Subjects, Moving Objects: Transnationalism, Cultural Production and Emotions*, Oxford: Berghahn.

Tarlo, E. (1996), *Clothing Matters: Dress and Identity in India*, London: Hurst & Company.

Taylor, L. (2002), *The Study of Dress History*, Manchester: Manchester University Press.

Thompson, J. B. (1995), *The Media and Modernity*, Cambridge: Polity Press.

Varadaraja, S. (2011), interview by author, 1 October.

Whisnant, D. (1983), *All That Is Native and Fine: The Politics of Culture in an American Region*, Chapel Hill and London: The University of North Carolina Press.

World Crafts Council (WCC) (2011), 'On the Road to Revival: Sungudi, the Exquisite Tie and Dye Craft of Madurai', poster for the *sungudi* exhibition at Apparao Art Gallery, Chennai.

World Crafts Council (WCC) (2013), 'What Is WCC', http://www.wcc-aisbl.org/, accessed 14 January 2014.

INDEX

Page numbers in **bold** refer to images.

Carlyle, T. 26
  Sartor Resartus 26
Carpenter, E. 11, 180–3, **183**, 184
Casey, J. G. 163, 175
Cassell's Family Magazine 103
Catharino, D. H. M. 67
Challis, D. 182
Chandler, J. 3, 17, 18
  Critical Inquiry 17
Chapman, J. 26
Cheang, S. 116
Chong, A. 113, 117, 118, 119, 121, 122
Clark, L. 50, 56
Clarkson, L. A. 37
Clifford, J. 93
Cloke, P. 168
clothing, definition of 2
Clunas, C. 93
Clynk, J. 9, 11
Cole, H. 88, 89, 94
Cole, S. 11, 150, 168
Coles, A. 16
Colombo, A. 78
Colonial Times 50
Comaroff, J. and J. 81
Comparative Sociology 4
Coombes, A. E. 92
Cooper, J. F. 26
  *Autobiography of a Pocket
    Handkerchief* 26
Coopey, R. 37, 40, 168, 169, 174
Corn, W. 113, 114, 123, 124
Cosbey, S. 11
Costume 4, 18
costume, definition of 2
Crane, D. 180, 193
Crane, L. 101
Crane, W. 101, 104, 107
creole clothing 65, 68
Crouch, D. 60
Crutchley, S. 190, 191, 192
Cumming, V. 2, 33, 35, 37, 39, 43
  Gloves 35
Cunningham, P. A. 99, 103, 104,
    180, 181
Cunnington, C. W. 19, 24, 30
  Art of English Costume 24
  The Perfect Lady 19, 24
Curtis, P. 137

Damgaard, M. 12
Damousi, J. 54, 57
Daniels, K. 54, 57
Das, V. 201
Davis, F. 188
de Abaitua, M. 181
de La Haye, A. 147
De Monchaux, N. 26, 27
  Spacesuit: Fashioning Apollo 26, 27
De Witte, M. 201
Dearmer, M. 182
Debret, J. B. 69, 71, 73, 74, 78
  'The Iron Collar' **71**
Deleuze, G. 23
design history 2
Devereaux, R. 104
  The Ascent of Woman 104
Dicks, B. 201
Diderot, D. 37
  Encylopédie 37
Dilley, R. 180
DiMaggio, P. 114
Dimant, E. 15
  Fashion and Minimalism 15
Dress and Identity (Eicher,
    Roach-Higgins and Johnson) 15
dress history,
  current practices 7–8
  interdisciplinarity 15–31
  see also dress thinking
  pioneers 25–31
  as a 'sub-discipline of history' 2
dress thinking 23–5
Dubuffet, J. 24
  'Asphyxiating Culture' 24
Dumas, A. 137
Duncan, L. 135, 139, 140
Duncan, R. 11, 127–41, **130**
  Prometeus 139
Dunlevy, M. 34
Durand, M. 136
Dyhouse, C. 166

Eden, W. 42, 43, 45
Edgeworth, M. 44, 45
  'The Limerick Gloves' 44
Edwards, N. 10
Ehrman, E. 100, 107, 147, 156
Eicher, J. 2, 9, 10, 82

Plankensteiner, B. 85
Plato 132
  'Republic' 132
Plumptre, A. 43
Pointon, M. 36
Pollen, A. 10, 11
Porter, G. 123
Pratl, C. 135
Preston, M. H. 49
Proctor, A. 37
Purbrick, L. 45

Quant, M. 168
Queen 101, 102, 103
Quinn, B. 26

radical shoemaking 179–93
  Carpenter's socialist sandals 180–4
  contemporary problems,
    solutions 190–2
  in historical context 184–6
  in revival 186–90
Rajiv Gandhi Handicrafts Bhawan 203
Ralph, S. 137
Ravenet, J. 54
Ravidat, M. 137
Raymond Duncan dress and textiles
    127–41
  the Akademia and 133–4
  designs 136–9
  production of 134–5
Reade, C. 59
Reibey, M. 61
Reilly, A. 11
Rendell, C. 186
Ribeiro, A. 12, 15
  Dress and Morality 15
  Fashion and Fiction 15
Richards, S. 40
Riello, G. 2, 3, 36, 37, 39, 62, 98, 180
  *Fashion History Reader: Global
    Perspectives* 2
Ritchie, R. 10, 164, 165, 168, 169, 174
Roach, M. E. 9
Roatcap, A. S. 129
Robinson, V. 180
Robson, L. L. 56
Rocha, M. 78
Rogoff, I. 98
Root, R. 9

Rosalind Jones, A. 35
Rose, C. 188
Ross, R. 9, 82
Rothstein, N. 108
Rowbotham, S. 181
Royal Ontario Museum (ROM) 127
Rubenson, S. 86
Rugendas, J. M. 69, 74, 78
Ruskin, J. 184
Rutschowscaya, M.-H. 137
Ryan, J. R. 87

Salter, M. 151
Samuel, R. 29
  Theatres of Memory 30
Santaolalla, I. 202
Schumacher, E. F. 186
  *Small Is Beautiful: Economics as if
    People Mattered* 186
Schwarcz, L. M. 69
Scott, J. W. 185, 186
Scott-James, A. 155
Sebba, A. 161
Sela, E. M. M. 69
Semmelhack, E. 192
Sensfelder, M. 185
shadow disciplines 3
Sherlock, A. 180
Shinkle, E. 12
Shreen, K. 9
Silver, K. E. 132
Skeggs, B. 174
Smith, B. 49
  Australia's Birthstain 49
Smith, W. 34, 35, 39, 49, 51, 52, 53,
  60, 168
Sorkin, J. 52
Spare Rib 179, 187, 190
Sparke, P. 115, 116
Splatt, C. 135
Spring, C. 82, 83
Spurling, H. 137
Stallybrass, P. 35
Stanford, J. 114
Steele, V. 10, 11, 192
Stein, G. 131
Stein, S. 66
Stengs, I. 198
Sterlacci, F. 37
Stern, R. 101, 180

PLATE 1 Pair of Limerick gloves, c.1800, leather, 18.5 cm, accession no. 0000.0503. Courtesy of Limerick Museum.

PLATE 2 Walnut etui, c.1860. Courtesy of Dawn Lewis, The Needle's Work Antiques, http://needleworkantiques.com/

PLATE 3 *Saia de crioula* [creole skirt], c. 1890–1910, printed cotton skirt with machine embroidery. Courtesy of Fundação Instituto Feminino da Bahia – Museu do Traje e do Têxtil, Brazil.

PLATE 4 *Saia de crioula* [creole skirt], c.1880–1900, printed cotton skirt with machine embroidery. Courtesy of Fundação Instituto Feminino da Bahia – Museu do Traje e do Têxtil, Brazil.

PLATE 5 Carlos Julião (1740–1811), 'Vendedoras' [Sellers], late eighteenth century, drawing/watercolour. Courtesy of Fundação Biblioteca Nacional, Brazil.

PLATE 6 Maria, Lady Callcott (1785–1842), 'Seller of sweetmeats: Bahia', probably early 1820s, drawing. Courtesy of Fundação Biblioteca Nacional, Brazil.

PLATE 7 *Kamis* [dress] belonging to Queen Terunesh, Ethiopia, mid-nineteenth century, cotton embroidered with silk, accession no. 399–1869. Courtesy of the Victoria and Albert Museum, London.

PLATE 8 Tea gown (front view), English, 1894–7, (ROM 959.63). With permission of the Royal Ontario Museum © ROM.

PLATE 9 Tea gown (back view), English, 1894–7, (ROM 959.63). With permission of the Royal Ontario Museum © ROM.

PLATE 10 Tea gown (front view), English, 1895, accession no. C003352, Farebrother Collection. Courtesy of Royal Pavilion and Museums, Brighton and Hove.

PLATE 11 Tea gown (detail of under bodice), 1895, accession no. C003352, Farebrother Collection. Courtesy of Royal Pavilion and Museums, Brighton and Hove.

PLATE 12 Photograph of the Titian Room with *Rape of Europa* and Worth gown beneath. Courtesy of Isabella Stewart Gardner Museum, Boston.

PLATE 13 Piero de la Francesca painting framed with textile. Courtesy of Isabella Stewart Gardner Museum.

PLATE 14 John Singer Sargent's 1888 portrait of Isabella Stewart Gardner installed in the Gothic Room. Courtesy of Isabella Stewart Gardner Museum.

PLATE 15 John Singer Sargent (1856–1925), *Isabella Stewart Gardner*, 1922. Courtesy of Isabella Stewart Gardner Museum.

PLATE 16 *Narcissus and Dryad* by Raymond Duncan. Block printed and dry brush on cotton tabby called *crêpon de coton*, 1920s, Paris, France (ROM 2010.102.4). Courtesy of Royal Ontario Museum. This acquisition was made possible with the generous support of the Louise Hawley Stone Charitable Trust.

PLATE 17 *Le Moissonneur*, a harvester, by Raymond Duncan. Block printed and dry brush repeat pattern on cotton tabby called *crêpon de coton*, 1920s, Paris, France (ROM 2010.102.5). Courtesy of Royal Ontario Museum. This acquisition was made possible with the generous support of the Louise Hawley Stone Charitable Trust.

PLATE 18 *Diana the Huntress with Dogs,* large shawl by Raymond Duncan. Block printed and dry brush cotton tabby called *crêpon de coton*, 1920s, Paris, France (ROM 2010.102.2). Courtesy of Royal Ontario Museum. This acquisition was made possible with the generous support of the Louise Hawley Stone Charitable Trust.

PLATE 19 Pyjama suit top. Courtesy of the Hartnell-Mitchison Archive.

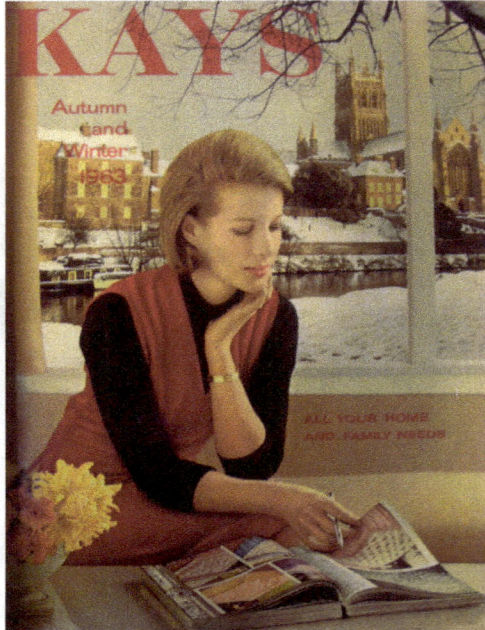

PLATE 20 Cover, Kay and Co. catalogue, autumn/winter 1963. Courtesy of the University of Worcester Research Collections and the Kays Heritage Group.

PLATE 21 George Adams, sandals, Letchworth Garden City, c. 1905. Courtesy of The Garden City Collection www.gardencitymuseum.org.

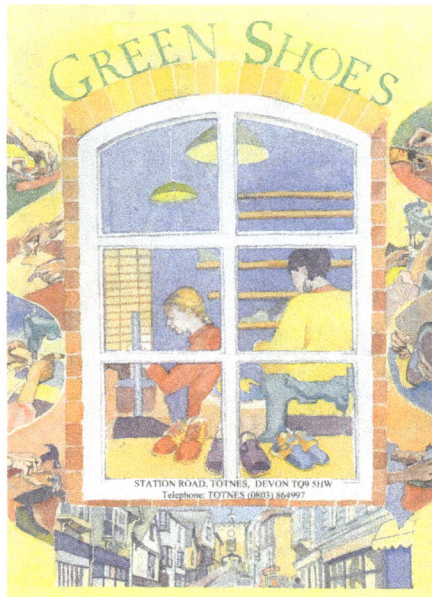

PLATE 22 Green Shoes, mail order brochure showing workshop, making processes and location, painted by Olivia Young, mid-1990s.

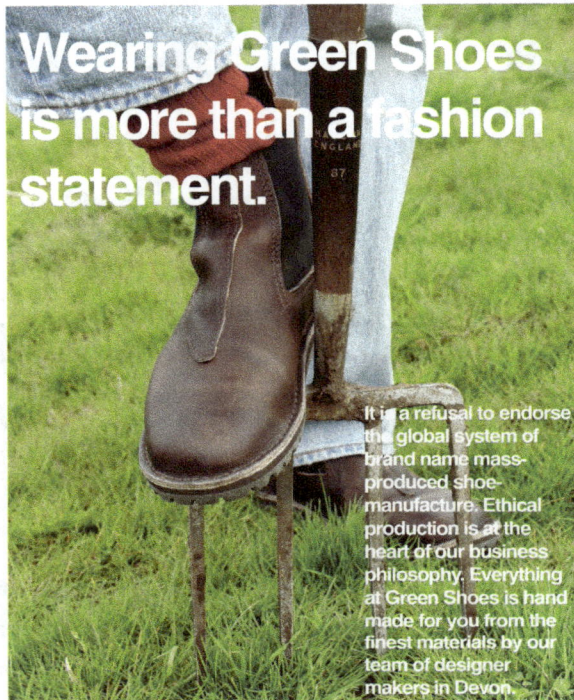

PLATE 23 Green Shoes advertisement, 2014.

PLATE 24 Display of *sungudi* saris, Apparao Art Gallery, Chennai, India, 1 October 2011. Photograph by Kala Shreen.

www.ingramcontent.com/pod-product-compliance
Lightning Source LLC
Chambersburg PA
CBHW071855270326
41929CB00013B/2239